Sharing Your Expertise with the World

This highly practical guide helps education experts of all levels share their knowledge, work, and research beyond their own field and colleagues. By pursuing the recommendations in this book, educators and researchers can increase the exposure of their ideas and impact more students' lives (which can also enhance readers' CVs and careers). Chapters cover the most effective and efficient ways to share readers' expertise with the world, such as:

- Branding (crafting your pitch and leveraging social media).
- Writing (landing book deals and succeeding in key writing opportunities).
- Speaking (giving TED Talks, delivering conference keynote presentations, appearing on NPR, landing interviews, and contributing to public dialogue).
- Participating and serving (making connections, influencing policy, and joining panels or advisory boards).
- Honors (winning awards and recognition to expand your platform).

Rich in tips, strategies, and guidelines, this book also includes downloadable eResources that provide links, leads, and templates to help secure radio broadcasts, podcasts, conferences, and other publication opportunities.

Jenny Grant Rankin, Ph.D., teaches the Post Doc Masterclass at the University of Cambridge, England, each year (as Lecturer) after having had a long career in education (teacher, administrator, and chief education & research officer). Dr. Rankin is a prolific speaker and writer and has been honored by the U.S. White House for her contributions to education.

Sharing Your Education Expertise with the World

Make Research Resonate and Widen Your Impact

Jenny Grant Rankin

Routledge
Taylor & Francis Group

NEW YORK AND LONDON

First published 2019
by Routledge
711 Third Avenue, New York, NY 10017

and by Routledge
2 Park Square, Milton Park, Abingdon, Oxon, OX14 4RN

Routledge is an imprint of the Taylor & Francis Group, an informa business

Library of Congress Cataloging-in-Publication Data
A catalog record for this title has been requested

ISBN: 978-0-8153-5935-7 (hbk)
ISBN: 978-0-8153-5936-4 (pbk)
ISBN: 978-1-351-12098-2 (ebk)

Typeset in Perpetua
by Deanta Global Publishing Services, Chennai, India

Visit the eResources: www.routledge.com/9780815359364

This book is dedicated to Dr. Gail and Rufus Thompson,

precious mentors and friends.

God bless you.

Contents

Meet the Author

Award-winning educator Jenny Grant Rankin, Ph.D., teaches the Post Doc Masterclass at the University of Cambridge, England (as Lecturer), once a year and spends the rest of her time living in Laguna Beach, California, writing books for educators and researchers (this is Dr. Rankin's tenth book, and the seventh book she has written alone). She has a Ph.D. in Education and served as an award-winning junior high school English teacher, teacher on special assignment, assistant principal/school administrator, primary and secondary school district administrator, and chief education & research officer before stepping into higher education and writing.

Dr. Rankin's media appearances include education broadcasts and National Public Radio (NPR). She is an active member of Mensa and many educational organizations, and she serves on multiple advisory boards and panels. Dr. Rankin's nearly 100 papers and articles have appeared in 31 different publications, including *Psychology Today*, *EdSurge*, *Education Week*, *Educational Leadership*, *Mensa Bulletin*, and other magazines and journals. She has delivered 172 speeches and presentations at 53 different venues in seven countries for organizations like the American Educational Research Association (AERA) and U.S. Department of Education, and her international speeches include a TED Talk at TEDxTUM. Dr. Rankin's many honors include winning Teacher of the Year and being honored multiple times by the U.S. White House for her contributions to education (for example, the American flag was flown over the U.S. Capitol Building in honor of Dr. Rankin). She regularly shares new research and resources at www.JennyRankin.com and can be found on Twitter at www.twitter.com/JennyGRankin (@JennyGRankin).

Preface

This is a book full of secrets and shortcuts. It contains all the tips and tricks I gathered on my journey to share my expertise and research with the world. These strategies and sources allowed me to share my work widely (internationally and with a massive audience). Though my goal was expanding my reach in order to help students, a side effect was that I quickly reached career goals I hadn't imagined possible. The most important reason for reading this book, however, is to make your expertise benefit more kids by reaching more of the folks who serve them.

The more time you have to devote to what you do best – like helping students, colleagues, and the field – the better for this world. So, this book is meant to save you time and introduce you to opportunities that can catapult your work's influence quickly and effectively.

Whether you are a researcher, teacher, instructional coach, school psychologist, librarian, principal, headteacher, non-profit trailblazer, district administrator, professor, or other faculty member in the education field, you likely have a vast store of expertise. While your skill and knowledge benefit students within your school or area of research, the education field requires widespread sharing of new strategies and ideas to support all stakeholders serving students within our rapidly changing world. Sharing your expertise outside the walls of your organization serves the field, students, and other educators, and provides you with validation beyond your immediate work environment. By sharing beyond the silos common in the education field (e.g., researchers sharing mainly with researchers, teachers sharing mainly with teachers, etc.), your work can reach varied audiences to improve decision-making, policies, research, and practices in more areas of the education arena, thus helping students on an expanded scale.

This book will guide you in winning opportunities such as book deals, radio and media interviews, conference presentations and keynotes, awards, consulting roles, panels, government involvement (such as at the White House), university-level teaching, magazine articles, journal papers, TED Talks, research, and more. This book won't just give you generalities; it will give you the specific web addresses, submission deadlines, contact information, and guidance to make it easy to share your voice in a variety of venues and formats.

Enjoy the contributions, connections, triumphs, and influence that come with these endeavors. Most of all, enjoy knowing your expertise will help as many students as you work to reach.

AUDIENCE

This book is for educators and others working within the education field. This book is written primarily for two groups:

- primary and secondary school educators (teachers, headteachers, instructional coaches, school psychologists, librarians, principals, district administrators, etc.);
- Other education professionals (higher education professors, non-profit gurus, researchers, etc.).

Professionals in related fields (like sociology) can also benefit from reading this book, as can professionals seeking to make complicated findings (such as those found in scientific research) accessible to varied audiences.

BOOK STRUCTURE AND CONTENT

The book's introduction provides a foundation that will help you with the other chapters' endeavors. Subsequent chapters focus on different means for sharing your expertise (media interviews, conference presentations, etc.). These chapters provide:

- **Descriptions** of opportunities (avenues through which you can share your work, such as the media, broadcasting, publication, events, panels, etc.).
- **Lists of specific opportunities** (such as being interviewed on National Public Radio) via the eResources that come with this book, including other details (web addresses, submission deadlines, etc.) you'll need to apply for each specific opportunity.
- **Tips and tricks** to land the opportunities.
- **Strategies** to improve performance of these endeavors (delivering a riveting keynote, writing a compelling article, etc.) so what you share has maximum impact.
- **Exercises** to help you apply key strategies shared in the chapter.

...and more.

TERMINOLOGY

Different terms are used in different countries to describe common fixtures in the education field and its settings. The term *practitioner* is typically used in this book to mean anyone who works directly with young students, whereas terms like *researcher* and *professor* stand in for those who don't work directly with young students.

Since terms are used interchangeably throughout this book, such as when presenting research findings from different countries, Table 0.1 can be used to understand their meaning, based on the countries referenced most frequently in this book.

Table 0.1 Terms Used for Practitioner Roles

Role	Terms Used
Based in a classroom, works with young students	schoolteacher (previously schoolmaster or schoolmistress), school teacher, teacher Assists teacher: teacher's assistant
Based at a school, works with young students	librarian, school counselor, school psychologist, speech therapist
Based at a school, works with young students (teaches) but is also in a leadership role	department chair, department coach, deputy head of house, deputy head of [subject], deputy head of year, director of [subject], grade level chair, grade level coach, head of department, head of house, head of year, second head of [subject]
Based at a school, leads staff (most of these terms have approximately the same meaning; thus if you commonly use the term *rector* but read the word *principal* in this book, you can assume the words share the same meaning)	head or headteacher (previously *headmaster* or *headmistress*), principal, rector, school administrator Assists school leadership: assistant headteacher, assistant principal, deputy headteacher, leadership team (includes all roles in this cell), vice principal
Based at a centralized location, leads and/or supports staff	director of [subject], district administrator, district/family liaison, district psychologist, [subject] specialist
Based at a centralized location, leads all staff	chief executive officer (CEO), executive headteacher, executive principal, superintendent Assists overarching leadership: assistant superintendent

TERMS FOR SCHOOL LEVELS

The "Terms for School Levels" eResource is also available to understand education terms used in Canada, the U.S., the U.K., and elsewhere. See the upcoming "eResources" section of this book for instructions on accessing this eResource online.

Since *public school* means different things in different countries, the term *public school* will only be used in this book when any country's interpretation is suitable. The U.S. term *school district* will be used to describe a collection of schools under the same overarching leadership, and it will often be paired with the U.K. terms *academy trust* and *local educational authority* (also used in the U.S. and other countries).

When referring to school levels preceding college, I will typically use terms like *primary and secondary school* or simply *school* (avoiding terms like "K-12") in order to use terms understood as the same in numerous countries. Terms for additional stakeholders (i.e., those involved) in the field of education are more similar from one country to the next. Figure 1.1 ("Stakeholder Silos") in "Chapter 1. Introduction" captures many of these terms.

Some readers of this book will be interested in sharing their knowledge concerning *practice* (e.g., classroom practice) with a wider audience, whereas others will want to share their *research* with a wider audience. This book's concepts apply to both cases, as well as other facets of education expertise. I will interchangeably use terms like your expertise, findings, knowledge, practice, research, subject, topic, and wisdom to describe what you are sharing with the world, but the book's concepts will apply to any of these.

For the sake of concision, I will use "Google" as a verb, as it's faster than "use a search engine to search for something on the internet". Likewise, to avoid long phrasing within sentences, I will alternate the use of male (in odd-numbered chapters) and female (in even-numbered chapters) pronouns when not writing of specific individuals. No favoring of either gender is intended in any of these uses.

BENEFITS

Applying this book's strategies will allow you to efficiently and effectively share your expertise with a wider audience in a variety of venues and formats. This will typically enhance your resume and career and will likely enhance your sense of professionalism and accomplishment.

However, the main benefit of this book is that sharing your expertise allows you to inform more people, and people in a wider spectrum of roles, in order to assist more students. Helping students – along with the effect on our world that the helping of children renders – is the most worthwhile goal any educational professional can aspire to reach. It involves an impact that few professionals outside our field can enjoy.

LOOK FOR BANNERS LIKE THIS THROUGHOUT THE BOOK

This book frequently mentions eResources, which are free resources available to you online. Many of these eResources serve as tools you can download and manipulate to suit your individualized use. Each eResource is described later in the book.

AVAILABLE eRESOURCES

You have access to the following eResources:

- Terms for School Levels
- CV Template
- Sample Bios
- Guide to Creating a Website
- List of Writing Opportunities (list of 239 places to publish articles, papers, op-eds, whitepapers, reports, chapters, and other written work)
- List of Book Publishers (list of 90 publishers of books within the education field)
- Sample Handout
- Bad Slide vs. Good Slide
- Countdown Timer Slides
- List of Conferences (list of 179 conferences and other events where education experts speak)
- List of Broadcasting Opportunities (list of 109 places to appear on radio, television, podcast, video, webcast, and more)
- List of Organizations (list of 220 organizations to join or subscribe)
- List of Serving Opportunities (list of 107 fellowships, programs, internships, panels, boards, calls for input or participation, and opportunities to be a judge or reviewer)

- List of Honors (list of 383+ awards, grants, and other honors; note some of these are award lists containing additional awards)
- Guide to Hunting and Harvesting

HOW TO ACCESS eRESOURCES

You can access these downloads by visiting the book product page at https://www.routledge.com/9780815359364. Once there, click on the "eResources" tab and then select the file(s) you need, which will download directly to your computer.

HOW TO USE eRESOURCES

Most of the eResources are lists of specific opportunities you can pursue to share your education expertise with the world. These Microsoft Excel files (indicated with "XLSX" after the file name) make it easy to:

- find opportunities (sort a list of events by type, location, when the conference takes place, or when submissions to speak are due; sort a list of publishing prospects by publication title or type; sort a list of award and involvement opportunities by category or application deadline; etc.);
- pursue opportunities (visit the provided website with a simple click, adhere to the given deadlines, etc.);
- track opportunities for which you apply (use manipulation-friendly fields).

After downloading any eResource with "XLSX" after the file name (as explained in the "How to Access eResources" section):

1. Save your downloaded copy of the eResource to your computer. Close the file and reopen it on your computer to ensure any modifications you make will be saved for your future use.
2. See Figure 0.1 to understand how to best use this type of file. The example provided in Figure 0.1 is a portion of the "List of Conferences" eResource, but the other eResource lists can be used in a similar way.
3. Use your own saved copy of the eResource to add details (as Figure 0.1 explains) on your own submissions (such as when you submitted an op-ed to *The New Yorker* and what that submission's status is).

Status (Enter Accepted)	Month to Apply (Can Change)	Month to Attend (Can Change)	Conference (When region-specific or university-specific, find the equivalent for your area or institution)
	1	5	4T Virtual Conference
	Varies	Varies	AACE (Events)
	7	12	American College Personnel Association (ACPA) College Student Educators International's,
	7	4	American Educational Research Association (AERA) Annual Meeting
	6	9	American Educational Research Association (AERA) Ed Talks
	10	3	Annual Computer-Using Educators (CUE) Conference
	11	11	Arizona Educational Research Organization (AERO) Annual Conference
	1	4	Arizona State University (ASU) Education Innovation Summit
	1	7	Artificial Intelligence in Education (AIED) Conference
	12	3	ASCD Annual Conference & Exhibit Show
	8	11	ASCD Conference on Educational Leadership
	8	6	ASCD Conference on Teaching Excellence
	8	3	ASCD Empower
	3	6	Association of California School Administrators (ACSA) and the Principals' Center at Harvar
	10	1	Association of California School Administrators (ACSA)'s Superintendents' Symposium
	10	1	BETT UK
	9	4	California Association for the Gifted (CAG) Conference
	1	4	California Association of School Business Officials (CASBO) Ann
	11	2	California College Personnel Association (CCPA) Conference
	8	10	California Council on Teacher Education (CCTE) Conference
	6	11	California Educational Research Association (CERA) Annual Co
	5	12	California EducationalTechnology Professionals Association (CETPA)
			nnel Islands (CSUCI) Conference for Social Justice in Educati
	7		vancement of Teaching Summit on Improvement in Educat
	12		) Orange Cou Technology Festival ("Tech Fest")
	ing		al Developme
			her 3 Ed. T
			Technolog

Figure 0.1 Top Portion of "List of Conferences" eResource (rows continue on next page)

Conferences' locations often change annually, whereas online conferences tend to remain online.

Dates can change from one year to the next. Sort by the 2nd column (Month to Apply) or 3rd column (Month to Attend) rather than these 2 columns.

Sample of a Previous Location (Future Places Can Vary)	Category	Info (if link no longer works, try dropping the URL's extension or u	Sample of a Previous Deadline to Apply (Future Dates Can Vary)	Sample of a Previous Conference Date (Future Dates Can Vary)	Applied for Event (Enter Date
Online	Edtech	http://www.fivtrsdliconc om/	1/20/16	5/20/17-5/22/17	
Varies	List to Check	http://www.aace.org/	Varies	Varies	
CA: Long Beach	Education	http://www.myacpa.org/ events/2016-leadership-	7/29/16	12/	
Washington, DC	Education	http://www.asra.net/cap d/10208/Default.aspx	7/22/16		
Washington, DC	Education	http://www.aera.net/che	6/10/15		
CA: Palm Springs	Edte		10/1/13		
AZ: Tempe	Educa		11/1/13		
AZ: Scottsdale	Edte		1/1/13		
TN: Memphis	Edte		1/1/14		
CA: Los Angeles	Educa		12/1/13		
NV: Las Vegas	Education		8/1/13		
CO: Denver	Educatic	http://www.ascd.org/conf erences.aspx	8/1/16	6/30/17-7/1/17	
CA: Anaheim	Education	http://annualconference. ascd.org/Default.aspx	8/1/16	3/25/17-3/27/17	
CA: Los Angeles	Education	http://www.acsa.org/Mai nMenuCategories/Profess	3/1/14	6/23/13-6/29/13	
CA: Monterey	Education	http://2013suptssymposi um.sched.org/	10/1/13	1/1/14-1/1/14	
ENGLAND: London	Edtech	http://www.bettshow.co m/	10/1/13	1/22/14-1/25/14	
CA: San Diego	Education	http://www.cagifted.org/ event/2016Conference	9/1/16	4/1/17	
CA: Long Beach	Education	http://www.myctap.org/i ndex.php/region/ctap9	1/1/14	4/1/13	
CA: Los Angeles	Education	https://docs.google.com/f orm/d/1GvcBd5X7kTEi0	11/30/15	2/19/16	
CA: San Diego	Education	http://sste.org/i1986r-10- 752	8/15/14	10/22/15-10/24/15	
CA: Sacramento	Education	http://cera- web.org/upcoming-	6/10/15	11/30/16-12/1/16	
CA: San Diego	Edtech	http://cetpa.net/ev file:///C:/Users/Je	5/16/15	12/1/15-12/1/15	
CA: Camarillo	Education	wnloads/SOJU%7	2/24/14	4/19/14	
CA: San Francisco	Education	http://www.ca	7/1/15	3/22/16-3/24/16	
CA: Santa Ana	Edtech	http://www.g t.blogspot.c	12/1/16	2/1/14	
Online	Education	http://www m/confer	Ongoing	Ongoing	

Feel free to add your own categories to your copy of this spreadsheet.

These are examples of *past* dates that give us a hint of what when the future deadlines will land. Future deadlines are usually within one week of past deadlines.

Conference organizers sometimes change the specific web address where conference information is located. If a web link no longer works, try the URL without its extension (i.e., only type through ".com" or ".org" and skip the rest of the web address) or google the conference to track down information on it. Once you find an updated web address, save it (on your copy of this spreadsheet) by replacing the nonworking URL.

When you apply to speak at an event, record the date you applied in the last column. This will be useful if you don't hear back about the outcome and need to follow up.

Figure 0.1 Top Portion of "List of Conferences" eResource (*continued*)

Because application pages vary from year to year, home page addresses are usually included on the eResource list. After visiting an opportunity's website, look for links based on what you seek to do (such as "Call for Speakers" or "Apply to Present" if you seek to apply to speak at a symposium, or "Author

ADD NEW OPPORTUNITIES

If you know of a great opportunity for readers that is not already featured on one of these eResource lists, please let us know at www.JennyRankin.com/opportunity. The opportunity you add could be included on an eResource list for future editions of this book.

Submission Details" or "Write for Us" if you seek to write for a publication). If you discover opportunities not already featured on a list, you can add them to your own copy of this spreadsheet by giving each new opportunity its own row.

Every time I apply for an opportunity, I store "P" (for Pending) in the spreadsheet's "Status" column for that opportunity's row, and I store my application date in the "Applied for" column. I then change the status to "A" (for Accepted) or "R" (for Rejected) when I hear back from the folks in charge (e.g., editors, organizers, or organization members). These cells will automatically change color based on the letter you use, which makes each status easier to spot.

When I sort the file by its "Status" column, I can then more easily spot all of the:

- Rejected opportunities, which I can copy entry information from (such as abstracts, papers, or session descriptions) to electronically paste into new prospects for which I apply.
- Pending opportunities, which I can follow up on (based on my noted submission date) to be sure my entry was received.
- Accepted opportunities, which I can add to my CV, promotion efforts, etc.

Do not fail to download these eResources and try using them. Any technical learning curve you encounter while using these files will be worth pushing through to enjoy the enhanced organization and efficiency they provide. As you share your expertise with the world, you'll come to enjoy this easy way to manage all the exciting venues that await you.

Acknowledgments

The inspiration for this book came from my own growth as an educator passionate about sharing my expertise and research with the world. I owe much thanks to those who opened doors for me along the way. One of these doors was opened by my wonderful editor, Heather Jarrow. I'll forever be grateful for her role in this book, those books that came before it, and those I'll write in the future. I thank Rebecca Collazo, editorial assistant at Routledge/Taylor & Francis Group, I thank Lisa Keating, who did a fabulous job overseeing the book's typesetting and production, and I thank photographer Michael Walker for his skill and kindness with a camera. Steve Waters helped with the U.K. terminology, for which I'm very grateful, as I am for those who generously offered early feedback on the book: Dr. Darlene Breaux, Dr. Colette Boston, Mariana De Albuquerque Simoes, Alex Alves Egido, Dr. Norman Eng, Dr. Bobbi Newman, Dr. Lisa Paisley, Gary Soto, and Dr. Gretchen Wright.

As always, I owe much gratitude to the tireless cheerleaders in my life: my family, Dr. Gail Thompson, Rufus Thompson, Vanessa Carroll, Dr. Margie Johnson, Dr. Colette Boston, Nancy Grant (my incredible mother), my loved ones at Illuminate Education, and my other dear friends. I thank my husband Lane Rankin for how he talks about me to others when he doesn't know I can hear, and how special and loved that makes me feel. I feel blessed beyond words for everyone's support.

Part I

Gearing Up

Part 1

Gearing Up

Chapter 1

Introduction

You wouldn't let someone who is not a doctor of medicine operate on your heart. You wouldn't ride in a plane flown by someone who is not a pilot. This is because it's unwise to put lives in the hands of folks who aren't specifically trained to look after those lives. Yet there are plenty of non-experts (non-educators, non-researchers, etc.) talking about what's needed in education.

The world needs education experts like you – knowledgeable heroes – to take the leading role in these conversations. Sharing your wisdom can enlighten decision makers, inform communities, help other educators improve practice, further research, and widen your impact on students.

Whether your expertise comes from working with students or from academic study, this book will help you share your expertise with a wider audience in a variety of venues and formats. Pursuing the opportunities in this book will also enhance your resume, CV, and career, and will likely increase your professional and personal satisfaction.

THE DANGER OF SILOS

Martin Rees (2017) of the University of Cambridge explains even fields tackling large matters, like astronomy, are far simpler than human sciences; black holes can be described precisely by simple equations, and a star's nature can be captured in a simple sentence. In the messy field of education, an overwhelming number of variables join with the complex natures of students and other stakeholders to make complete understanding difficult to achieve. Fundamental questions like "Does this intervention help children learn?" and "What is best for this child?" are daunting to answer with certainty. Yet answer (or at least get a likely notion of the answer) we must if we are to act in providing students with what they most likely need.

It is often noted that education stakeholders communicate most fully in silos. This means they usually communicate with people in the same role (such as teacher to teacher) or at the same site (such as working within the same school) when sharing knowledge, seeking knowledge, making decisions, and collaborating. Compacting this problem is "the gradual disappearance of program

> ## DEFINITION OF SILO
>
> A *silo* is a structure within which content is contained. When people, such as within the education field, communicate in silos, it means they are communicating with people like them (e.g., headmaster to headmaster) and not (or rarely) with others, even when those other stakeholders know much that can inform and benefit their efforts in the field.

evaluators from the district office staff" (Rees, 2018, p. 3) and other support personnel, largely for budgetary reasons, which eliminates people who help link practitioners with research.

Sometimes sharing does not even occur regularly and fluidly *within* silos. These same-silo and restricted-sharing paradigms provide education stakeholders, as a whole, with limited awareness of knowledge available elsewhere in the field.

To meet this noble challenge, knowledge gained in all corners of the field must be shared with the other corners. Teachers cannot share their discoveries only with their teacher colleagues, or policymakers will make decisions that don't benefit from those discoveries. Researchers cannot share their discoveries only with readers of an academic journal unread by practitioners, or school leaders will make decisions that don't benefit from those discoveries. Additional examples can pair any stakeholder with any other stakeholder to the same effect. Figure 1.1 features 37 (not an exhaustive list of) stakeholders who influence students, and who possess knowledge that can help students.

Transcending the boundaries of traditional silos in the field is best for students. It's also best for education experts, who enjoy expanded knowledge and improved success as we learn from others in all areas of the field. This transcendence can occur if stakeholders make efforts to share their expertise with stakeholders of all natures, within their own traditional silos and outside their silos. As you share with varied constituents, you can also learn from varied constituents to serve as an even stronger champion for kids.

THE (SCRAPPY) PATH YOU TAKE

Your workplace, specialties, preferences, and personality are all aspects that make your journey very individual. Thus, the way you use this book should be very

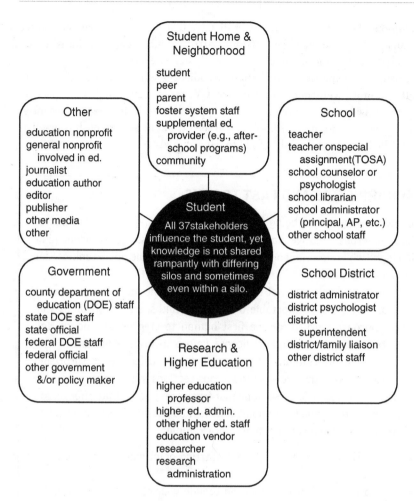

Student Home & Neighborhood

student
peer
parent
foster system staff
supplemental ed.
    provider (e.g., after-
    school programs)
community

Other

education nonprofit
general nonprofit
    involved in ed.
journalist
education author
editor
publisher
other media
other

School

teacher
teacher onspecial
    assignment(TOSA)
school counselor or
    psychologist
school librarian
school administrator
    (principal, AP, etc.)
other school staff

Student

All 37stakeholders influence the student, yet knowledge is not shared rampantly with differing silos and sometimes even within a silo.

Government

county department of
    education (DOE) staff
state DOE staff
state official
federal DOE staff
federal official
other government
    &/or policy maker

School District

district administrator
district psychologist
district
    superintendent
district/family liaison
other district staff

Research & Higher Education

higher education
    professor
higher ed. admin.
other higher ed. staff
education vendor
researcher
research
    administration

Figure 1.1 Stakeholder Silos

individual. Not a fan of writing? Then spend less time tackling this book's writing recommendations than you do on speaking and other endeavors. Not able to live away from home for a White House fellowship? Then do not apply for one. Just want to try a few new things without setting up a webpage or brand? Then start small.

Use this book for your individual circumstances. However, note that stepping outside your comfort zone and pursuing a variety of opportunities is most beneficial. For example, public speaking increases writing opportunities and exposure, and writing increases public speaking opportunities and exposure. Social media presence and speaking engagements are something you put on your book proposal to get a book deal. All opportunities covered in this book are likely to increase other types of prospects, which will benefit the reach of your work.

In addition, the mere exposure effect dictates that the more people encounter something, the more they like it (Grant, 2016), so increasing your ideas' exposure could increase the acceptance of them by stakeholders.

Sharing your expertise with a variety of audiences and in a variety of ways will result in a more well-rounded resume or CV, more well-rounded experience, and a much wider net to catch additional opportunities. This, most importantly, benefits students. So, use this book as you see fit, but be sure to push yourself as you do. Be brave, and don't be afraid to get scrappy.

SCRAPPY TIPS AND FAST TRACKS

Being *scrappy* means being determined and thinking outside the box to find numerous, creative ways to seize opportunities. It also means aiming high (while simultaneously seizing more accessible opportunities) for maximum impact.

Some call this moonshot thinking: shoot for the moon — ten times as high as might feel comfortable or typical — and see where it lands you. That approach worked for the first human to step on the moon: Neil Armstrong acquired his pilot's license *before* his driver's license.

This book offers many "scrappy tips" that offer clever, surprising ways to achieve a goal related to various sections in the book.

This book also offers "scrappy fast track" text boxes that offer action plans to get from point A to point B as fast as possible. This will help you hit your mark when you aim high. For example:

- Publish a book even though your starting point includes no published writing experience.
- Give a TED Talk or keynote even though your starting point includes no notable speaking experience.
- Appear on NPR even though your starting point includes no radio experience.
- Be honored by the White House even though your starting point includes no previous awards
- Gain lots of exposure even though your starting point includes limited branding and social media presence

You'll have to scale up your skillsets quickly to achieve lofty goals (something this book will help you do), but these scrappy routes will open those big doors for you. The payoff — helping more students — is too important to not pursue and walk through such doors.

HONESTY AND INTEGRITY

As you follow your path to maximum impact and career growth, commit to maintaining honesty and integrity. This means never lying on your CV, never taking credit for someone else's work, never throwing a colleague or acquaintance under the bus, etc. Even if an underhanded move appears to have a positive result in the short term, it will likely damage you in the long term, such as by hurting your reputation. You can still be scrappy (as covered in the previous section) but do so honorably.

You will feel your best if you operate with honesty and integrity, and people will respond better to you. You will also set a good example for others in the field, and this will trickle down to the students our work affects. Plus, people are well connected within the field of education, and it serves you well to have good conduct shared in relation to your name.

RESOURCE TIP

The Committee of Publication Ethics (COPE) (www.publicationethics.org) can help you navigate topics (such as authorship and publishing) with integrity.

UNFAIR, BUT BE AWARE

This book celebrates the need for all education experts to share what they know so our field and students can benefit from their wisdom. Yet women, people of color, and LGBT+ individuals face discrimination in their efforts to share their expertise within our professional arena. It is important to be aware of unfair obstacles, and how they manifest themselves, so we can all find ways to ensure the field benefits from diverse voices.

See Rankin (2018) for a three-part series in *Psychology Today* that shares statistics and suggestions related to this topic. The series provides a glimpse at the added hurdles traditionally marginalized groups face in the Education departments of higher education, working in primary and secondary schools, and when seeking to publish their work.

I hate that statistics on bias surround us, yet they fire me up to find opportunities for improvement. Please get fired up with me, and hold this issue close to your heart as you seek to share your expertise with the world. Speak up for yourself, knowing you have a value too great to be quieted, and speak up for others so their voices can be heard loud and clear. Apply any added creativity and scrappiness it takes to circumvent obstacles. As Congresswoman Shirley Chisholm said,

"If they don't give you a seat at the table, bring a folding chair" (Vaidyanathan, 2016, p. 5).

Areas of inequity will never improve without courageous dialogue and conscientious actions. As educators we have a moral obligation to lead this charge.

CRITICS

When it comes to using social media and other avenues promoted in this book to widen the reach of your work, you might encounter critics. For example, as you share your work:

- People in the higher education sphere might accuse you of debasing the profession or assume you think digital download metrics equate to the value of research and scholarly writings.
- Your loved ones, colleagues, or supervisors might discourage you from working on projects not directly related to your professional advancement (for example, if you teach at a university that rewards publishing in journals but views your magazine articles and documentary film as unnecessary).
- People in the primary and secondary school sphere might erroneously assume your motives are self-promotion and a narcissistic love of the spotlight, or that you have "sold out" as a practitioner.

I don't mean to scare you. I just want to caution you that these slights arise so you can nip misunderstandings in the bud or brace to let them roll off your back. It can take a tough skin to share on a large scale. For 26 years Nicolaus Copernicus refused to publish his discovery that the earth revolves around the sun because he feared ridicule. His discovery was only published when someone submitted the work just before Copernicus's death. Astronomy was stagnated when Copernicus held back from sharing, but it is arguably worse that kids could be hurt (or at least not helped as much) if you keep quiet about information you know can help them. Share in ways likely to make a difference in our field, even if some criticize you for doing so.

The reality of our world is that the way people get their information has changed in substantial ways. The internet, in particular, has opened countless new channels to reach and help others with your knowledge. For example, "every day scholarly articles receive 12,000 new mentions across social media, news, and blogs. That's 1 mention every 7 seconds" (Elsevier, 2018, p. 1). Ignoring this reality is like the teacher who says, "I shouldn't have to entertain my kids to teach!" and continues to lecture his bored students from a lectern while scoffing at the teacher next door who engages his students in fun learning activities (more learning probably happens in the latter classroom).

With all the opportunities for information exchange at our fingertips, it's commendable and encouraged that you use these avenues to share your wisdom with the world. Engaging with the public and with experts in varied roles and in varied locales within the education field will multiply your impact on students. If you know something that is dramatically helping kids in your classroom or kids in a classroom that reflects your research, why stop there? Why not let it dramatically help the students of people who read an article you wrote, hear you on National Public Radio (NPR), or watch your TED Talk? …and let it dramatically help the students of people who *those* people's new understanding reaches? If you imagine the enhanced impact that these (merely three!) new avenues for sharing can have, then you can imagine the enormity of the difference you can make by seizing many of the couple of thousand sharing opportunities waiting for you in this book.

If you are in a higher education faculty, your organization might be one that frowns upon "non-academic" contributions, or it might be one that actively encourages the exchange between researchers and others (shout out to University of Pennsylvania's Graduate School of Education's CPRE Knowledge Hub; Harvard Graduate School of Education's Usable Knowledge; Universities of Delaware, Pennsylvania, and Minnesota's Center for Research Use in Education; and UMass Amherst's Public Engagement Project). Either way, which is more important: that you impress university colleagues and ease your journey to tenure, or that you help more kids? For me, the latter objective is far more worthwhile. Plus, you can be part of the movement to modernize what it means to be a scholar. Badgett (2016) found:

> Many … professors have gotten new research questions, new perspectives, new ideas, new sources of data, and occasionally even new funding opportunities by interacting with the broader public. That can all add up to better research as well as even more engagement.
>
> (p. 8)

Whatever opposition you encounter, let it *fire you up*. Don't let anyone turn you away from your goal of helping more students through the wider sharing of your expertise. This book you're reading is my tenth book to be published. When I was writing my first book three years ago, a loved one told me, "You're wasting your time on that book. It will never be published. You're a nobody." He didn't want me to get my hopes up, only to have them dashed (and yes, he had a wretched way of communicating this).

I didn't think, "He's right. I should abandon this project and not seek to share outside of my current work bubble." No way. I cared too much about my knowledge and findings' potential to help children. I thought more along the lines of the movie *Dirty Dancing*, in which Patrick Swayze declared, "Nobody puts Baby in the

9

corner." I thought, "Nobody knows this stuff I've learned, and this unawareness is hurting kids! I have to get this out there! I *will* get this out there!"

Your work is just as important as mine. People need to know about it. Don't let anyone put you in the corner. Push to get up on that stage, push to put your words into readers' hands, push to shape professional and public dialogue, push to share your work on a national or international scale, push to have a massive impact on students and the world. If you keep pushing, it is only a matter of time before you break through common obstacles to reach any goals you set. You're really the only one who can hold you back, so don't listen to anyone foolish enough to suggest you stay in the corner.

DOMINO EFFECT

A single domino can knock down multiple dominos, or even a domino 50% larger than itself. This is an example of geometric progression: If you started with a regular-sized domino, the 18th domino to be knocked down could be as tall as the Leaning Tower of Pisa, and the 57th domino could reach from here to the moon (Keller & Papasan, 2013). As Malcolm Gladwell (2000) says of geometric progression, "Sometimes big changes follow small events, and ... sometimes these changes can happen very quickly" (p. 11).

Brace yourself for the domino effect to knock open opportunities for you. When one door of opportunity falls open to you and you walk through it, this leads to more open doors of increasing stature. Walk through any of those, and yet more doors of ever-greater opportunities await you.

Even opportunities that seem minor can have an unexpectedly huge payoff. For example, maybe you speak at a fledgling conference but happen to influence a government official who will take your idea region-wide, or you sit next to someone who connects you with a BBC reporter through which your message reaches thousands.

Teacher Karen Wagner was interviewed for an article in *Chalkbeat* following her participation in the Colorado Teaching Policy Fellowship. After I was booked to present at an ASCD conference, the organizers asked that I arrange to have a practicing teacher present with me. I Googled the conference location, the word "teacher", and the session's topic and found the *Chalkbeat* article profiling Karen, who I then invited to present with me. At the conference, Karen and I discussed her desire to write books, and I plan to introduce her to my editor when she is ready. After our session, an ASCD representative from the audience approached Karen and asked her to present at another event.

Karen's speaking engagements were rolling in, and it all began with a fellowship, which led to an article, which led to a single conference session, which led to more and might eventually lead to a book. To quote a lyric from *The Sound of Music*: "Nothing comes from nothing." Every time you "step out" in the field and share in some way, you increase the likelihood of more great things happening. In this case, it's more chances to share your work and impact more student lives.

BALANCE AND CHOICE

That said, be cognizant of how you allocate your time. As you follow this book's strategies you will likely get excited as you land more keynotes or book deals or whatever avenues you pursue to share your wisdom with the world. Be conscientious about striking a balance between time spent sharing versus time spent on your actual research or practice. You don't want to sacrifice the quality of your work in your pursuit of widening the audience that benefits from it.

Also, you don't have to do everything recommended in this book. This book is written for education experts of all roles and backgrounds, so some opportunities might not feel like the right fit for what you, specifically, are trying to do. That's OK. If a particular engagement or strategy doesn't fit your goals, then I'm not suggesting you do it. I encourage you to pick and pursue what's right for you.

FIND YOUR MESSAGE

Sharing your expertise with the world is easier when you have a strong message to share. Before you elaborate on your ideas, identify your core message. Heath and Heath (2008) found that a concept is more memorable when it is simple and has been stripped down to its core, making the message as compact as possible. Identifying your primary message will help you ensure it stands out in all your communications.

If you have a few messages (if you research different areas or practice different teaching specialties, for example), you might have a different message for each book segment or each hour in a course you teach, or for different articles you write. For this chapter's exercises, think of your message as the main piece of news you want to share with the world, such as the main thing you'd want to get across (in the interest of helping students) if you were interviewed in a 30-second radio clip or had a chance to make a quick impression on educators.

For example, in the early days of an educational technology company called Illuminate Education, our message centered on promoting student and educator success. Thus, when I planned our first conferences, I scheduled them at Soka

University (which is known for its philanthropy), so registration funds went back to helping students instead of conference centers. Instead of topping table centers with flower arrangements, the "decorations" were backpacks stuffed with school supplies so educator attendees could later give them to students in need. Rather than intangible conference themes like "Help Kids Succeed", each theme was a quote meant to inspire benevolent efforts, like Margaret Mead's "Never doubt that a small group of thoughtful, committed, citizens can change the world. Indeed, it is the only thing that ever has" (Keys, 1982, p. 79). All of these decisions tied in with our message (promote student and educator success), because our message touched all our actions, choices, and communications, just as your message should guide you.

Your message can be an important lesson or idea you wish to share with others, or even just an area of work within which you have expertise to offer. Here are some sample messages:

- Student teachers can make experienced teachers' jobs easier.
- The [Name of Program] is boosting the achievement of previously-disengaged students.
- Community centers should be persuaded to provide free tutorial services to students.

Notice the above messages are simple. The education expert sharing one of these ideas likely has many ideas related to it, and many important aspects of the idea to share. However, a long paragraph or list (not to mention a multi-page discourse) conveying the idea would not be neatly packaged to pass to someone else.

Imagine we are playing the telephone game, where someone whispers a message in someone's ear, who then whispers the same message in the next person's ear, and so on, until we all get to hear what the last person in line heard whispered. If the message were, "I'm on fire," that message would likely pass perfectly to the last person unchanged. However, if the message were, "My pant leg came into contact with a bonfire, and now the flames have consumed my pants and are burning me," the message would likely morph in ways its originator can't control.

The shorter and less convoluted your message, the better. Whittle your ideas down to their essence. When considering what your message might be, draw inspiration from any of the following:

- A powerful strategy or solution you employ in your classroom, school, district, academy trust, or organization (such as a way you offer rigor to English learners, or how you get the community actively involved in the school).
- A major accomplishment (such as cutting your school's or school district's suspensions by 50%).

- A new movement you are part of (such as the student entrepreneurship movement).
- A new technology or tool you incorporate into your practice (such as virtual reality).
- A unique perspective you have (for example, if you're a new teacher, or have just moved from the secondary level to the primary level).
- Whatever your colleagues ask (or should ask) for your help concerning.
- A problem you're trying to solve (such as children of color being underrepresented in college preparatory courses).
- A cause about which you're passionate (such as getting more girls involved in computer programming).
- Research findings from a study you conducted or were part of.
- A special collaboration you're part of.
- A unique population you work with.
- A university think tank you're part of.

Whatever your message, it should be something about which you feel passion. If you don't feel passion for what you have to share, it is unlikely others will. Finding and maintaining that passion is easier when you know the answers to the questions in Exercise 1.1, so spend some time thinking about (and then writing) the answers.

You might have more than one message, or you might tweak your message for different audiences. For now, pick one message and your most typical audience to complete Exercise 1.1. This will help you get to know your main message and its merits. As you share your message with others, let it evolve based on what resonates with people. One reason for *The Daily Show*'s success is that co-creator Lizz Winstead tweets possible jokes on Twitter and posts longer bits on Facebook, then sees which ones get a lot of likes (Grant, 2016). As you share your message widely, pay attention to what phrasing and context seems to work best. Likewise, your message will likely evolve over time as awareness of your message evolves in the field, media, and public over time.

EXERCISE 1.1: MESSAGE

1. **Start thinking about your message in generalities.**
   Some words or phrases that might relate to my message are ...

2. **What might your message be?**
   A single message I have to share is ...

3. **What is so special about your message?** It can help to consider how your work is unique or addresses something traditionally overlooked. My message is special because ...

4. **Why should people care about your message?** It can help to consider how your work can have a massive impact or offer important benefits.
People should care about my message because ...

5. **How will people be able to apply what you share?** Messages become more powerful when benefits can be replicated.
People will be able to apply what I share by ...

Note your message might be the same as others'. For example, maybe you're part of a non-profit that unites you and your colleagues behind a shared message.

Sharing the same message as others is fine. In fact, people's acceptance of new messages improves when they hear the same message at different times and in different ways. Charles Darwin sat on his theory of natural selection for two decades, not publishing for fear of backlash, before Alfred Wallace shared his similar discoveries with Darwin. They published both of their papers together in 1858, and each naturalist's ideas bolstered acceptance of the other's to where the theory of evolution by natural selection became widely accepted. We should treat our field as a collaboration rather than a competition; touting the same message as others does nothing to hurt our value to students.

CRAFT YOUR PITCH

Sharing your message with the world is easier when you have narrowed it down to one sentence that both:

- summarizes your message; and
- communicates its merit.

You might think of this as your *elevator pitch*, meaning: If you had someone's attention for the span of an elevator ride, how would you get that person to believe in your concept?

Here is a sample pitch based on a sample message provided in the previous section:

- Veteran teachers' job satisfaction quadruples when they get three months of student teachers' help.

As with your message, you might opt to develop different pitches for different audiences. Reflect on your message from Exercise 1.1. Then draft and shape your pitch in Exercise 1.2 until you have a concise, compelling sentence.

EXERCISE 1.2: PITCH

1. What is your "elevator pitch" that summarizes your message and its merit? Rework it until each word has maximum impact and superfluous words are absent.

   Draft 1:

   Draft 2:

   Draft 3:

If your pitch doesn't make you want to jump onto a soapbox and share it with the world, keep reworking your pitch until it sounds stronger. If you still feel underwhelmed, return to this book's "Find Your Message" section to consider a different starting point. This task might even inspire you to try some new things in your classroom, school(s), or study.

Your *message* will remain the heart of what you want to share (for example, upon completing a speech or publication you'll think, "I hope I got my message across"). Your *pitch* serves as the way you'll communicate your message when you have limited time or space, with the hope this leads to a chance to share more (you'll think, "Since I only have this person's attention for seconds right now, I'll share my pitch).

CRAFT TALKING POINTS

As you successfully share your pitch, you will earn the luxury of saying more (such as when a journalist likes your pitch and wants to hear details, or when a presentation proposal leads to giving a speech, or when your article proposal is accepted). At those points you'll want to be ready with two to eight key talking points that support your message. Just as you did with your message and pitch, strip these points down to the key information you need to get across.

Assign a general rank to your points (maybe it's most important to share points 1–3, and to share points 4–6 if time or space allows). Sometimes this rank will depend on your audience (for example, I share points 1–3 when I speak to parents, whereas I share points 1, 2, and 4 when I speak to policymakers).

You might already have talking points on hand, or you might jump straight into opportunities covered later in this book (such as speeches or articles) and glean talking points from the work you develop then. Either way, Exercise 1.3 can help you keep a list of talking points close at hand. As you write numerous works, deliver numerous speeches, get interviewed in numerous broadcasts, and more, you will apply these talking points in different ways to sway different audiences.

EXERCISE 1.3: TALKING POINTS

What are key points you will communicate with your message or pitch? Write them in order of importance or else renumber them after you write them.

1.

2.

3.

4.

5.

6.

CONSIDER PACKAGING

For the 2016 U.S. presidential election, former Secretary of State Hillary Clinton's slogan was "I'm with Her," and President Donald Trump's slogan was "Make America Great Again." Both candidates had bumper stickers, signage, commercials, many appearances, and more to spread these slogans. A phrase just as memorable at the time, however, came from First Lady Michelle Obama in a single speech at the 2016 Democratic National Convention. She talked about raising her daughters to not stoop to the level of a bully, including any public figure who uses hateful language. After leading up to the moment with rich storytelling, Obama shared her family's now-famous motto, which is, "When they go low, we go high." Though also used for her family, this aphorism perfectly captured what Obama was implying about the presidential candidates (one going low and one going high in the moral sense), and reporters continued to reference this unforgettable phrase following the speech. Obama didn't need bumper stickers, signage, commercials, or frequent appearances to spread her "slogan"; rather, the statement was so perfect that it spread all on its own and might have helped Clinton win the popular vote. Two years later I even heard the aphorism used in an episode of *Will & Grace*.

We often see concepts packaged in creative ways when remembering them means life or death. We know to "stop, drop, and roll" if we catch fire, without having to remember a full essay on what to do in that emergency. We merely have to remember the acronym CAB to recall the order in which to perform cardiopulmonary resuscitation (CPR) steps: compressions, airway, and breathing.

Just reading a list of talking points will do little to move an audience. The way you put together and present your ideas will determine whether or not they engage listeners and readers, whether or not they are memorable, and whether or not the ideas spread from one person to another to increase their benefit to students. This book's "Writing" and "Speaking" chapters cover many ways to effectively share your ideas. However, as you apply those chapters' strategies, it can also help to neatly package your message within a term, image, classification, or description.

Consider whether one of this section's packaging approaches will help you communicate an idea as you pursue speaking and writing. We'll look at ways other education experts have packaged their discoveries to help them resonate with people and spread (approaches and examples to follow). If none of these are appropriate for communicating your ideas, that's fine. Packaging is simply an option to consider.

TERMINOLOGY

The field of education is notorious for embracing new terminology, often when new terms are unnecessary. Giving an old movement a novel name as if it is new or giving a strategy a confusing name when a single verb or noun could have captured it well, are undesirable pet peeves in the industry and a disservice to the concept you want to teach.

The time for selecting a term to describe something comes under the following circumstances:

- Your concept is new or complicated (such as a multi-step process or a specific combination of factors).
- Your concept has not been captured with a simple phrase or term before.

In the above cases, finding a term that gets to the heart of a concept and clearly evokes the concept's meaning (for example, by bringing an image to mind for those who hear the term) can assist understanding, memorability, and communication. For example, FrameWorks Institute has helped nonprofits inform public opinion and move important issues through Congress by crafting buzzwords that clarify messages, such as coining the term "toxic stress" to communicate how trauma and volatility disrupt a child's mental development (Joslyn, 2016).

Consider how carefully selected terms make these concepts easier to capture and communicate:

- Imagine if Robert Havinghurst had regularly used the phrase "when an educator can intervene to build upon a situation at hand in a way that leads to reflection and learning" to summarize his concept and had never, instead, simply used the term "teachable moment".
- Imagine if Carol Dweck had regularly used the phrase "belief that one can acquire any ability with enough effort and study" to summarize her concept and had never, instead, simply used the term "growth mindset".

17

- Imagine if P. David Pearson and Margaret Gallagher had regularly used the phrase "the pedagogy behind transferring the learning responsibility from the teacher to the increasingly independent learner" to summarize their concept and had never, instead, simply used the term "gradual release of responsibility".

You are likely familiar with what someone means when he says, "teachable moment," "growth mindset," or "gradual release of responsibility," as well as countless other terms used in our field. These terms evoke the heart of each concept in a succinct way that is easy to communicate to others. This helps these concepts to spread, which helps more people adopt your concept to help learners. You'll still want to explain terminology you use, but your audience will walk away with a succinct way (through this neatly packaged term) to call to mind all that you've taught them.

Note some terms survive because the movements they describe are major, historical, or rich in controversy, and thus spread as "hot topics", but the terms themselves tell us nothing of what they describe. For example, *affirmative action* (U.S. term) and *positive action* (U.K. term) are weak terms that would have been easily forgotten if they hadn't described a major proposal. Think about it: If you hadn't learned those terms' meaning, you'd have no idea what kind of action they described. The term affirmative action was pulled from executive orders signed by John F. Kennedy and Lyndon B. Johnson and lacked the design considerations that go into a term meant to stand alone. Any term you design to spread should be well thought out and reveal something about what it describes.

IMAGES

The visual cortex in the back of the brain is extremely fast and efficient, whereas cognition (handled primarily by the cerebral cortex in the brain's front) is much slower and not as efficient; because of this, visualizing information takes fuller advantage of the brain's abilities (Few, 2014). In a Stanford University study on cognitive methods for information visualization, Kessel (2008) found visualizing information enhanced cognition, schematized and reduced complexity, assisted problem solving, enhanced memory, and facilitated discovery, but only if the visualizations were applied effectively.

TECH TIP

If you use Microsoft Word or PowerPoint, use the SmartArt function (versions differ, but you can typically click "Insert" and then "SmartArt") to see the multitude of arrangements available to express your ideas.

Figure 1.2 Maslow's Hierarchy of Needs

This section of the book concerns a single image, such as a graphic organizer, that neatly packages your entire concept (as opposed to the multiple images used in slides to communicate various talking points). Some education experts are known largely by the images packaging their core findings.

For his studies and books on Visible Learning, John Hattie (2009, 2015) synthesized an increasing number of meta-analyses (culminating in 1,200) relating to influences on student achievement. One could dig through these comprehensive texts and make notes concerning the 195 interventions and the extent to which they each impact student learning. However, Hattie's ranking of these interventions, sorting them by effect size, and displaying the interventions in a single bar graph offered an easy way for readers to instantly understand which types of attempts to improve student achievement held the most potential. Even critics can easily communicate their suggested revisions using this single graphical image to frame the discussion.

Hattie's phrasing also helps here. When people hear the term "Visible Learning," they inevitably think of this ranked display that helps make learning visible. It's a phrase and visual that work well together, and the pairing is far more powerful than the text would be if it lacked these elements.

For Abraham Maslow's (1943) Hierarchy of Needs, the mere description of human motivation patterns was not as neatly packaged as the pyramid that has been used to portray the human needs' hierarchy (see Figure 1.2). Even though experts have since suggested changes to Maslow's hierarchy (Heath & Heath, 2008; Villarica, 2011), they can easily communicate their revisions by applying them to this visual construct (such as by redrawing the pyramid levels as overlapping waves, or by renaming the pyramid levels). We remember the needs within a hierarchy because the visual arrangement embeds itself in our memories, in line with Kessel's findings. The pyramid visual makes the entirety of Maslow's concept easier to understand, easier to remember, and easier to share with others.

CLASSIFICATION

Simplifying ideas into a list or hierarchy, or further arranging the ideas into groups, is a useful way to communicate a large amount of information in an easy-to-process way (the Microsoft Word SmartArt tool can help here, as well). The Hattie and Maslow examples described previously also involve classification.

One of the most well-known classifications in the field is a taxonomy of educational objectives developed by Benjamin Bloom (1956) and colleagues, commonly known as Bloom's Taxonomy. Despite its merit, Bloom's Taxonomy would hardly have made such a strong mark on students if it hadn't been packaged so neatly (for example, if it had remained solely in academic speak). Consider how the following elements have assisted the spreading of Bloom's ideas:

- The taxonomy fits on a single page, making it an inviting read and easy to hand to someone.
- Teachers and other educators can quickly and easily understand the taxonomy's nature and recognize how to apply it for improved instruction.
- Most parents can understand the taxonomy's basics, and the document can easily be translated into various home languages (even crude translations accurately convey most of what Bloom created).
- Academics can easily communicate their criticisms or revisions in simple terms (for example, by swapping "Synthesize" with "Evaluate"), which also spread easily.

Those wanting to know more about the taxonomy have plenty of academic discourse available to inform them, but they are *drawn in* to read more because they have a tool that classifies the ideas so clearly.

In the field of education, we often see classifications in the form of "standards". Examples include the Common Core State Standards (CCSS) and New Teacher Center's (NTC's) Teacher Induction Program Standards (TIPS), though examples abound.

When I conducted one of my studies on how to best communicate data to educators, the "research paper" was so big it was published as a book. If I wanted all education data providers and educator leaders to follow these standards, I could not just sit back and expect them all to read the 50,000 words within the book *Standards for Reporting Data to Educators: What Educational Leaders Should Know and Demand* (Rankin, 2016). I thus created a packet with eight pages of standards (see www.jennyrankin.com/s/OTCDStandards.pdf) data providers and communicators can follow to make data easy to use. Though the book can be read to better understand the standards and the research behind them, the packet can function well on its own as a checklist of best practices to follow when displaying or communicating data to educators or others. Since most of the book's readers are researchers and educators, the standards also give these readers something to hand to edtech vendors who create many of the data tools educators use, as these vendors are less likely to read the research-heavy book.

When you need to communicate a long list of best practices or other information, standards and other classifying formats allow you to convey the meat of your ideas without losing much detail. The grouping also gives readers a straightforward framework to understand how the ideas relate and differ. Furthermore, if you can rid your standards of jargon or at least define any field-specific terms used, then you can expand the variety of audiences that can understand and use your ideas.

DESCRIPTIONS

Anecdotes, analogies, metaphors, and other literary constructs hold lots of potential to make concepts resonate with audiences. Such words can evoke associations and emotional responses that make ideas more memorable, as long as the description is highly appropriate to the concepts you seek to communicate. For example, an anecdote used to introduce a research question enhances memorability, unless it is too unrelated to the paper's actual topic, in which case the reader can struggle to recall what the anecdote related to, even though he recalls the anecdote well (Madan, 2015).

I research, write, and talk about the need to better display data for educators so they can use the data more easily and appropriately. Yet that idea (and the best practices that go with it) might not resonate strongly or memorably with readers. Consider the following less-than-striking delivery of this idea:

> When student data is displayed better, educators are able to better understand and use the data. In a study of more than 300 studies and texts from experts in related fields, best practices for the reporting of student data were identified. These best practices were synthesized as a set of 60 standards to which education data reports (such as a graph of student attendance) can adhere. These 60 standards call for:
>
> - better **labeling** on data reports (such as annotations that succinctly explain the data within the report and warn of common misunderstandings);
> - accompanying data with **supplemental documentation** (such as reference guides that offer details about the reported data and illustrate what educators should look for in data displays);
> - access to an online **help system** (with easy-to-follow lessons that help educators access and interpret data);
> - better **display** (such as clearer data visualization, and display formats that encourage proper interpretation); and
> - effective **content** (offering educators the exact data they need, without being overwhelming, in a timely fashion).

The above explanation is informative, yet dry and forgettable. I solve this by explaining these same best practices in conjunction with the "over-the-counter" concept that inspired my research. Imagine if the above text were replaced by the following analogy:

> You would never take flu medicine from a container merely reading, "Flu," with no indication of how to best use the contents. You'd be left to wonder, "How many pills should I take and when? Of what possible side effects and dangers should I be warned? What kind of flu does this treat?" Such a lack of support from the product would be dangerous, and thus we don't see unmarked medicine containers on drugstore shelves.
>
> Rather, you're able to use over-the-counter medicine properly on your own because a **label** tells you exactly what you need to know. If you require further explanation, you can reference **supplemental documentation** tucked inside the box, or search online for a **help system** like www.WebMD.com. You can also guess a product's nature from its packaging and **display** (for example, a colorful label with a crayon drawing of a smiling child indicates medicine appropriate for children to take, and the label would be grossly misleading if this product was only for adults). Also key to the medicine's success is its appropriate **contents** (your flu symptoms would not get better if the medicine only contained sugar and food coloring, or if a year had passed since the expiration date).
>
> Just like medicine, data can help or hurt lives — depending on the efficacy of its use. Yet most data reports given to educators lack embedded supports to make it easy to understand and use the data. These inadequate data reports are dangerous to student lives, just as unmarked medicine containers would be. Imagine if we made data "over-the-counter" for educators using data to inform decisions that impact students. The 60 research-based best practices known as Over-the-Counter Data Standards improve student data reports with:
>
> - **labeling** that explains the data's implications;
> - **supplemental documentation** that walks educators through the use of each data report;
> - an online **help system** with lessons on interpreting data;
> - effective **display** (such as data visualization that encourages proper interpretation); and
> - appropriate **content** (that helps data reports do what they're meant to do).
>
> This way educators can use the data properly and easily, without a statistician needing to be present…just as you don't need a physician standing beside you when you take over-the-counter medicine.

The above comparison helps the audience recognize how ridiculous and dangerous it would be to give educators data without over-the-counter supports.

This helps the audience understand the importance of the standards and the research behind them. Organizing the best practices (in this case the study findings) within succinct standards makes the knowledge accessible, easy to share, and easy to apply. Calling them Over-the-Counter Data Standards helps the audience remember the over-the-counter concept (and — with it — the importance of the standards) without having to provide this lengthy description every time.

The description is also efficient in that it taps into people's preexisting knowledge (of what it means to be over-the-counter), so less description is needed. When it comes to selecting words while trying to remain succinct, Heath and Heath (2008) suggest the strategy of using a concept people already know: "You tap the existing memory terrain of your audience. You use what's already there" (p. 52). For example, they could describe the various attributes of a pomelo to help you understand what a pomelo is, or they could instead tell you a pomelo is like a supersized grapefruit. The latter description builds on what you already know and is far more potent, just as "horseless carriage" helped people understand what an automobile was in the late nineteenth century.

YOUR TURN

Your pitched concept might be served by a term, image, classification, or figurative description. Consider how you might package your concepts to make them digestible and memorable. What language will make your ideas easy to remember and evoke their importance? Complete Exercise 1.4 to play with some ideas.

Remember: the whole purpose of packaging is to make it *easier* for people to understand and spread your concept to help students. Avoid packaging that makes things impossible to remember. If you expect people to remember "The 16 A's of Teaching: acceptance, authenticity, assessment, etc." you will be let down. That package is too long, too complicated, and with too many possible variations.

EXERCISE 1.4: PACKAGING

It could be that your concept requires no special packaging, so don't feel forced into using whatever you develop in this exercise. However, it is worth playing around with some ideas to see if clever packaging can help your concept spread (so more students are helped by it).

1. **Reflect on your pitch from Exercise 1.2 and the concept you are hoping to spread.** Which of the following are likely to be your concept's biggest challenges?
   ❏ Being memorable
   ❏ Being easy to understand
   ❏ Being communicable (easy for people to share with others)

> Effective packaging aims to help with all of the above challenges. Keep these in mind as you complete the rest of this exercise.
>
> 2. **Write some terms that succinctly capture your concept.** Read the "Terms" subsection of this chapter for assistance (and to determine if a term is recommended).
>
> 3. **Draw an image or begin a classification that could make your concept clear.** Read the "Images" and "Classification" subsections of this chapter for assistance.
>
> 4. **Write a description or phrase that could cleverly capture your concept.** Read the "Description" subsection of this chapter for assistance.
>
> Consider if using one of the above packaging ideas will help your ideas impact the field. If so, place a star next to it and use it as you apply this book's concepts.

In the "Writing" and "Speaking" parts of this book you will learn much more about making your concept attention-grabbing, interesting, and memorable. However, all sharing endeavors should be built around what you learned in this chapter.

- Remember your primary message.
- Deliver your message in a concrete pitch when you have only a moment to sway someone.
- Share compelling talking points when you have the space or time to drive your message home.
- Cleverly package your whole message or key findings if it will help your ideas resonate and spread.

Keep this core information ready. It will give you a solid starting point for any time or way you seek to share your expertise.

REFERENCES

Badgett, M. V. L. (2016). *The public professor: How to use your research to change the world.* New York, NY: NYU Press.

Bloom, B. (1956). *Taxonomy of Educational Objectives: Cognitive and affective domains.* New York, NY: David McKay Company.

Elsevier. (2018). *Get noticed: Increase the impact of your research.* Retrieved from www.elsevier.com/_data/assets/pdf_file/0014/201326/GetNoticed_A4_factsheet_2017.pdf

Few, S. (2014). Data visualization for human perception. In Soegaard, Mads and Dam, Rikke Friis (Eds.), *The Encyclopedia of Human-Computer Interaction, 2nd Ed.* Aarhus,

Denmark: The Interaction Design Foundation. Retrieved from www.interaction-design.org/encyclopedia/data_visualization_for_human_perception.html

Gladwell, M. (2000). *The tipping point: How little things can make a big difference.* London, United Kingdom: Abacus.

Grant, A. (2016). *Originals: How non-conformists move the world.* New York, NY: Penguin Books.

Hattie, J. (2009). *Visible learning: A synthesis of over 800 meta-analyses relating to achievement.* New York, NY: Routledge.

Hattie, J. (2015). The applicability of Visible Learning to higher education. *Scholarship of Teaching and Learning in Psychology*, *1*(1), 79–91. doi:10.1037/stl0000021

Heath, C., & Heath, D. (2008). *Made to stick: Why some ideas survive and others die.* New York, NY: Random House.

Joslyn, H. (2016). Words that change minds. *Chronicle of Philanthropy*, *2016*(9), 20–24. Retrieved from www.frameworksinstitute.org/assets/files/PDF/chroniclephilanthropy_wordsthatchangeminds_2016.pdf

Keys, D. (1982). *Earth at Omega: Passage to planetization.* Boston, MA: Branden Press.

Keller, G., & Papasan, (2013). *The ONE thing: The surprisingly simple truth behind extraordinary results.* Austin, TX: Bard Press.

Kessell, A. M. (2008). *Cognitive methods for information visualization: Linear and cyclical events* (Doctoral dissertation). Retrieved from ProQuest Dissertations and Theses. (3313597)

Madan, C. R. (2015). Every scientist is a memory researcher: Suggestions for making research more memorable. *F1000Research 2015, 4*(19). doi:10.12688/f1000research.6053.1

Maslow, A. H. (1943). A theory of human motivation. *Psychological Review*, *50*(4), 370–396.

Rankin, J. G. (2016). *Standards for reporting data to educators: What educational leaders should know and demand.* New York, NY: Routledge/Taylor & Francis.

Rankin, J. (2018, April 1). Educators battle discrimination in the field. *Psychology Today.* Retrieved from www.psychologytoday.com/us/blog/much-more-common-core/201804/educators-battle-discrimination-in-the-field

Rees, M. (2017, December 6). Is there a limit to scientific understanding? We can measure black holes, but we still can't cure the common cold. *The Atlantic.* Retrieved from https://aeon.co/ideas/black-holes-are-simpler-than-forests-and-science-has-its-limits

Rees, S. (2018, February 21). Make room for young analysts in your district's team. *School Wise Press.* Retrieved from www.schoolwisepress.com/blog/make-room-for-young-analysts-in-your-districts-team

Vaidyanathan, R. (2016, January 26). Before Hillary Clinton, there was Shirley Chisholm. *BBC News.* Retrieved from https://www.bbc.com/news/magazine-35057641

Villarica, H. (2011, August 17). Maslow 2.0: A new and improved recipe for happiness. *The Atlantic.* Retrieved from www.theatlantic.com/health/archive/2011/08/maslow-20-a-new-and-improved-recipe-for-happiness/243486

Chapter 2

Image

If you're like me, you'd only recognize a fraction of the names on a list of the world's 100 greatest tennis players of all time. You'd know Billie Jean King and Arthur Ashe, who broke barriers; Andre Agassi, who sported a heavy metal mullet and wore acid-washed jean shorts on the court; Serena and Venus Williams, who wear bold fashions and manicures, and sometimes purple hair; Anna Kournikova, who starred in her boyfriend Enrique Iglesias' music video; and John McEnroe with his infamous tantrums. These seven aren't the very top players, but their image (based on breaking barriers, personality, style, or other markers unrelated to their skill with a tennis racquet) is what makes them so memorable. Agassi even said in a 1989 commercial, "Image is everything."

Image might not be *everything*, but it counts for a lot if you aim to lodge yourself in people's minds. I'm not suggesting you wear acid-washed jeans and a mullet to your next education conference (though you would be memorable). I'm suggesting you find ways for your online, on-paper, and in-person profile to help you be perceived and remembered as a go-to expert in your specialty area.

Before you reach for the opportunities discussed in this book, you'll want to have some tools ready that will highlight your expertise and contribute to your polished, professional image. For example, if you submit an article for an education publication or apply to give a TED Talk, those contemplating your acceptance will Google you to get a sense of your credibility, and they will want to see a bio, resume, or CV that communicates your experience on the subject.

Some readers will want to develop all the tools discussed in this chapter, whereas others might only want a bio or a single social media account. It is fine to start with only those tools you know to be vital to your immediate goals. You can always build more of these tools later as you see fit. Knowing this chapter can be used with such flexibility should prevent you from feeling bogged down with "too much preparation", since it is important to ultimately move on to the prospects discussed in subsequent chapters. Just remember that a more polished presence online and on paper can significantly boost efforts to share your expertise.

BIO

You will use a bio extensively when applying this book's strategies. A professional bio "is the short summary of relevant background you need to introduce yourself in a variety of settings" (Jacobs, 2014 p. 1). According to brand and marketing strategist Alex Honeysett (2017), it is the most important text you will ever write concerning yourself. Your bio, if well crafted, can open a lot of doors for you.

SAMPLE BIOS

Download the "Sample Bios" eResource to see examples of a single bio written for four different length requirements. See the "eResources" section near the start of this book for details. Note how the most impressive and pertinent accomplishments show up in all four examples. Common bio details include:

- Full Name (including post-nominal letters, such as PhD)
- Job Title
- Place of Employment
- Past Roles of Note
- Major Awards and Honors
- Website (leading the reader to your online resume or CV)

When you apply for different opportunities, you will be asked for bios of different lengths. Sometimes a word count will be established (such as when an online submission form's field only allows for 200 words), and sometimes you will need to judge what is appropriate (such as when your online article is followed by an author bio that must range from 20 to 40 words in length).

TIME-SAVING TIP

As you adjust your bio for different lengths and purposes over time, save all your bios in a single place, ordered by word count. This will save you time when you pull bios to meet different needs in the future

What you include in your bio (see the "Sample Bios" text box for details) will be shaped by how many words you are allotted, but longer is not always better. Your bio should drive home who you are and why someone should pay attention to you … and thus what you share. Complete Exercise 2.1 to play with some ideas.

SCRAPPY TIP

Tailor your bio to the environment where it appears. For example, when I wrote *First Aid for Teacher Burnout: How You Can Find Peace and Success* (2017), my back-of-book bio mentions I won a Teacher of the Year award, which would appeal to my audience of teachers. However, when I wrote *Designing Data Reports that Work: A Guide for Creating Data Systems in Schools and Districts* (2016), I instead used this space to note my previous role as chief education and research officer of an educational technology data systems company, which would appeal more to my audience of edtech and data specialists.

EXERCISE 2.1: BIO

1. List 4-8 key details (such as a specific award you won) that should appear in your own bio for a use of your choosing (such as at the end of a magazine article you wrote).

2. Craft a short bio in which you include the above details.

RESUME AND CV

Sharing your expertise through new outlets requires first establishing your credibility. It's thus important to polish your resume or CV and keep it current with new accomplishments.

A solid resume is needed when applying for a job in a primary or secondary school, school district, or academic trust. There are many great books and online sources that can guide you through resume development.

However, in the field of education , an impressive curriculum vitae (CV) tends to open more doors for you than a simple resume will. In some countries, *CV* means the same thing as resume. In other countries, *CV* describes a much more detailed document outlining your academic and professional history but also your publications, presentations, research, awards, honors, grants, fellowships, and other achievements of note. This book uses the term in the latter sense.

TIME-SAVING TIP

Even if you will not need a CV to show others, maintaining a CV for your own purposes will be a huge time saver. You can just electronically copy and paste information from its various sections whenever providing such information is required to secure an opportunity. For example, when a conference organizer wants you to list all your previous speaking engagements before she books you for a keynote, you will not have to dig through old files to find each date, location, session title, etc. It is much easier to simply save these details on a CV as each new accomplishment occurs.

I maintain a longer-than-recommended CV (see www.JennyRankin.com/bio) because I often use it to electronically copy and paste requested information (as captured in the "Time-Saving Tip" text box), and I can easily remove sections if necessary before submitting the CV to someone in static form. Choosing your own CV's length will also be an act of weighing pros and cons to determine what best suits your needs.

SCRAPPY TIP

If you are actively on course to complete an achievement (such as earning your doctorate), it is ethical and advisable to mention this. For example, you could list your PhD or EdD in the Education section of your CV with its expected completion date (just make sure its "To Be Completed" nature is clear, and that you are honest and realistic about the expected date).

I put together my CV for the first time (having previously always just used a resume) when I started looking for a university teaching job. I was surprised to find it was just as useful for non-university contacts. So often when I'm communicating with someone about my research or a collaboration, I give her the link to my CV.

Having the CV helps establish my credibility. For example, if I tell someone about myself I only communicate a few key things, but it's more powerful to see all of a person's accomplishments in one place: in the CV.

CV TEMPLATE

Download the "CV Template" eResource for a Word document which you can use to build your own CV. See the "eResources" section near the start of this book for details on accessing and using the template. Common CV segments include:

- Bio (if your CV gets large and unruly, add this to the beginning of your CV so your proudest moments stand out)
- Employment
- Education
- Awards and Honors (if you have many honors within a specific category – for example, grants – consider making that its own segment)
- Volunteering
- Publications
- Media Interviews
- Presentations and Seminars
- Research
- Professional Affiliations and Memberships
- Technical Proficiencies (for those with edtech specialization)
- Social Media
- Resume (to include a link to your resume, if you also maintain one)

When I first looked at a sample CV, I was mortified by how few awards, publications, etc. I had to include on my CV at the time, even after a long career as a primary and secondary school educator. However, using the strategies shared elsewhere in this book, my CV looked great within its first year. If you feel disheartened by your achievements when crafting your first CV draft, know that this book's tips will lead you to all sorts of accomplishments in a matter of weeks or months, depending on your efforts. Complete Exercise 2.2 to start building your own CV if you don't yet have one.

EXERCISE 2.2: CV

1. Preplan your CV. Referring to the CV Template text box, list the categories that will make strong segments on your CV (for example, if you have won many impressive awards, include the "Awards" category). When you start putting together your CV, start with these categories.

2. Referring to the CV Template text box, list the categories within which you have few or no accomplishments. As you pursue the opportunities featured in this book, try improving some of these areas first.

3. Using the "CV Template" eResource (or another tool), start building your own CV. Your CV is meant to make you look your best, so modify it to suit your expertise. For example:

   - If your education is more impressive than your employment history, put the "Education" section before the "Employment" section.
   - If you don't have a research background and haven't volunteered, take out the "Research" and "Volunteering" sections.

   ...and so on. When you have a website (which will be discussed later), post your CV online.

PERSONAL BRANDING

When you think of the company Apple, you might imagine their products (such as a MacBook or an iPhone) or their logo (an apple), but its "brand" relates to the feelings and impressions you associate with Apple. Common associations with Apple's brand include cutting-edge technology, creativity, underdog, streamlined design, and thinking differently. These associations are proliferated by what Apple does (its products satisfy people's need for streamlined, effective technology), what others write and say about Apple (which relates to what Apple does), and what Apple tells us about Apple (for example, the impression its advertising leaves).

Personal branding is similar to branding, except you are proliferating a mental association with a person (you) rather than a product or company. For educators, your personal brand is the essence of what you offer your profession and students. As you pursue opportunities to spread your knowledge, efforts to communicate a

> ### DEFINITION OF PERSONAL BRANDING
>
> Personal branding is essentially what you are known for and what people seek you out for (Tannahill-Moran, 2016, p. 1)

clear personal brand will help others understand what you can offer them. For example, no one will ask you to speak at a differentiation symposium if your expertise in differentiation, your professionalism, and your polished communication are not known to people. Your website, conduct, social media sites, handouts, literature, logo, slides – anything you put out into the world – can communicate these kinds of qualities as your brand.

Branding is important to helping you stand out to successfully share your ideas (Arruda, 2016), yet a strong personal brand can also limit you to whatever niche you brand yourself as having (Hartley, 2016). How specific a brand you establish will depend on how sure you are that your specialties will never change.

Determining this is no easy task. I say this as someone whose first website was www.OverTheCounterData.com, which was one of my focus areas as an educator and in my first studies and books. Though that concept of sharing education data effectively relates to this book's concept of sharing education research and strategies effectively, the website was very data-specific.

At the time I thought this emphasis would never change, but it did. My expertise expanded to encompass additional topics unrelated to data. Eek! I then had to change my web address, social media account names, details on repeatedly used slides and handouts, business cards, and more to reflect my name instead of a single one of my specialties. This took time away from my work and risked confusing my contacts.

To avoid a similar mistake, err on the side of caution. If you have a long career devoted to special education, opened a center for students with disabilities, and are certain that will remain your specialty, you can establish that clearly (such as with a web domain that bears your center's name). However, if you are passionate about your makerspace specialization right now, but you've always been a Renaissance woman with varied interests, proceed as if your expertise will fundamentally change someday to something that might not even be on your radar right now. In this case (and in most cases), I recommend using a website domain and social media account names that simply reflect your name (instead of a topic) and possibly your doctorate. Use a design style that communicates a polished presence (and anything else that matches you as a person), and nods to your current topic without limiting you to it. For example, my logo at www.JennyRankin.com alludes to a bar graph (as my initial expertise I shared with the world was how to best display data for educators), but also suits my additional areas of expertise (the logo hints at growth, since my other niches relate to helping students and educators be their best). Let your business card reflect your specialty, but limit your order so future cards can reflect a change in focus.

Of course, if you start a center, organization, education consulting company, or other movement, you can get highly specific branding for a website, social media accounts, and other materials devoted solely to that endeavor. Maintaining two "identities" (that of you as a person and that of your endeavor, such as through different websites and social media accounts) can be taxing, so this arrangement works best if more than one person is involved in the movement. This chapter and book applies to the marketing and spreading of your endeavor, just as it applies to sharing your ideas as an individual person, but I suggest looking at the "Branding for a Movement" text box for additional considerations.

BRANDING FOR A MOVEMENT

There are additional branding considerations if you seek to brand a center, organization, company, or other movement (in other words, something other than a person):

- Consider if you want your brand to also appeal to fields outside of education, for example, business or science. If you do, select terms for the organization name and literature that will be as easily understandable in those fields as they are in the education sector.
- Be sure any terms you use ("PD", for example) will still be in use, current, and recognizable 10 years from now, given how fickle education terms and movements can be.
- If picking a concept for your brand, try to find one that lends itself well to a visual. If your brand triggers an image in people's minds, this can help them understand and remember the brand. This also makes it easier to come up with a brand icon or logo.
- Conduct Google searches to be sure no one is already using that term, particularly in any trademarked or copyrighted form. This is especially true if you pick a name for your brand (rather than using your own name), like Wolpert-Gawron's "Tween Teacher". Even if you use your own name as your brand you'll want to be sure it's not already in use. If it is, consider a twist on your name or brand to avoid confusion.

Boiling yourself down to a specific concept lets people instantly understand the essence of what you're mainly all about. People are busy, particularly in the field of education, and branding's shorthand helps you to be noticed, included, and remembered. However, keep your brand open enough to evolve, such as with a web address that matches your name. Complete Exercise 2.3 to plan some aspects of your brand.

EXERCISE 2.3: PERSONAL BRAND

1. What are six words or short phrases you want people in the field to associate with your name? These traits or topics should be true to who you are. For example, don't write "good with people" if you are socially awkward. Rather, aim for a brand that reflects your best qualities.

2. Now circle the three most important associations you wrote above. Then place a star next to the single most important. As you judge importance, keep your expertise-sharing goals in mind (for example,

do you aspire to shape policy, engage in public debates, or inform educators from behind the scenes?).

3. Google "modern color schemes" to investigate possible color schemes to use for resources you'll produce in the future (such as slides, handouts, logo, etc.).

The color scheme best suited for me is (or can be found at) ...

WEBSITE

A website offers people an easy way to find you and your work in one centralized location. It also helps you establish your brand. If you are in an early stage of your career, a website can help people understand you are serious about communicating your ideas. "Crafting an online scholarly identity ... exposes you to a level of public engagement with your ideas that simply is not feasible through other modes of dissemination" (Stewart, 2016, p. 81).

You have many website and webpage options. Regardless of which you choose, the site should allow you access to personally edit and add extensive and varied content. The following guide will help you establish the best webpage for you.

GUIDE TO CREATING A WEBSITE

See the "eResources" section near the start of this book for details on accessing the "Guide to Creating a Website". Two different approaches for your web presence are detailed in the guide. Option 1 is to host your own website and Option 2 is to maintain a web*page* within an existing website, such as one hosted by your institution, organization, company, or publisher, including bio and profile pages. Think carefully about which option will work best for you. If you choose Option 1, however, you should *also* utilize Option 2 whenever the scenario is available to you. The guide offers a shortcut that makes it fast and easy to maintain multiple webpages.

IMAGES

Today's communication is largely visual, and images play an important role in branding. The more you promote your work, you'll find yourself needing a range of images, most of which you can use repeatedly. These images should fit well with your brand and with one another.

Logo

You might decide to use a logo. It's not necessary to hire a professional (or a talented student) to create one for you, as you can create one yourself. While tools like Adobe Illustrator offer limitless possibilities, there are plenty of tools that are free and don't require much tech skill. Consider tools such as the following:

- The *Insert*: *Shape*, *WordArt*, and *Text Box* tools in Microsoft Word are more robust than most people guess. I used two of these to design my logo, but I've also used Word for complex diagrams and infographics.
- Sites like www.graphicsprings.com, www.logomaker.com, and www. logomakr.com can help you create a logo.
- Infographic makers like www.canva.com, www.visme.co, www.pik-tochart.com, and www.venngage.com can be used to create logos or other branding-friendly images.
- Sites like www.bitmoji.com, www.thecartoonist.me, and www.cartoonify. de can be used to turn your portrait into a cartoon.

If you don't have a good design sense, it's especially important to get feedback from people you know who do. You should also show your potential logo to people who work in your field (and will thus be one of your target consumers) for input so you can improve your logo as necessary.

Headshot

Select a single headshot to use for everything (your website, social media sites, "about the author" section of articles, etc.). Some educators I know hired a professional for beautiful headshots. My photo of choice was snapped by my friend's father at a party.

Consider these tips for whatever photograph you select:

- A beefy border (such as the surrounding foliage in my headshot) will give you more cropping options when different sites have different proportion requirements for your headshot.
- The background should either be blank, free of distractions (for example, the foliage behind me in my headshot is blurred), or should highlight a key accomplishment. For example, some educators are able to fit in the lectern or signage of a noteworthy event at which they are speaking. As long as the photo leaves enough room to make your face clear, these images can help communicate your merit.
- Are you known for being happy and energetic, or for being serious and intense? Your headshot should reflect your nature.
- The photo should clearly look like you. It might be tempting to pick a photo taken when you were younger or fitter, or a photo in which you look stunning but not your usual self, but such images will not aid your recognition as you mingle at conferences and forge relationships.

35

Stock Photos and Illustrations

If you use stock images (such as for your website), you'll want to do so carefully, and without violating copyright. See the "Slide Images: Stock Images" section of "Chapter 7. Preparing Slides for Anywhere" for support.

SOCIAL MEDIA AND PRESENCE

Social media facilitates fast, easy, and concise communication well suited to busy educators. We are experiencing a revolution of scholarly communication through social media platforms that represents a shift toward giving research and ideas greater visibility (Sugimoto, Work, Larivière, & Haustein, 2017).

Social media provides a direct avenue to the public, where you can inform non-experts concerning education. Sixty-nine percent of Americans use social media to get news, connect with one another, and share information (Pew Research Center, 2018). Contrary to the popular belief that Millennials dominate social media, Generation X (aged 35–49) spends the most time on social media, at nearly seven hours per week, with the average hours per week spent on social media for all adults being over five hours (Casey, 2017). By joining dialogue on social media and sharing links to relevant work, you can help shape the content and tone of education news.

Education experts also reach out to students through social networks. Since 52% of Generation Z use Twitter, the American College Application Campaign (ACAC) ran a social media marketing campaign to inspire students to apply for college; within one week its #WhyApply hashtag reaped 2,367 uses and 5.3 million impressions (Shop, 2017).

SCRAPPY TIP

Right before you give a presentation (with your social media sites displayed on a slide), tweet and post a special resource or handout. Ask attendees to take out their cell phones and find your post. Many will use that moment to "follow" you online, whereas they might not have otherwise set themselves up to stay updated on your work via social media.

You don't have to be a massive organization or celebrity to reach many viewers. LinkedIn's Top Voices list of 2017, which used varied metrics to determine whose posts engaged professionals and got them talking, included an assistant professor, a director of curriculum, and a student success coach, pulled from a membership of more than 530 million members (Anders, 2017; Roth, 2017).

More examples follow of education experts significantly expanding the reach of their work through social media.

Primary and Secondary School Educators

Educators who work with children have long shared quick tips, resources, and insights on social media platforms. A survey of 1,000 school teachers' weekly social media use indicated 82% of teachers use Facebook weekly, 69% Pinterest, 49% Google+, 40% Instagram, and 32% Twitter (Devaney, 2016). These are teachers you could be reaching with your social media posts.

Sharing via social media can also lead to a strong following, where school educators can reach many peers. For example, "Cool Cat Teacher" Vicki Davis (@coolcatteacher) has 149,000 Twitter followers. Secondary educator Nicholas Provenzano (@thenerdyteacher) joined Twitter to promote his educational blog (Pannoni, 2015) and already has well over 60,000 followers. Having more followers means more people are likely to see the updates you share (tips on what works in schools, links to articles you've written or admire on best teaching practices, etc.), learn from you, and use your wisdom to help students.

On Twitter alone, 4.2 million *daily* posts (known as tweets) relate to education (Stevens, 2014). Primary and secondary educators know they can turn to social media for professional learning and collaboration, and you could use social media to reach them there. These online tools also offer educators convenient interaction with stakeholders outside of school circles.

Education Researchers

Academics are increasingly sharing and discussing research on social media platforms such as Twitter rather than in the faculty lounge (Priem, 2013). LinkedIn is used by 65% of researchers for professional purposes, and scholarly articles are mentioned on social media and other online sites once every seven seconds (Elsevier, 2018). Using social media helps researchers combat the isolation common in their field while simultaneously increasing the impact of their work (Reeve & Partridge, 2017).

"The old adage 'publish or perish' could soon go digital as 'clicks or canned'" (Brown, 2017, p. 1). Social media is changing the way academics disseminate research, and academics are expected to have a professional online presence, which is increasingly recognized in determining tenure and promotions (Espinoza Vasquez & Caicedo Bastidas, 2015; Gruzd, Staves, & Wilk, 2011). Richard Reddick (2016), Associate Professor in Educational Administration, announces his new publications through Facebook and Twitter and notes, "As a scholar wedded to seeing my research impact people in the communities that I research, it's imperative that I spread the word outside the ivy walls of academe" (p. 60).

Social media is important for authors of books, papers, or other works. "As an author, you are the face of your work, and the information you share on social media can help you gain exposure, convey crucial information in real-time, and foster genuine, direct connections with your readers" (Routledge, Taylor & Francis Group, 2017).

Value

I cannot stress enough the value of establishing a presence on social media and using it to:

- ❑ share your expertise (directing traffic to your blog posts, presentations, etc.);
- ❑ connect with others;
- ❑ learn of valuable opportunities (not to mention all of the other things you'll learn; new teaching strategies, links to newly released studies, and more are waiting for you on social media).

SCRAPPY TIP

Keep an eye out for the expertise-sharing opportunities regularly announced on social media. When I landed my lecturer gig of the Post Doc Masterclass at University of Cambridge, one of my career highlights, it was made possible by social media. I saw a Twitter post about the position, and that post linked to the class's Facebook page, where I found the University of Cambridge's application instructions.

The Basics

Even non-techies can find the standard social media tools to be easier to use than they anticipated. The following social media tools are particularly popular amongst educators and important for your branding:

- Facebook (www.facebook.com); consider adding a group to your personal website (this allows you to publicly share your professional content on the group page while keeping your Facebook page personal and private); WeChat (https://web.wechat.com) is a similar tool used widely in China.
- Google+ (plus.google.com).
- LinkedIn (www.linkedin.com); in addition to setting up your professional profile, consider creating a group devoted to your brand or topic of interest.

- Pinterest (www.pinterest.com); primary and secondary teachers use this professionally more often than other education stakeholders.
- Twitter (www.twitter.com); this is where the field of education is currently most active; Weibo (www.weibo.com) is a similar tool used widely in China.

For each tool you use, create a profile that will be easy for others to find. For example, a good Twitter handle for someone who goes by Maria Cho Patel is @MariaChoPatel.

RESOURCE TIP

These guides can help you get started with social media:

- The Educator's Guide to Social Media (www.connectsafely.org/eduguide)
- The Twitter Guide for Teachers (https://elearningindustry.com/the-twitter-guide-for-teachers)

As I write this, Twitter is currently reworking its process for verifying accounts, which displays a blue badge beside your name to indicate yours is an authentic account of someone "of public interest". This can enhance your credibility and thus improve people's acceptance of your ideas (expressed through retweeting your comment, asking to interview you, etc.). Check https://verification.twitter.com for future verification instructions.

Educator Social Networking Sites

Some social media sites are designed specifically for educators, particularly school teachers. These include:

- Administrator 2.0 (www.admin20.org)
- Classroom 2.0 (www.classroom20.com)
- EdWeb (http://home.edweb.net)
- EdModo (www.edmodo.com)
- Edutopia (www.edutopia.org)

These sites allow you to network and collaborate with other educators. Academics looking to share with primary and secondary school educators can look into having their research-based tools and articles shared on sites like these, as well.

Academic Social Networking Sites

Another form of social media is specific to scholars. Academic social networking sites (ASNSs) include:

- Academia (www.academia.edu)
- Bepress (www.bepress.com)
- Faculty Row (www.facultyrow.com)
- Mendeley (www.mendeley.com)
- ResearchGate (www.researchgate.net)
- Scholabrate (www.scholabrate.com)
- Zenodo (www.zenodo.org)

These sites allow you to network with other academics, and to discover and share new research. ASNSs improve scholarly communication, facilitate collaboration, and facilitate the development of an online academic identity (Jordan, 2014).

There is some controversy concerning these types of sites, particularly when it comes to uploading one's own research. See the "Exposure for Your Other Writing: Research Repositories" section of "Chapter 13. Multiply Your Impact" for details and determine how you want to use these tools.

Posting

Posting valuable content brings you more followers, which will cause more people to see your own work when you post about it (such as when you post a link to an article you wrote). Thus, when you read online education news and research your topics of interest online, it helps to post links to that content. Sharing links to others' work that you deem valuable is part of using your voice to better our field.

To use Twitter as an example, these guidelines can increase the visibility of your tweets and you:

- ❏ When sharing others' work, include the author's Twitter handle (example: @BillGates) and source's Twitter handle (example: @NYTimes). This often prompts that person or organization to favorite and retweet the tweet, which can bring you new followers. This encourages exposure to the work you want to share.
- ❏ Include one or two hashtags (example: #EdData) per tweet or post. Many people use hashtags to search for content, so hashtags expose people who don't know you to your posts. Tweets with at least one hashtag are retweeted 55% more often and increase post engagement by up to 100% (Cooper, 2013).
- ❏ Engage in some of the many edchats (see https://sites.google.com/site/twittereducationchats/education-chat-calendar), explained in "Chapter 10. Connecting". If the conversation fits, include a link to one of your articles or presentations as you post a related comment.

❏ Stick to professional content, as people you don't know will likely unfollow you if you clutter their news feeds with coverage of *The Real Housewives of Orange County*, photos of your meals or cats, or other subjects in which they aren't necessarily interested. In a study on educators' Twitter use, Alderton, Brunsell, and Bariexca (2011) found that 82% of the time educators chose to follow other educators or content experts when it would be meaningful to their professional needs, as opposed to non-educationally focused interests.

TECH TIP

Some social media provide data analytics. For example, if you click your profile icon in Twitter and select "Analytics" you can view "Tweet Activity" and see which of your tweets had the most views and engagements (such as retweets and link clicks). Use such information to inform how you craft future posts.

❏ Add social media icons to your website and other bio or profile webpages to give people easy access to your social media accounts. If these pages don't allow you to add icon links, you can always add a statement like "Dr. Margie Johnson can be found at www.twitter.com/MargieLJohnson3 and..." to your bio.

❏ Sync your social media accounts. For example, I've synced my social media accounts with my SquareSpace website so that whenever I post a new blog entry it automatically appears as a post on each of my social media sites.

❏ Maintain an open, positive, and constructive tone, as educators are most likely to engage with tweets that reflect these qualities (Alderton, Brunsell, & Bariexca, 2011). On that note, do not post when you are drinking alcohol or when your emotions flair.

❏ Add an image to your post when appropriate. Tweets with images get clicked 18% more, liked 89% more, and retweeted 150% more frequently (Smith, 2016).

RESOURCE TIP

Andrew Ibrahim offers free tools to help researchers create visual abstracts for their own studies and tweets (see www.surgeryredesign.com/resources).

❏ When tweeting about research, include a "visual abstract" that summarizes a study's key findings. Tweets with visual abstracts were seen by 7.7 times as many people, retweeted 8.4 times as often, and clicked (to read the paper) 2.7 times as often (Ibrahim, Lillemoe, Klingensmith, & Dimick, 2017).

As long as you don't let social media time detract from your main work, the more active you are with any social networking tool (posting quality content regularly), the better. Of those who made LinkedIn's Top Voices list of 2017, which includes an Education category, 71% published posts monthly at a minimum (four posts per month was the average) (Roth, 2017). I don't mention this to emphasize what you have to do to win that honor; rather, I mention it because of the degree to which such posting can expand your audience, allowing your wisdom to benefit more people and the students they serve:

> Compared to all members writing and sharing in 2017, the Top Voices received on average 5x more comments, 72x more likes and 7x more shares on their posts, articles and videos. Each of our Top Voices generated over 120,000 new follows this year — almost 330 new followers a day.
>
> (Roth, 232017, p. 2)

The more you post quality content bearing wisdom that can help people help students, the more followers are likely to read and learn from it, and the more likely you are to have followers who can benefit from your future shares, as well.

EMAIL SIGNATURE

Use your email account's settings to add links to your signature (text that will appear automatically at the end of every email you send). Mine looks like this (each underlined word can be clicked to acquire the item mentioned, and "TED Talk" appears in red):

EMAIL SIGNATURE

Jenny Grant Rankin, Ph.D.
Bio & CV / Twitter / TED Talk
Books

Upon breaking into the email service industry, Hotmail automatically added a short message and link to the bottom of every email its users sent anyone. Berger (2013) credits this practice with causing Hotmail to acquire 8.5 million subscribers in just over a year and then being bought by Microsoft for $400 million. In other words, people pay attention to the information at the bottom of emails and follow the links there.

REFERENCES

Alderton, E., Brunsell, E., & Bariexca, D. (2011, September). The end of isolation. *Journal of Online Learning and Teaching*, 7(3), 1–14.

Anders, G. (2017, December 12). *LinkedIn Top Voices 2017: Education*. Retrieved from www.linkedin.com/pulse/linkedin-top-voices-2017-education-george-anders

Arruda, W. (2016, April 26). Effective branding is in the details. *Forbes*. Retrieved from www.forbes.com/sites/williamarruda/2016/04/26/effective-branding-is-in-the-details/#5a54f9fd4a6a

Berger, J. (2013). *Contagious: Why things catch on*. New York, NY: Simon & Schuster.

Brown, J. L. (2017, August 1). Will 'publish or perish' become 'clicks or canned'? The rise of academic social networks. *EdSurge*. Retrieved from www.edsurge.com/news/2017-08-01-will-publish-or-perish-become-clicks-or-canned-the-rise-of-academic-social-networks

Casey, S. (2017, January 17). *2016 Nielsen Social Media Report*. Retrieved from www.nielsen.com/us/en/insights/reports/2017/2016-nielsen-social-media-report.html

Cooper, S. (2013, October 17). Big mistake: Making fun of hashtags instead of using them. *Forbes*. Retrieved from www.forbes.com/sites/stevecooper/2013/10/17/big-mistake-making-fun-of-hashtags-instead-of-using-them/#548ed65928f0

Devaney, L. (2016, July 29). 14 surprising facts about educators' social media use. *eSchool News*. Retrieved from www.eschoolnews.com/2016/07/29/14-facts-about-educators-social-media-use

Elsevier. (2018). *Get noticed: Increase the impact of your research*. Retrieved from www.elsevier.com/__data/assets/pdf_file/0014/201326/GetNoticed_A4_factsheet_2017.pdf

Espinoza Vasquez, F.K., Caicedo Bastidas, C.E. (2015). Academic social networking sites: A comparative analysis of their services and tools. In *iConference 2015 Proceedings*, 1–6.

Gruzd, A., Staves, K., & Wilk, A. (2011). Tenure and promotion in the age of online social media. In *Proceedings of the American Society for Information Science and Technology*, 48(1), 1–9.

Hartley, D. (2016, May 20). Stop trying to build your "personal brand": Trust me - I'm in marketing. *Psychology Today*. Retrieved from www.psychologytoday.com/blog/machiavellians-gulling-the-rubes/201605/stop-trying-build-your-personal-brand

Honeysett, A. (2017, January 26). The professional bio template that makes everyone sound accomplished. *Forbes*. Retrieved from www.forbes.com/sites/dailymuse/2017/01/26/the-professional-bio-template-that-makes-everyone-sound-accomplished/#3c2198ba7cb2

Ibrahim, A. M., Lillemoe, K. D., Klingensmith, M. E., & Dimick, J. B. (2017, August 1). Visual abstracts to disseminate research on social media: A prospective, case-control crossover study. *Annals of Surgery, [Epub ahead of print]*. doi: 10.1097/SLA.0000000000002277

Jacobs, D. L. (2014, June 3). What to do when you need a bio, rather than a résumé. *Forbes*. Retrieved from www.forbes.com/sites/deborahljacobs/2014/06/03/what-to-do-when-you-need-a-bio-rather-than-a-resume/#7307fc8b284f

Jordan, K. (2014, November 3). Academics and their online networks: Exploring the role of academic social networking sites. *First Monday: Peer Reviewed Journal on the Internet, 19*(11), doi:http://dx.doi.org/10.5210/fm.v19i11.4937

Pannoni, A. (2015). High school educators share how they became Twitter rock stars. *U.S. News.* Retrieved from www.usnews.com/education/blogs/high-school-notes/2015/07/06/high-school-educators-share-how-they-became-twitter-rock-stars

Pew Research Center. (2018, February 5). *Social media fact sheet.* Retrieved from www.pewinternet.org/fact-sheet/social-media

Priem, J. (2013, March 28). Scholarship: Beyond the paper. *Nature: International Weekly Journal of Science, 495*(7442), 437–440. doi:10.1038/495437a

Rankin, J. G. (2016). *Designing data reports that work: A guide for creating data systems in schools and districts.* New York, NY: Routledge/Taylor & Francis.

Rankin, J. G. (2017). *First aid for teacher burnout: How you can find peace and success.* New York, NY: Routledge/Taylor & Francis.

Reddick, R. J. (2016). Using social media to promote scholarship. In M. Gasman (Ed.), *Academics going public: how to write and speak beyond academe,* (pp. 55–70). New York, NY: Routledge, Taylor & Francis.

Reeve, M. A., & Partridge, M. (2017, September 6). The use of social media to combat research-isolation. *Annals of the Entomological Society of America, 110*(5), 449–456. doi:10.1093/aesa/sax051

Roth, D. (2017, December 12). *LinkedIn Top Voices 2017: Meet the all-stars driving today's professional conversations.* Retrieved from www.linkedin.com/pulse/linkedin-top-voices-2017-must-know-people-inspiring-todays-roth

Routledge, Taylor & Francis Group. (2017). *Author directions: navigating your success in social media: 5 key tips for authors using social media.* Boca Raton, FL: CRC Press.

Shop, A. (2017, November 29). How the 6 'e's of social can get more traction to your tweets. *EdSurge.* Retrieved from www.edsurge.com/news/2017-11-29-how-the-6-e-s-of-social-can-get-more-traction-to-your-tweets

Smith, K. (2016, May 17). 44 Twitter statistics for 2016. *Brandwatch.* Retrieved from www.brandwatch.com/blog/44-twitter-stats-2016

Stevens, K. (2014, April 30). Twitter exec reports that educators dominate the Twitter-sphere. *EdSurge.* Retrieved from www.edsurge.com/news/2014-04-30-twitter-exec-reports-that-educators-dominate-the-twitter-sphere

Stewart, D. (2016). Crafting an online scholarly identity. In M. Gasman (Ed.), *Academics going public: how to write and speak beyond academe,* (pp. 71-85). New York, NY: Routledge, Taylor & Francis.

Sugimoto, C. R., Work, S., Larivière, V. & Haustein, S. (2017). Scholarly use of social media and altmetrics: A review of the literature. *Journal of the Association for Information Science and Technology, 68*(2017), 2037–2062. doi:10.1002/asi.23833

Tannahill-Moran, D. (2016, September 23). 3 examples of great personal branding. *Work It Daily.* Retrieved from www.workitdaily.com/personal-branding-examples/#!RWk7E

Part II

Writing

Chapter 3

Writing Anything

In *On Writing: A Memoir of the Craft*, Stephen King (2010) wrote, "The scariest moment is always just before you start. After that, things can only get better" (p. 269). The blank page or screen can be daunting for anyone. Fortunately, in the field of education, we have a compelling reason to push through any hesitations: the more we write, the more we can change students' lives and this world for the better.

Writing leads to speaking gigs and other opportunities you won't want to miss. For example, one of my early keynote presentations resulted from the conference organizer reading my book and then finding me online. He invited me to deliver a keynote on my book's topic at his organization's next conference, allowing me to reach an audience with 1,200 teachers. Even if you don't want to write a full-length book, there are many, varied outlets for your writing, and any one of them could lead to prospects for greater impact.

The more you write, the better your ideas (and your communication of them) will be, and in our field that means increased benefit to kids. "The most prolific people ... generate their most original output during the periods in which they produce the largest volume" (Grant, 2016, p. 37); for example, Albert Einstein wrote 248 publications, Thomas Edison filed 1,093 patents, and Martin Luther King, Jr. wrote over 350 speeches in the single year of his most iconic speech. It's a matter of statistics: The more darts you throw, the more likely you are to hit bullseye. Your bullseye can be an idea, publication, or speech that shifts the whole education field for the better.

In addition to volume, your work will be especially impactful if you write for different audiences and different types of publications, as you will cast a wider net and reach people through one avenue who you might not have reached through another avenue.

Consider dating. If you were single and visited the same bar once per month hoping to meet a quality partner, you could easily remain dateless. If you began visiting that bar every single night, you would likely meet more prospects, but you still might not find that special someone. However, if you recognized there were all sorts of places to meet people (the dog park, yoga class, a National Geographic cruise, a friend's party, etc.) and "got out there" more, you would meet a wide range of people, some of whom possessed the qualities of a partner you were hoping to find.

The same is true when sharing your expertise via writing: "get out there." Write plenty and vary your writing outlets. The three chapters in this "Writing" part of the book will provide you with many, varied opportunities to pursue. Even if writing displeases or even scares you (which the next chapter addresses), options abound.

HOW THIS CHAPTER WORKS

(You Need It for the Next Two Chapters)

While this chapter's title "Writing Anything" is hyperbolic, it means this chapter will provide you with the fundamental guidelines that apply to all writing opportunities described in this book. For example, considering one's audience (meaning the reader, along with his role, frame of reference, and background) is just as important when crafting a blog post as it is when writing a journal paper. Depending on what you need to submit prior to publication, you may follow some parts of this chapter out of order.

The subsequent two chapters in this "Writing" part of the book will offer additional guidelines specific only to certain types of writing. For example, you'll need to write an abstract if you write a journal paper, but not when you craft a magazine article. Though this chapter is broken into subsections ("Before Writing Anything", "While Writing Anything", etc.), it is most beneficial to read the entire chapter before your next writing project and then return to it throughout your writing endeavors.

This chapter contains no exercises. Instead, the next two chapters feature exercises where you can apply what you learn in this chapter, combined with what you learn in those chapters. Those chapters will also lead you to choose publications to write for, which you'll want to have in mind as you consider your audience, purpose, and other aspects introduced in this chapter.

SCRAPPY FAST TRACK

If you want to ascend quickly to authorship (for example, you have no published writing experience but are anxious to author a published book), I recommend you use the information in the "Writing" chapters of this book (including their eResources to find opportunities) to take this route:

Step 1. Though you can skip ahead to Step 3, this first step will help you achieve steps 3 and 4. Submit articles to short-form publications. Begin with outlets you frequently read (your familiarity with them will make it easier to write an appropriate piece). When you ultimately complete a book proposal, it will help to be able to list multiple publications on your CV. When you ultimately write the 2–3 book chapters that must typically accompany a book proposal, you can use these articles' ideas as a starting point (using new verbiage to form chapters in your book). If you have conducted a study or academic literature review *and* you plan to write an academic book, it can help to have some journal publications under your belt. However, be aware of Step 3 before submitting all your papers to journals.

Step 2. Use Chapter 2's "Resume and CV" section to make your CV as impressive as possible and show off your published writing. Your CV will accompany your chapter and book proposals. Begin pursuing an assortment of this book's opportunities (media interviews, TED Talks, etc.), which will increase your appeal as a potential author, and continue to pursue those opportunities as you move on to the next steps.

Step 3. Submit content to write a chapter for a book (see the "Book Chapters" section of this chapter). When that book is published, you'll be a published author, which will look great on your proposal for a full-length book to a publisher. If the book is sold through popular vendors, the book can also appear on your "author page" with these booksellers (like the author page you'll reach if you visit www.Amazon. com, search for me, and then click my name when it appears as a link beside my books). This means that even if you have not written an entire published book, you can still set up an author page (book proposals look better when you provide proof of a strong online presence).

Step 4. Submit a proposal to write a full-length book (the "List of Book Publishers" eResource, which will be discussed later, provides web links for submissions). For two expedited ways to produce a book (such as a short book or monograph), see the next chapter's "If You Hate Writing" section.

BEFORE WRITING ANYTHING

Have you ever bought a gift for someone you didn't know very well? Maybe it was a hostess gift for your partner's friend, a holiday gift for your new mother-in-law, or a birthday gift for an estranged sibling's kid. It's hard to pick great gifts for people you don't know well. The chances they'll like the presents are slimmer, and they're more likely to want to return the gifts that don't meet their needs.

This is because knowing people and circumstances up-front and using that understanding to shape what you select and deliver gives you a major edge on success. The same is true of writing. Considering your audience, circumstances, and submission norms up-front will help you select words and shape your work so it best meets your audience's and publisher's needs, as well as your own.

Determine Circumstances

The following strategies will help you know the writing waters you're about to sail so you can plan accordingly:

❑ **Plan to write for publications that will land in the hands of the right audiences.** Think of who is in a position to *do something* with what you teach him, and target those audiences first and primarily (adding others over time). This perspective will help you maximize your impact (it's not writing the words that matters; it's how many students are helped as a result of your writing).

For example, if I'm writing about ways teachers can prevent bullying, I'll submit to publications like *Teaching Tolerance* that are read by teachers seeking to establish a culture of respect in their classrooms. When I write about decisions made at the multi-school level to improve how data is shared with staff, however, I'll submit to publications like *The District* that are read by superintendents and their office staff.

❑ **Plan to write for publications that match your purpose.** The websites of journals, magazines, and publishing houses typically have an "About" section where you can learn about their intent and get a feel for their priorities. Knowing this information can also help you craft more personalized pitches and proposals.

❑ **Read your chosen publication's current articles.** Note published pieces' topics, voice, tone, style, format, and more. Note which of these aspects vary from one article to the next, versus which aspects seem to be the publication's established norm. Crafting a piece that "fits in" as it covers something new will increase your odds of receiving acceptance and make your piece more digestible for readers, whose expectations have been shaped by previous experiences with the publication.

SCRAPPY TIP

You might see "deadline extended" for an opportunity (like submitting a paper for a special journal issue, a chapter for a multi-author book, or an application to present a paper at a conference). This often means not many people applied, or not enough of those who did apply were deemed worthy of selection. In such cases, it's likely there will be reduced competition if you apply, which increases your odds of being selected and thus reaching new readers.

❑ **Consider time of year.** When I was eager to share findings from a book I'd just written on teacher burnout, I considered how the topic related to what stage schools were in at that very moment. Since summer was just ending, I wrote an op-ed that approached the topic of teacher burnout through a back-to-school lens and submitted it to the *Los Angeles Times*.

My op-ed was published so immediately I learned of its publication from its readers on social media before even hearing back from the editor. If I hadn't applied my concept to the time of year, the piece might not have received the same consideration or speedy publication.

❏ **Consider publication theme.** Many writing venues, particularly magazines, designate themes for issues well in advance of their release. ASCD's *Educational Leadership* magazine (www.ascd.org/Publications/Educational-Leadership/Upcoming-Themes.aspx) and the National Association of Elementary School Principals' (NAESP's) *Principal* magazine (www.naesp.org/editorial-calendar) exemplify this practice. Even journals sometimes have special issues devoted to particular topics.

Before writing for a publication, learn whether or not themes are established. If they are, cater your submission to clearly address a theme that suits your ideas. Submit well before that issue's deadline and clearly state the piece is intended for that issue.

❏ **Consider current events.** In 2017 when the world was plagued with unusually numerous and severe natural disasters, I wrote a piece for ASCD's *Inservice* blog on how gifted students are affected by trauma in unique ways. If I had submitted a piece on an aspect of giftedness unrelated to the time's most current events, its publication would have been less likely.

You can also relate your concept to upcoming events, holidays, or anniversaries of historical events. "Media outlets like to run advance opinion articles that help set up an upcoming event, or alternatively, op-ed pieces that are released in parallel with breaking news stories" (Heller, 2016, p. 26). The same applies to other types of articles, such as those sharing factual information that helps readers understand an upcoming occasion.

SCRAPPY TIP

Due to the holiday season, December deadlines are notoriously hard for people to meet. If you can apply for an opportunity (writing, speaking, or otherwise) that has a December deadline, you might benefit from reduced competition. This means better odds for getting your ideas out there.

❏ **Plan to contribute something new**. You should provide new information to the field, even if this means communicating an established concept in a new and improved way. Search a range of field literature to see if your concept has already been covered and how. Be sure your submission stands out from those already published. A piece is not likely to be selected for publication if it covers an issue that was already covered extensively or if it is similar to a column that was already run (Heller, 2016).

The newness requirement is particularly rigid in the scholarly arena (such as for journal submissions). In this case, you will need to argue (with cited support) in the work itself that you are filling a gap in field literature with findings of significance. Pitching your concept to experts in your area of specialty can help you identify whether your direction is a new one.

Consider Your Audience

As with planning a speech, before you write you should contemplate your audience. Your vocabulary, examples, explanations, style, and more should cater to the type of person reading your work. Use Table 3.1 to consider aspects of your potential readers. Note how these aspects help you estimate what your audience members already know and what they might want or need to know.

Only some of Table 3.1's questions will apply to your piece, and your answers to them need not be certain. You merely want to consider likely possibilities concerning your audience's backgrounds, roles, and environments. This will help you plan an appropriate piece and keep you more aware (such as knowing when to add a particular example or clarification) as you write. Determining who your primary audience is makes subsequent writing steps easier. It's ideal to have one main audience (such as urban school teachers), but you can certainly reach a highly mixed audience: determine main groups, and plan to relate your recommendations and examples to them all or else cater to each in different points of the piece.

Determine Purpose

Now that you know your audience, determine your purpose for writing something. For example, maybe your primary purpose is to inform policymakers about a multi-faceted problem in education, but your secondary purpose is to prompt them to improve their student-impacting decisions. Identifying all of your key purposes will help you write and revise with your goal in mind. In the example just provided, these purposes would encourage you to include facts and stories that inform and would also remind you to include a call to action for policymakers.

Draft a Title

Draft a title, knowing you can rework this during and after writing your piece. The title is your best chance to grab a reader's attention. Your audience will largely base its first impression of your work on the title. Whether or not your

Table 3.1 Consider Your Audience

Your Reader	Consider Answers to Questions Like These Before Writing
Background	• Will most of your readers have experience working at the primary and secondary school level? Will they be familiar with any practitioner lingo you want to use? Will such language make them uncomfortable? For example, a researcher might know what "circle time" is but not have experience conducting circle time and juggling the elements at play. • Will most of your readers have doctorates? Will they be familiar with any research lingo you want to use? Will such language make them uncomfortable? For example, a principal who wrote a dissertation but doesn't regularly conduct research might have used terms like "regression analysis" yet still feel insecure about their full meaning.
Role	• Will your main readers be teachers? If so, will they teach a mix of grade levels and subject areas, or one in particular? If they are principals, what school level do they serve? Etc. If roles are mixed, how will your recommendations and examples relate to them all, or cater to each at different times, or be written exclusively for one role? • Will your main readers be academics? If so, what are their specific roles and related interests? Will they use what you share to perfect a research study, enhance a course, etc.? If roles are mixed, how will your recommendations and examples relate to them all, or cater to each at different times, or be written exclusively for one role?
Environment	• Will your practitioner readers' student and school demographics be mixed, or will they all be from urban schools with a high percentage of English learners? Will their leadership teams take progressive approaches to professional development, and will they have adequate access to educational technology? Considering how your topic intersects with practitioner readers' environments, how will you help all readers understand and relate to your work? • Will your higher education readers' institutions have supportive and collaborative cultures? Will they have authentic, sustained dialogue with primary and secondary school educators? Considering how your topic intersects with researchers' and higher education readers' environments, how will you help all readers understand and relate to your work?

title intrigues people enough to read the rest of your piece impacts whether or not they learn what's contained there, but it also impacts whether or not future readers – brought in by citations and recommendations that initial readers spread of your work – learn what you have to share.

Consider an article on school shootings. For its title you might ask a compelling question:

- "Do We Love Our Children Enough to Stop School Shootings?" by Dan Weisberg

...or pique readers' curiosity or fears:

- "Thresholds of Violence: How School Shootings Catch On" by Malcolm Gladwell

...or promise to break things down simply:

- "Four Truths About the Florida School Shooting" by Adam Gopnik; "many of the most viral articles on *The New York Times* and other websites have a similar structure ... short lists focused around a key topic" (Berger, 2013, p. 174)

...or say something unexpected:

- "Teachers Are Already Armed" (the media was awash in responses to President Trump's suggestion to arm teachers with guns as a solution to school shootings; in this article for *Psychology Today* I argued teachers are already armed to the hilt ... with compassion, knowledge, grit, etc. – see how I spun that? – and too overloaded with current responsibilities to add guns to their arsenals).

The trick is to catch viewers' attention and make them want to keep reading. Saying something unexpected draws people in, but it also cements your idea in their memory (Heath & Heath, 2008). Get inspiration from Mental Floss's (www.mentalfloss.com) clever titles; most make you realize there's a tidbit of intriguing information you don't know, and a quick read will quench your kindled curiosity.

Your title can evolve through the writing process, but you still want to begin with something that captures the heart of what you want to say. This way you'll have a guide post during the writing process.

Determine Solutions to Share

Plan to share solutions, not just problems. Your readers should not finish your article or book with a mere understanding of a problem. They should put down your work understanding one or more of the following:

- how to apply specific strategies to combat the problem (or at least know *about* the strategies);

- what causes the problem (so causes can be targeted);
- leading theories regarding solutions;
- recommendations for future research;
- what stakeholders should *not* do.

Otherwise, what's the point? Your primary purpose in sharing your work should involve helping kids, and solutions make that possible.

Dream up Magic

Do not start outlining just yet. Once you outline a written piece, you end up with clear sections and direction. However, it can then be hard to insert some magic (defined in the text box) into something already planned. Instead, give your writing ideas time to marinate. I like to dream up ideas for a piece when I exercise, shower, walk the dog, and try to fall asleep (hence my insomnia).

Dream up some magic "wow" segments, which help readers connect to your content and are typically the parts readers remember most. Magic moments also make your ideas more likely to spread. When ideas are communicated in a way that is interesting, surprising, or entertaining, people are more likely to tell others about them (like social currency) (Berger, 2013).

Magic increases your piece's impact if you weave it around the more matter-of-fact necessities. For example, there are plenty of areas in this book where straight-

> ### DEFINITION OF HOOK VS. MAGIC
>
> A hook is meant to grab your audience's attention, introduce your topic, and set the tone of your speech or written work. I dislike the term "hook" because it's often portrayed as only occurring at the start of a piece. This implies once you initially catch someone's attention you need not worry about losing it, just as a fish can't easily get off a hook.
>
> Conversely, attentions are actually slippery escape artists. We are well served to plan multiple ways to catch and hold attention throughout the course of our delivery.
>
> This is where magic comes in. "Magic" conveys more power and wonder than a hook. Truly magic segments ignite readers' imaginations, make your audience care about what you have to say, make concepts come to life and connections snap into place, and take your readers on an unforgettable ride.

forward strategies must be listed but note the magic that begins or pops up within every chapter to make content more digestible and memorable. If you have a lot of information to communicate (such as the many strategies in this book), you can't afford to bury every tip in magic, but you can identify key concepts or moments that can use magic's added boost. If you determine some of these magic moments up front, you can then produce an outline that incorporates them.

You can devise additional magic moments when your writing process is in full swing. You can add, remove, or change magic portions during this process with an eye to what will best serve your purpose and your readers' needs. You might also revisit the "Consider Packaging" section of "Chapter 1. Introduction" for inspiration; clever packaging of the lessons you give readers can certainly inject magic into your work. You can think of these memorable moments as hooks, but only if you remember they can occur throughout your work (not just near the beginning), such as each time you introduce a new concept within your piece.

You'll notice that many types of magic segments can also be characterized as stories. Embedding stories throughout your work is a great way to hold the audience's attention and make your message memorable. It is far easier for people to remember stories than facts because the human brain processes experiences we are told about in practically the same way it processes experiences that really happen to us (Gillett, 2014).

Ideas for explaining concepts in magic ways (as long as each clearly illustrates your idea) are detailed below. See Table 3.2, shared on the next page, to inspire magic in your own work before writing, and also for when you reach the outline and template stages. Most of the magic examples in "Chapter 6. Speaking Anywhere" can also be adapted well for writing.

Also determine how you'll make the impact on students resonate with readers. For example, if you argue that teachers should learn to pronounce students' names correctly, how will you convey how doing so (or not doing so) affects how students feel about themselves, connect with their teacher and peers, perform, or other measures?

Sharing the impact on specific children (while keeping the identities of minors private) is highly effective. The reason why charities mail us photos of individual children, and why the single photo of a dead toddler moved previously-unmoved countries and donors to help Syrian refugees, is that:

> identifying a single victim of a tragedy arouses us more than faceless multitudes do. We'll be concerned by the plight of the girl trapped at the bottom of a well, but give far less thought to millions of children dying of hunger or caught up in genocide.

> (Alda, 2017, p. 129)

Heath and Heath (2008) note statistics — even relating to the suffering of millions — shift people into an analytical and non-emotional frame of mind, whereas

Table 3.2 Ways to Insert Magic into Your Writing

Magic/Hook	Example
Analogy, Metaphor, or Simile	In "Chapter 1. Introduction" I described how I package the idea that student data needs to be displayed in easy-to-use ways when given to educators. If I simply make this statement, people tend to think, "Sure, data should be well displayed. That's a no-brainer, so I'm sure it's already being done." If I simply share statistics indicating most teachers misunderstand most data they view, even after expert-recommended training, people often erroneously assume this is some failing of teachers'. People *really* understand the concept, however, when I compare student data to over-the-counter medicine:

> You would never take medicine from an unmarked container. For over-the-counter medicine to be used properly and help lives, it contains specific supports like a label offering directions and warnings, packaging that accurately indicates its nature, supplemental documentation for instructions that won't fit on the label, etc.

> Meanwhile, we give teachers data graphs that lack all of these supports: graphs with no other annotations than the title, poor graphing (i.e., poor packaging) that doesn't encourage accurate interpretation of the data, no supplemental documentation to walk teachers through the meaning of data displays, etc.

> Such a lack of support is dangerous for students affected by data-*mis*informed decisions, just as ingesting medicine from an unmarked container is dangerous. We need to make data "over-the-counter" (thoroughly labeled, etc.) for the educators using it.

Consider how metaphors or extended analogies can illuminate a concept you present. Accompanying your writing with a related image can clarify the relationship (such as between data and a medicine bottle) and make it memorable.

| Case Study or Confession | In the book *Yes, You Can!: Advice for Teachers Who Want a Great Start and a Great Finish with Their Students of Color*, Gail and Rufus Thompson (2014) introduced new issues with sections like "Meet Michaela: A Frustrated New Teacher" (p. 2), "Meet Jamel: A Troubled Student" (p. 72), and "Meet the Parent(s) Part 4: A Single Mother's Dilemma" (p. 135). These sections told true stories that helped the reader step inside the lives of varied stakeholders, including teachers with whom he might identify. These experiences helped the reader drop his defenses so the book's lessons could take root in the reader's heart and mind. |

(*Continued*)

Table 3.2 Continued

Magic/Hook	Example
	I began each chapter of the book *First Aid for Teacher Burnout* with one or two real teacher confessions related to the problem each chapter would help solve. This helped readers relate to chapter topics and illustrated problems the chapter would address. The stories also disarmed the reader as he learned of other teachers who shared the same private fears and thoughts that he might. Consider how case studies or confessions might help your reader understand different perspectives and circumstances.
Comparison	When discussing how students of color are disproportionately suspended and expelled from school, former U.S. Secretary of Education John B. King (2018) said, "We would never say to a kid who got a bad grade on a math assignment, 'So, no more math for you!' but we do respond that way on behavior" when we remove kids from class due to perceived misbehavior. Though spoken rather than written, this comparison would work well in an article. The contrast allows the audience to notice the paradox of current student discipline practices and consider alternatives.

Comparisons can also humanize concepts to make them more tangible. For example, Stephen Covey (2004) describes *Harris Poll* industry findings indicating problems in companies, but the statistics are overwhelming until he writes:

> If, say, a soccer team had these same scores, only four of the eleven players on the field would know which goal is theirs. Only two of the eleven would care. Only two of the eleven would know what position they play and know exactly what they are supposed to do. And all but two players would, in some way, be competing against their own team members rather than the opponent.
>
> (p. 3)

Heath and Heath (2008) analyze this quote and note it joins the abstract statistics with a human comparison (drawing on our understanding of soccer teams), which makes the statistics much more vivid and powerful.

When writing about education, feel free to relate a scenario to something outside our field. The world is rife with comparisons people can connect to, and taking your reader outside the field for a moment can help him recognize something within the field for the first time.

(*Continued*)

Table 3.2 Continued

Magic/Hook	Example
Contrast	When writing about the importance of displaying data appropriately (a topic related to student data), I told stories of how effective data displays ended a cholera epidemic and won the Crimean War. Then I told the story of how faulty data displays are blamed for a poor decision to launch the Challenger Space Shuttle despite rocket defects. The shuttle exploded, killing all crew members. Contrasting how appropriate data displays saved lives with how poor data displays likely lost lives established the gravity of the topic so readers would embrace the research-based recommendations that followed. Contrast can highlight differences and give readers added insight.
Example	Eng (2017) wrote about scholars' tendency to overestimate what their audience knows. He provided a clear example of how unfamiliar terms impact an audience:

> Think of it like giving directions. I think I'm being clear when I tell a tourist on the New York City subway to "go to the other side of the platform and take the downtown R train to SoHo." Yet the other person's probably thinking, *First of all, what do you mean by "the other side"? Does the R train only go downtown or are all downtown trains R trains? What stop is SoHo?*
>
> (p. 19)

	Empathizing with the confused tourist helps us embrace the need to baseline assumptions about our audience's prior knowledge. Notice how we could also consider this example a comparison or simile; magic can fit more than one of this table's categories.
Fable or Parable	A fable or parable can demonstrate a relevant moral or norm that draws the reader in while simultaneously helping the author make a point. For example, consider this introduction to a piece on educators' need to prepare students to make our country globally competitive in the future. Debby Lauret (2014) shares the story of the gazelle who wakes every morning knowing it must outrun the fastest lion or be killed, and the lion who wakes every morning knowing it must outrun the slowest gazelle or starve. The moral is that whether you are a gazelle or a lion, you have to be running each day to survive. This fable establishes a sense of urgency that primes the reader for the rest of the article.
Humor	Corcos (2016) writes of the No Child Left Behind (NCLB) Act, which declared all U.S. students would be academically proficient by 2014:

(*Continued*)

Table 3.2 Continued

Magic/Hook	Example
	Steven Lauridsen of the *New York Times* ridiculed NCLB by suggesting that there should be a "No Dental Patient Left Behind" plan, guaranteeing that America will be 100 percent free of tooth decay in, say, the year 2020. His ridiculous plan outlines how American residents would be assigned to a public dental clinic, which would be financed primarily by local property taxes. Patients' teeth would be thoroughly tested each year, and any dentist who does not adequately reduce her patient's rate of dental failure will face escalating sanctions.
	(p. 85)
	This humorous parody underscored NCLB's shortcomings. Consider how a joke, funny story, or other humor might disarm and enlighten your readers.
Mystery	When I was an assistant principal, I often corresponded with others about how my students' financial hardships affected their ability to attend school regularly, remain at the same school consistently, and succeed while there. I could rattle off stats like our students' use of the National School Lunch Program (NSLP) for free lunches, but I got my message across more memorably with this story (I've changed names to protect privacy):
	It was mid-year when Ms. Garcia's two sons were newly enrolled at our junior high school. She came to our front office with one of these sons (Max) to get their school schedules and take care of other logistics. When her other son (Dale) was mentioned, Ms. Garcia sent Max from the office, and Dale entered the office in his place a couple of minutes later. A bit later some questions pertaining to Max were raised, so Ms. Garcia sent Dale from the office, and Max entered the office in his place a couple of minutes later. This pattern persisted in which only one son at a time was directed to be with us in the office. Ms. Garcia shook off our inquiries, clearly uncomfortable explaining why she would send one son away before the other could join us. My fellow assistant principal, the amazing Chuck Meyers, learned what was going on when he left the building. He saw Max and Dale in the school parking lot as they traded places...and a single pair of shoes. The family only owned one pair of boys' shoes, so Max and Dale had to take turns wearing them, which Ms. Garcia felt they must do to be properly dressed in the school office.

(*Continued*)

Table 3.2 Continued

Magic/Hook	Example

What challenges might Max and Dale face when it came to attending school regularly, remaining at the same school consistently, and succeeding while there? Rather than hit you over the head with facts, this mystery puts you in my place to guess, as the story progresses, why the boys kept trading places. When listeners realize there is a gap in their knowledge – which a story can deliver – they tend to be hooked until that gap is filled (Heath & Heath, 2008). This story also humanizes the families behind the statistics; Ms. Garcia's insistence that her sons not break propriety when on school grounds reminds listeners to treat underprivileged families with dignity.

Those sharing research or practitioner findings can often benefit from a mystery. By introducing the problem you were trying to solve in your study or in your classroom, you can put the reader in your shoes to discover the solution "with" you. This invests the reader in your topic while also communicating its nature. In a study of books written by academics for non-academics, Cialdini (2005) found the books that were most successful "each began with a mystery story. The authors described a state of affairs that seemed to make no sense and then invited the reader into the subsequent material as a way of solving the mystery" (p. 23). This approach can be adapted successfully for other forms of writing, as well.

Personal Anecdote

I often write about how to make data "over-the-counter" for educators. When it's time to define the term and describe the five components to making data over-the-counter, I sometimes tell of the experience that inspired my study. My daughter got sick with a flu. She didn't need a doctor, but she did need over-the-counter medicine. I was able to easily understand which medicine was appropriate for her, the medicine's nature, and how to use the medicine safely due to components that allow medicine to be used effectively (explanatory label, clear packaging, effective content, etc.). I then detail how these same components can be easily applied to the way data is displayed. Through this anecdote, the reader acquires an understanding of the term "over-the-counter" and how it applies to student data, and the reader recognizes the life-or-death importance of each component explained.

Personal anecdotes, such as the human struggle or mental journey behind one of your findings or efforts, humanizes concepts to help audiences connect with them. Such anecdotes can also be about others. Consider this title of an NPR story:

(*Continued*)

Table 3.2 Continued

Magic/Hook	Example
	• Dolly Parton Gives the Gift of Literacy: A Library Of 100 Million Books (Pao, 2018, p. 1).

That's super impressive (way to go, Dolly!) but isn't very relatable. However, consider how much more inviting the story is when a personal anecdote is introduced, even though it's short enough to fit in this Tweet:

- "Dolly Parton's father never learned to read. She started her nonprofit, Imagination Library, to give children what he didn't have: early access to books" (NPR's Education Team, 2018, p. 1).

While the title likely touches you on an analytical level, the tweeted anecdote likely touches you on an emotional level. Touching people on an emotional level is more likely to make them connect, care, remember, and act than touching them on an analytical level will (Heath & Heath, 2008).

Quiz   I began an article on teacher burnout for ASCD's *Educational Leadership* like this:

Grab a pen or pencil and fill in the blanks:

- Less than 15% of _____ would recommend their profession to others.
- 91% of _____ suffer from stress.
- 15% of _____ leave the profession each year (this statistic rises to 20% for those working in high-poverty areas).
- More than 41% of _____ leave their jobs within five years of starting.

If you stopped people on the street and gave them this quiz, they might guess things like *police officers, emergency room nurses, attorneys,* or *warzone doctors.* Who else could be shouldering such pressure and fleeing the profession in droves?

However, if you're an educator, you probably know the answer because you lived it. The professionals who serve as the quiz answer to complete all four of the above sentences are *teachers.*

(Rankin, 2018, p. 1)

Quizzes actively involve the reader and help him feel invested in what you share. Imagine if the above passage had instead spoon-fed the statements to the reader as facts. That reader would have taken on a much more passive role. Even if a reader gets the whole quiz wrong, you have actively involved him in your content and instilled a desire for the correct answers.

(Continued)

Table 3.2 Continued

Magic/Hook	Example
Relate Material to the Reader	While second person point of view (using words like "you" and "your") is typically discouraged for scholarly writing like journal papers, it is more welcome in less formal publications and can be highly effective. Writing "you" helps readers imagine you are conversing with them more intimately and allows them to step into your written world.
	Consider this opening to a book on the learning brain (something very clinical) and how it draws you in as the reader:
	> The oddest thing is that you're not quite the same person as you were a few minutes ago. You have a memory of picking up this book, and this memory has joined others held somewhere in your biology: how you came to be here today, who you are and even how to read these words. Something must change amongst the atoms and molecules of your body for you to learn and remember these things. > (Howard-Jones, 2018, p. 1)
	Try replacing words like "people" and "someone's" with "you" and "your" to see if your written piece improves.
Story	In the book *If I Understood You, Would I Have This Look on My Face?: My Adventures in the Art and Science of Relating and Communicating*, Alan Alda (2017) of the Center for Communicating Science tells an alarming-yet-funny tale of a dentist's malpractice on his mouth. Miscommunication led to the operation, which removed Alda's ability to smile until a follow-up surgery. The story is highly memorable (it's hard to forget a botched dental job) and helps readers understand the value of communicating and listening (Alda's topics). People are more likely to tell others about a concept when it is an integral component of a specific story people will want to tell; 70% of story details get lost after 5-6 retellings but the main point sharpens (Berger, 2013). If people are able to tell your "cool story" without including your crucial message, then it isn't the right story for you to tell.
	The field of education is full of gripping stories. Tales of survival, triumph, or overcoming adversity all introduce a human element that helps readers connect with your content and grasp its gravity. The stories you choose to share should convey your message and should also be short enough to maintain the reader's attention and leave room for your related points.

(*Continued*)

Table 3.2 Continued

Magic/Hook	*Example*
	If you want to find an *inspiring* story to use, Heath and Heath (2008) suggest looking for three key plot types, depending on your purpose: "Challenge (to overcome obstacles), Connection (to get along or reconnect), [or] Creativity (to inspire a new way of thinking)" (p. 289). To use student-related movies as examples:
	<ul><li>*Stand and Deliver* is a Challenge plot in which a teacher inspires his academically-failing students to learn calculus.</li><li>*Dangerous Minds* is a Connection plot in which a retired marine becomes a teacher who connects with her inner-city students of different backgrounds.</li><li>*Dead Poets Society* is a Creativity plot in which an unconventional teacher inspires his students to view poetry and life in new ways.</li></ul>
	Consider how you might use a story to help readers connect with your message.
Surprising Statistic or Fascinating Fact	A surprising statistic or fact can seize a reader's interest if it is unusual (such as a little-known aspect of a historical event), extreme, emotional, or hard to believe. For example, in an article on developing hope and resilience in disengaged students, Chris Balow (2017) writes, "by grade 12 about two-thirds of all students are either not engaged or actively disengaged" (p. 1).
	Yikes! Disengagement among a solid majority of students is far too huge a problem to ignore. Balow's fact positions the audience to care about the details shared in the rest of the article, and also to download the whitepaper the article introduces. Any stories of individual students' disengagement that follow this statistic will be especially impactful, as the reader is primed with the knowledge that such stories are plentiful.
Voices of Those Involved	Our recommendations are meant to help students (and often educators, too), but their voices are frequently missing from our conversations. Consider including quotes from students or educators to communicate your message. For example, rather than claim your new program helps students learn to read, include quotes from three students describing how this phenomenon happened for them. See the Education Writers Association's reporting guide to interviewing children (www.ewa.org/sites/main/files/file-attachments/ewa-reporter-guide-interviewing-children.pdf) for legal guidance in quoting minors.

describing a single person's plight primes people to care about, remember, and act on a concept. Whether or not you classify a particular classroom practice as a tragedy, a win, or somewhere in between, sharing its impact on a single life can help readers care about the many more lives it impacts.

In education we have countless real-life stories to draw from: how a new policy deterred Dahye from becoming the first college graduate in her family, or how Juan's face lit up when a teaching strategy helped him understand fractions for the first time. Good or bad, true stories help audiences feel the impact that initiatives have on students.

Consider how you can add such stories to your writing. You might focus on one child as an introduction, or devote a few-sentence account to a different youth each time you describe a new facet of your idea. If you also share statistics or wide-sweeping facts, try doing so after you've primed your reader with a more personal story. Scholarly writing is not off limits for such stories, which can illustrate whatever concepts your reader must understand.

Create a Template

Setting up an organized structure for your words will make writing easier, whether your brilliance spills rapidly onto the page or you struggle to drag the words out. A template can even be the place where you craft your original outline.

Open a new file in your word processing software (I prefer Microsoft Word) and type any headings you are required to include. Add your title (knowing it can change), name, affiliation, bio, and other staples. Format the pages to match any publisher specifications (common for journal submissions). If there are no format requirements, you can aim for a standard approach (double-spaced lines with size 12 Times New Roman font) or use a format that matches what your targeted venue uses for published work (for example, electronically copy text from an online article, paste it onto your template, and use its font and spacing for your work).

Having a template will help protect your writing flow. If you are working on the Introduction and think of something you don't want to forget including in the Conclusion, you can quickly throw a reminder (just a few words, without elaborating) into the Conclusion section yet get right back to what you were writing in the Intro.

Outline

You can then outline (list brief notes and ideas in the order you plan to write about them) directly on your template. Just be sure you've already spent time dreaming up compelling ways to share your ideas (covered earlier in this section). Otherwise, if you try to outline before you spend time daydreaming, you might find yourself locked into a lackluster delivery.

Reflect on your audience and purpose. Record key talking points in your outline in the order you plan to share them. Fill in needed information and transitions you'll need to make. Don't feel the need to get too specific in your outline (sometimes that limits you once you're in the flow of writing, whereas you want to be able to follow your gut as you write when it tells you what's needed).

SCRAPPY TIP

Getting discouraged by rejections? Look at the CV or publication list of someone whose career you admire and note which publications were his earliest. Early-career publications sometimes signify venues that are easier to break into, and the author you admire obviously got accepted there *before* all of his later successes. Consider which of those magazines, radio shows, etc. fit your work and then apply there.

WHILE WRITING ANYTHING

Now you can flesh out your outline directly on your template, turning ideas into complete sentences and working your magic. In other words, it's time to write.

Little Things That Add Up

Keep the following tips in mind as you work. They might seem like little things but missing any one of them can throw a wrench into your process or product.

❏ **Adhere strictly to submission guidelines.** Publications often provide clear parameters for:
  • The submission (word count, line spacing, section subheadings like "theoretical framework" to include, bio location and length, etc.).
  • The submission process (what the subject field of your email should state, what questions you should answer in your cover letter, how your submission's electronic file should be named, etc.).
  Yet ignoring publishers' requirements is a common submitter's mistake. For example, "Some [journal] publishers report that one paper in five does not follow the style and format requirements of the target journal" (Shaikh, 2016, p. 3).
  Follow all guidelines closely. Though you can ask for clarification if you're unsure about something, you can avoid bothering editors in many cases

by reviewing pieces they already published and mirroring the format you find there.

❑ **Establish order through formatting.** Headings, subheadings, text boxes, bullets, checkboxes, and other formatting conventions can help you organize material in a way that's easier for readers to digest.

❑ **Don't get bogged down with precision** (spelling, edits, etc.) while writing your initial draft. If you used the word "trajectory" but don't think it fits quite right, just put "@@" in front of the word for now. That will be your signal to investigate and correct something later ("@@" is easy to spot, and an electronic search for those two characters side-by-side will bring up a list of places you need to revisit) so you can continue writing for now.

❑ **Don't be afraid to write out of order.** If you are eager to flesh out examples of your theory's application in classrooms before writing your Introduction, seize that excitement and skip ahead. You can write sections in any order and can catch any transition or cohesion problems during revision.

❑ **Use an appropriate and consistent style.** Do you want your piece to read like you're speaking to the reader in a familiar, casual way? Do you want to be humorous? Do you want to be blunt or formal? The answer to questions like these is a very personal one. Think hard about what you want your writing voice to sound like, and use a style that will fit your nature, audience, and purpose.

Beware the Shoulder Chip

Some of your audience members will have preexisting grievances that cause them to look for particular weaknesses or claims in your work...and to find those weaknesses or claims, whether or not they actually exist in your work. This can trigger confusing reactions to your writing, such as someone accusing you of blaming teachers for a problem when your article is specifically about how teachers are *not* to blame for the problem.

Grievances have often developed because someone feels disrespected on a regular basis or sees a topic mishandled frequently. By anticipating shoulder chips some readers might have, you can be sure your work clearly sidesteps related misunderstandings so your real message can be heard. Table 3.3 provides examples of how you can do this, though your piece's purpose and space allowance will impact which of these are appropriate.

Address Inequity

Unless you are writing a very short piece, there will be room to address aspects of equity that impact your topic. Nearly every education topic merits addressing

Table 3.3 Problems for Which Readers Search

Reader's Grievance	Ways to Prevent Grievance or Misunderstanding
You are blaming or belittling teachers.	• Beginning in your introduction, use language that applauds teachers and acknowledges the difficulties and impact of their work. • If appropriate, mention (early) your own teaching experience.
Your findings aren't backed up by sound research, or you are jumping to conclusions (like you claim causation when there is only correlation).	• Detail how you arrived at a conclusion. • Cite others' research (not just your own). • Detail how you accounted for secondary variables (such as how you know it wasn't family income that accounted for students' added support). • If space doesn't allow for these details, provide a link or web address readers can follow to get them.
You are misusing terms.	• If there is common confusion surrounding a term, define the term early. • As an alternative, provide a footnote with explanation. For example, when I write "data is" I commonly add a footnote explaining how data can be used as a singular or plural noun (otherwise I'll lose readers who mistake the former tense as grammatically incorrect, since the term's singularity did not used to be universally accepted). This might seem excessive, but some people go a little crazy when they think they spot an error.
You are implying non-teachers (such as researchers) know more about teaching than school teachers.	• Detail how school teacher input was an integral part of your process and reasoning. • Acknowledge on-the-job variables. For example, if you recommend teachers give each student personalized feedback, give examples of how a teacher with 224 students (7 class periods with 32 students each) manages this.
You are treating an old movement (like direct instruction) as if it is something brand new.	• Acknowledge related movements of the past and describe how the new movement builds upon these. • Explain the specific ways in which the new movement differs from the old.

(*Continued*)

Table 3.3 (Continued)

Reader's Grievance	Ways to Prevent Grievance or Misunderstanding
You are ignoring major variables (for example, success at a charter school where students must pass a rigorous test to attend will have limitations translating to other schools).	• Be upfront about pertinent characteristics (such as those of the school where a study took place, those of students whose feedback you collected, etc.). • Address how your findings might apply to other environments and underscore important conditions.
Your recommendation is flawed or unrealistic.	• Spend time in classrooms and speaking with varied teachers to understand the constraints involved when teaching. For example, a recommendation that each student receive 30 minutes of uninterrupted one-on-one time with the teacher to maximize reading progress is unrealistic for a teacher who must engage 35+ students of varied levels simultaneously. • Recall or speak with very different educators or very different students. Consider how your recommendation would apply to and help them all. Adjust your recommendations as necessary, or stipulate limitations (example: the strategy only works well with students who exhibit high intrinsic motivation).
No one else is saying what you're saying, so you must be wrong.	• Demonstrate how your theory is a natural extension of past research or movements. • Emphasize concrete evidence (such as study findings) supporting your stance. • If replying to this criticism, politely mention that many norms accepted in the field today were initially deemed preposterous (such as the belief that spanking a child does not teach a child a helpful lesson).

how some student populations are underrepresented or underserved, in order to also provide strategies to combat the disparity.

For example, if you write about how to ensure more students go to college, you'll be ignoring major barriers if you don't address the huge discrepancies between different races, ethnicities, and socioeconomic statuses of students being enrolled in college preparatory classes. If you write about grooming students to be future scientists, you'll be writing only on behalf of boys if you don't address how girls' interest and confidence in science plummets the longer they are in school. If you write about improving early education discipline, you won't be addressing the topic properly if you don't share that students of color are expelled from preschool significantly more than any other group. Let these insights shape the solutions you recommend so your writing works to close gaps in our schools and society.

Too often, education experts fail to address disparity unless they're writing exclusively about that topic. White, male, and straight people worry they'll say "the wrong thing" when promoting equity for those in groups other than their own. But that fear stands in the way of dialogue that can improve our field and thus advance the lives of kids.

I'll tell you a story that involves presentations but could just as likely have occurred in written form. At the same education symposium, I once heard an invited speaker argue against desegregation efforts (reasoning they communicate one's neighborhood has nothing worthy to offer, which she felt as a child being transplanted to a faraway school, rather than focusing on improving local schools), and immediately after that I heard another invited speaker argue that school desegregation is the single most important answer to ending racial inequity in our nation. Both speakers were highly regarded experts, both speakers were women of color, and both deemed the other presenter's stance as wrong. But only by hearing these views were we, as an audience, informed of the complexities involved in this issue and more invested in finding the best solution while mitigating its shortcomings. Don't act like you have all the answers (a rich, straight, White, Christian, male American shouldn't claim he knows as much about experiencing discrimination as those in traditionally marginalized groups, and someone in a traditionally marginalized group should not assume that group has a single perspective on everything) but share diversity-related facts and ideas you have investigated so we can all move our understanding forward through vital discourse. Knowing you don't have all the answers is a blessing when it comes to equity, because it keeps you studying and speaking with others to continually advance your understanding. Can you imagine if every education expert took ownership of the quest to end disparity in our world? It's a powerful goal, and it also makes coverage of any other topic more comprehensive in the process.

Whatever topic you've chosen, I challenge you to find where equity intersects it. If you struggle in this endeavor, see "Chapter 6. Speaking Anywhere" for added support.

Don't Lose Your Core Message

Remember your pitch from "Chapter 1. Introduction"? Be sure it stands out clearly in your work. Sometimes we get so busy explaining something in detail that we forget to hit the reader over the head with statements that capture the essence of what we are saying. Summarizing your points in single sentences will make your message clear and also make it easier for others to cite direct quotes from your work.

Be Very Clear

Craft straightforward sentences, use jargon sparingly, establish context (for example: when you say "teachers" in your abstract, do you mean primary and secondary school teachers of public schools?), and define terms to avoid confusion. While sentences like "The study's purpose was…" might seem clunky or mundane, their straightforwardness is actually helpful for the reader.

Sentence structure also impacts clarity. I could have written the previous sentence as *How clear something is can be affected by the way that sentences within it are structured*, but that would not be as straightforward or clear. Trim unnecessary words and rearrange overly complicated sentences.

Those used to academic writing, in particular, struggle with clarity. See Pinker (2014) for the many reasons for this. Scholars tend to pad sentences with qualifiers that weaken prose, and with jargon that complicates prose. The more difficult sentences are for the reader to process, the more they produce *cognitive strain*, which is a state involving discomfort, lack of trust, and disbelief in what you are saying (Kahneman, 2011).

Worse than the crimes of jargon and complicated prose, however, is what many experts call The Curse of Knowledge. This curse involves forgetting what it was like to not know something we now know. The audience reads something to gain something new, yet we often forget the audience doesn't already share our knowledge or perspective. If left unchecked, The Curse of Knowledge makes us use terms while erroneously assuming the reader already knows what they mean, or we explain how to apply an idea without fleshing out what the idea is made of and looks like (Pinker, 2014). To trump The Curse of Knowledge, we must maintain awareness (throughout the planning, writing, and revision processes) of our audience's nature and needs.

Part of clarity is establishing context. Once when I read an article on writing an effective proposal, it wasn't until six paragraphs in that I could begin to guess the author meant a business proposal, though nowhere in the entire article was the phrase "business proposal" ever used. The meaning of "proposal" could have alternately been a book proposal, an op-ed proposal to a problem, a marriage proposal, a grant proposal, or something else. Ideally your reader should know your piece's focus from your title, and your introduction should unequivocally communicate what the written work will be about.

In our industry, we get used to the shorthand we use with our closest colleagues. Yet we cannot presume our audience accepts our terms to mean the same thing we do. Like "proposal", words can mean different things in different contexts. Even if your readers understand a term can be used in a particular way, they need confirmation that is the way you are using the term.

When you write for an international audience, be extra wary of misunderstandings. For example, in the U.S. the leader of a school for children is commonly called the principal, whereas in England this person is commonly called the headteacher. Editor-in-chief Hugh McLaughlin notes, "We get people who write from America who assume everyone knows the American system – and the same happens with U.K. writers. Because we're an international journal, we need writers to include that international context" (Higher Education Network, 2015, p. 3).

Consider your range of readers and provide context clues and definitions as needed. Online, terms can feature hyperlinks that lead to definitions, and longer forms like books can include a glossary, definition text box, or an explanation of terms that appears in the book's introduction.

Write Confidently

Don't use phrases like "I think…" or "In my opinion…" that qualify your statements. First of all, your name is on the piece as its author, so the reader already knows these ideas are coming from you as opposed to someone else. Second of all, you are an expert. You are backing your statements up with citations, case studies, examples, concrete facts, and other supports. Verbiage that makes you sound unsure or alone in your beliefs undermines your message.

However, check self-absorption at the door. Being confident doesn't mean mistaking a writing project as an opportunity to ramble about yourself. I am shocked by how many education experts cross the "let's talk about me" line.

Providing examples from your own experiences and efforts is helpful for readers and highly recommended. What *isn't* helpful or recommended is devoting large sections to things like, "Let me tell you my history…" or "My list of accomplishments…". There are exceptions (such as the "Meet the Author" section in a book, an author bio accompanying an article, or stories that illustrate strategies or findings). Otherwise, focusing predominantly on yourself for multiple paragraphs is generally self-indulgent, off-topic, and wastes space that could be spent informing and engaging your reader.

When sharing your own experiences, only include those pieces that propel your message about your topic. If your piece reads like a memoir, consider reworking it.

Don't Overload Your Reader

We are experts on the topics we write about, so there is *much* we can share. We often get carried away in our excitement: "Ooh – since I mentioned ___, I should also mention ___! I have so many great examples of ___ I can throw in, too!" But readers can only take so much. Even if they're interested in your topic, readers can miss your core message amid excess verbiage.

In describing what the Center for Communicating Science wants from scientists sharing information, Alda (2017) writes, "Sometimes, telling us just enough to make us want to know more is exactly the right amount. We gag on force-feeding. We're uncomfortable feeling like geese getting our livers fattened" (p. 73). This is especially true of short form writing, whereas readers are expecting more information in a book.

When stopping short of overload, you can always point readers to resources for more information when they're ready. Online articles can include links to more information, and printed pieces can feature web addresses and other details for those interested.

Cite Recent Work

As a general rule, all sources should be from within the last six years, with few exceptions. If you do cite older work, there should be a reason for it. For example, something like, "In a seminal study...", "In an often-cited paper..." or "...established the foundation for..." can help justify the source's inclusion. Pair the finding with any follow-up evidence that helped advance the previous source's merit.

AFTER WRITING ANYTHING

- ❏ **Proof and edit meticulously**. Use your word processing software's spell check and grammar check tools. Print your piece and proof read it for errors, clarity, and recommendations given in this chapter and others. Turn the submission requirements into a checklist (I add a to-be-checked box next to each required item) and ensure you've met every demand.

❏ **Step into your audience's shoes.** Is the "big picture" conveyed? Does the flow work for readers? Are you sure your sentences and explanations are clear? Are you too wordy or do your descriptions ramble? Try to view your work with an honest mind and fix any fumbles.

❏ **Check with people you mention** in relation to personal experience (as opposed to repeating what you see in print), as there's a chance you'll get details wrong. Whenever I mention someone I know or someone for whom I'm unsure of a detail, I share the verbiage with him (prior to submission and publication) to ensure details are accurate. Sometimes I hear back, "Actually, I'm leaving that position this week; here's my new job title..." or "That's great, but did you know I also..." I've had my qualifications and words misprinted plenty of times, whereas this practice keeps my sharing of others' information accurate.

Those I contact are usually excited to be mentioned and want me to keep them posted when the piece is published. They often become the biggest sharers of those works, which helps me reach more readers. Folks you mention will likely do the same.

❏ **Revisit and finesse your title.** Revisit the "Before Writing Anything: Draft a Title" section of this chapter and ensure your title will capture readers' attention and draw them into reading the rest of your piece.

Also make sure your piece delivers on what the title promises. If it doesn't, you can either rework your title or rework your piece. Otherwise, your title primes readers with expectations of what they believe your writing will deliver, and a piece that fails to deliver this will disappoint. Your reader will be distracted by thoughts like, "When is he going to cover __?" Though the "Writing for Journals" section of this chapter pertains to journal papers, its segment on titles offers many tips you can apply to other forms of writing, too.

❏ **Write compelling cover letters/emails and proposals.** These should stick to the publisher's specifications (does he want a cover letter or cover *email*?), avoid jargon (editors are rarely practitioners or experts in the field and their understanding of your topic is likely less deep than yours), and win over the editor or journalist. Have at least one item that will make your proposal jump out from the rest (for example, if you assisted President Obama in addressing your topic, you'd better slip in that fact).

In order to be succinct, an email or its attachment can use hyperlinks that lead to more information. I did this on the sample cover email shown on the next page (each underlined word was a link the editors could click), which resulted in acceptance.

One approach is to craft your cover letters and proposals before writing your actual submissions, which can help you identify your purpose before tackling the writing process. Whenever you wrote your cover email or proposal, review what you prepared and be sure the cover letter or proposal accurately reflects the written work you are submitting. Edit each item as needed until these two pieces are well matched.

SAMPLE COVER EMAIL THAT LED TO A PUBLICATION

Dear *Los Angeles Times* Editorial Team,

I have attached a timely 612-word submission for the Commentary section. The op-ed relates to this "back-to-school" time of year and the pandemic of <u>teacher burnout</u>.

    I live in Southern California writing <u>books</u> for educators. My perspective on this submission's topic stems from being a former teacher (honored by the U.S. White House for my dedication to students), assistant principal, school district administrator, and chief education and research officer. My CV and bio (with long list of publications) can be found at <u>www.JennyRankin/bio</u>.

Thank you very much for your consideration.
Sincerely,
Dr. Jenny Grant Rankin

❏ **Provide (or consider providing) images.** In most cases you won't be *expected* to provide images to illustrate your work, yet editors often appreciate being offered a copyright-free image they can consider using. See the "Slide Images" section of "Chapter 7. Preparing Slides for Anywhere" for assistance in preparing or selecting copyright-free images.

AFTER RECEIVING VERDICT

Your work will typically be reviewed prior to its publication, and you will often receive reviewers' and editors' feedback, to which you are expected to respond. Sometimes this process is handled in a formal way (example: "Review comments on the Reviewer Feedback Form and use the form's last column to respond to each line item, such as indicating how you will change your work to reflect a suggestion"), and sometimes the process is as informal as fielding a few suggestions or questions from an editor. No matter the conditions, this section's tips can help you make the most of this stage so that each written piece is shaped into its best possible self.

Consider Feedback

You could receive reviewer feedback whether or not your work is accepted. Acceptance might hinge on the condition that you respond to the reviewer's feedback and make requested changes.

Usually there is something to learn from each piece of feedback, and some change to make whenever a change is requested. This need not necessarily be the same change that was requested, but it should be a change that solves the problem at the root of the feedback. For example:

- The reviewer writes, "The qualitative aspects of the paper were communicated, but the quantitative aspects were not addressed."
- You immediately think, "That reviewer is crazy! My paper wasn't a mixed methods study. It was only a qualitative study and thus there were no quantitative aspects to address."
- After further consideration you think, "The reviewer misunderstood that my paper was mixed methods. I'll revise the abstract, introduction, and methodology sections of the paper to make it clear this is a qualitative study." You can incorporate this reasoning into your response to the reviewer's comment and describe the change you made. Thus, you are making a change that solves the true problem (confusion) that triggered the reviewer's response.

If your initial impression of the feedback is outrage or a feeling the reviewers "got it wrong", return to that feedback later when you feel calmer. Even if a reviewer is off-base, this usually means he was confused in some way. You can at least consider ways to make your concept clearer (such as by making its context clearer) so future readers don't get lost.

Clarify Changes

Indicate exactly where you made changes (example: "second sentence in the first paragraph of the "Recommendations" section) so editors don't have to hunt for them. When editors embed feedback directly on the draft (such as by using Word or Adobe Acrobat's comment features), use that same system to add your responses.

When a piece is extensive, such as a dissertation, and its feedback is provided in a separate document, use a system that makes it clear you are addressing every comment. In these cases, I create a table with a row for each request. Requests go in the first column, my explanations of resultant changes go in the second column, and descriptions of the exact location of each change go in the third.

Once I left out such details and it cost me a project. I'd spent a year of back-and-forth with changing editors (whose requests contradicted one another) on an article for a publication known for mistreating freelance contributors. In my final email to the newest editor, I noted I made her requested changes but – for the first time – did not detail where they lay. What I got back was a curt, late night email from the editor that she couldn't spot the changes, my article had become "too much work", and she was canceling its scheduled publication. What a waste of a year and the potential good that could have come from the piece, all because I didn't provide details I could have easily offered.

Speak Up

Speak up early if major problems are brewing. Egido (2018) found that during the feedback stage, the reviewed may not feel at ease and are uncomfortable expressing their thoughts to the reviewer, yet open exchange is necessary to arrive upon the best decisions for authors' work. While you want to be agreeable to work with, your main priority must be the quality of your work, as this will shape its impact on students.

One of my books (not with this publisher) was assigned a copy editor I later learned was brand new to the publishing house and to education books. For her first round of feedback, she edited my draft without turning on the "track changes" feature in Word (which shows where edits were made), and she only told me of a fraction of her changes to the manuscript. Once I spotted some alterations and additions she hadn't mentioned, which misused field terminology and would have embarrassed me if published, I talked to her about how vital this feature was and why I needed to know about changes being made (I also reread the whole book from scratch to catch her other changes). She used the feature from that point forward and ended up doing a great job. If I had remained silent about this major problem, however, we would not have worked successfully together and the book (with its impact) would have suffered.

Thrive Despite Rejection

Learn from a rejection. Reviewers' comments and the justification for your rejection can be golden pieces of information. They can help you improve your paper, achieve acceptance on your next try, and improve future work. In an international survey of more than 4,000 paper writers and reviewers, 91% of authors indicated the peer review process improved their papers (Mulligan, Hall, & Raphael, 2012).

Though helpful, reviews are also subjective. You might even find reviewers sometimes contradict one another. Consider the highest-grossing movie of 1985, *Back to the Future*. Disney passed on the script because it was "too sexually perverse," whereas Columbia Pictures rejected the script because it was not "sexual enough" (Conradt, 2016, p. 4-5). Madeleine L'Engle's *A Wrinkle in Time* is one of the most frequently banned books as it's sometimes perceived as being "anti-Christian", yet other critics argue the award-winning book is "too religious" (Parr, 2018, p. 7).

Different reviewers have different backgrounds, goals, and impressions. Do your best to glean helpful recommendations from the feedback you receive, even if it means finding alternate ways to improve the work (like an approach more likely to meet the needs of all readers), and your work will likely benefit.

Remember that rejection is common. Academics list and talk about their book, elite periodical, and journal publications, but they rarely reveal the longer list of rejections they received on their journey. Rejection is part of the publication process and does not mean you or your ideas are unworthy.

I've found there to be a domino effect when it comes to getting published: the more I got published, the more "previous publications" I got to mention when submitting new pieces to get published elsewhere, and then it seemed like I had an easier time breaking in to new publications than I had when I was new to all this. So, have heart: gaining acceptance will get easier!

Be proud of your courage and initiative in putting yourself out there. Though rejection stings, students are lucky that someone such as you is braving that discomfort for the sake of bettering education. You owe it to them and yourself to dust yourself off, rework your piece, and submit again.

REFERENCES

Alda, A. (2017). *If I understood you, would I have this look on my face?: My adventures in the art and science of relating and communicating*. New York, NY: Random House.

Balow, C. (2017, December 1). *Developing hope & resilience in disengaged students*. Retrieved from www.illuminateed.com/blog/2017/12/developing-hope-resilience-disengaged-students

Berger, J. (2013). *Contagious: Why things catch on*. New York, NY: Simon & Schuster.

Cialdini, R. B. (2005). What's the best secret device for engaging student interest? The answer is in the title. *Journal of Social and Clinical Psychology*, 24(1), 22–29.

Conradt, S. (2016, April 30). 8 hit movies that were originally rejected by studios. *Mental Floss*. Retrieved from http://mentalfloss.com/article/79197/8-hit-movies-were-originally-rejected-studios

Corcos, A. F. (2016). *Affirmative action for all our children: And why college education should be free*. Tucson, AZ: Author.

Covey, S. (2004). *The 8th habit: From effectiveness to greatness*. New York, NY: Free Press/Simon & Schuster.

Egido, A. A. (2018). *Students' presupposition, prejudice, and discrimination in an English language class*. Londrina, Brazil: State University of Londrina.

Elsevier. (2018). *About SSRN*. Retrieved from www.elsevier.com/solutions/ssrn

Eng, N. (2017). *Teaching college: The ultimate guide to lecturing, presenting, and engaging students*. New York, NY: Author.

Gillett, R. (2014, September 18). Why we're more likely to remember content with images and video (infographic). *Fast Company*. Retrieved from https://www.fastcompany.com/3035856/why-were-more-likely-to-remember-content-with-images-and-video-infogr

Grant, A. (2016). *Originals: How non-conformists move the world*. New York, NY: Penguin Books.

Heath, C., & Heath, D. (2008). *Made to stick: Why some ideas survive and others die*. New York, NY: Random House.

Heller, D. E. (2016). Writing opinion articles. In M. Gasman (Ed.), *Academics going public: How to write and speak beyond academe*, (pp. 21–37). New York, NY: Routledge, Taylor & Francis.

Higher Education Network. (2015, January 3). How to get published in an academic journal: Top tips from editors. *The Guardian*. Retrieved from www.theguardian.com/education/2015/jan/03/how-to-get-published-in-an-academic-journal-top-tips-from-editors

Howard-Jones, P. (2018). *Evolution of the learning brain: Or how you got to be so smart*. New York, NY: Routledge/Taylor & Francis.

Kahneman, D. (2011). *Thinking, fast and slow*. New York, NY: Farrar, Straus and Giroux.

King, J. B. (2018, February 18). Future forward: Ending educational inequity in our lifetime. *New Teacher Center National Symposium*. Keynote panel conducted from the Hyatt Regency San Francisco Airport, Burlingame, CA.

King, S. (2010). *On writing: A memoir of the craft: 10th anniversary edition*. New York, NY: Simon & Schuster, Inc.

Lauret, D. (2014, October 21). An education parable: Survival of the fittest. *Daily Herald*. Retrieved from www.heraldextra.com/news/community/business/chambers/an-education-parable-survival-of-the-fittest/article_0fd5991f-298c-58ad-bdd0-4bf10a6099d6.html

Mulligan, A., Hall, L., & Raphael, E. (2012, December 4). Peer review in a changing world: An international study measuring the attitudes of researchers. *Journal of the Association for Information Science and Technology*, *64*(1), 132–161.

NPR's Education Team. [@npr_ed]. (2018, March 1). *Dolly Parton's father never learned to read. She started her nonprofit, Imagination Library, to give children what he didn't have: early access to books*. [Twitter moment]. Retrieved from https://twitter.com/npr_ed

Pao, M. (2018, March 1). Dolly Parton gives the gift of literacy: A library of 100 million books. *NPR Ed*. Retrieved from www.npr.org/sections/ed/2018/03/01/589912466/dolly-parton-gives-the-gift-of-literacy-a-library-of-100-million-books

Parr, A. (2018, February 27). 12 fantastic facts about A Wrinkle in Time. *Mental Floss*. Retrieved from http://mentalfloss.com/article/62736/12-fantastic-facts-about-wrinkle-time

80

Pinker, S. (2014, September 26). Why academics stink at writing. *The Chronical of Higher Education*. Retrieved from https://stevenpinker.com/files/pinker/files/why_academics_stink_at_writing.pdf

Rankin, J. (2018, Summer). How administrators can help teachers win the burnout war. *Educational Leadership, 75*(9), 1–6.

Reddick, R. J. (2016). Using social media to promote scholarship. In M. Gasman (Ed.), *Academics going public: How to write and speak beyond academe*, (pp. 55–70). New York, NY: Routledge, Taylor & Francis.

Shaikh, A. A. (2016, April 4). 7 steps to publishing in a scientific journal: Before you hit "submit," here's a checklist (and pitfalls to avoid). *Elsevier*. Retrieved from www.elsevier.com/connect/7-steps-to-publishing-in-a-scientific-journal

Thompson, G. L., & Thompson, R. (2014). *Yes, you can!: Advice for teachers who want a great start and a great finish with their students of color*. Thousand Oaks, CA: Corwin.

Chapter 4

Writing Short-Form (Articles, Papers, Etc.)

Quick quiz:

1. Would you rather read a *book* on how Laotian teaching strategies differ from Thai teaching strategies, or an *article* on the same topic?
2. Would you rather read a *book* on how the brain stem supports cognitive function, or an *article* on the same topic?
3. Would you rather read a *book* on how to speak Dothraki, or an *article* on the same topic? (And if you already speak Dothraki, you're one of the few people in this world nerdier than I; *me nem nesa!*)

Chances are, you selected "article" for most of the above questions. I read a lot of books. You probably do, too. But for every book we read, we read countless more articles, papers, blog posts, or other assortment of short-form writing. We are also more likely to read outside our usual genres and topics when the reading commitment is only a handful of pages. The shorter works' higher consumption rate means you can introduce far more stakeholders to your ideas – and thus help more students – if you embrace short-form writing. Even if short-form writing limits you to sharing only a taste of a complex topic, that taste leads people to seek the rest you have to share.

Some short pieces are for other education experts and decision-makers, and some are for the general public. The latter group is often neglected by folks like us yet has huge potential to touch lives. Julian Tyson decided to write an article for *The Conversation*, a site for which articles – exclusively by professors and researchers – are written for the general public. The article "reached more readers than the scholar had in *all the preceding decades* of work" (Lynch, 2016, p. 7). Our work is relevant for students, parents, and other family members. When we write for these audiences or the public at large, we can offer these folks information that helps kids and makes it easier for educators to do their jobs. Plus, educators are included among readers of non-field publications, too.

HOW THIS CHAPTER WORKS

(You Need Chapter 3)

"Chapter 3. Writing Anything" provided you with the fundamental guidelines that apply to all writing opportunities described in this book. The writing guidelines provided in this chapter are supplemental and are meant to be considered *with* the guidelines in "Chapter 3. Writing Anything".

IF YOU HATE WRITING (OR EVEN IF YOU LOVE IT)

Some of the smartest people I know struggle with writing. Others write well but doing so takes them a lot of time. The following tricks can help those who hate writing but want to publish their work. These tips happen to be useful for those who love writing as well.

- ❏ Submit short answers to publications. See the "Short Answer and Reference Sites" section of this chapter for opportunities like the "Tell Me About" column in ASCD's *Educational Leadership*.
- ❏ Co-write with a colleague. If you pull your weight by offering bullet points, disparate snippets of content, sources to cite, etc., a colleague who writes with ease can pull it all together. If she ends up with the greater workload, place her name before yours in authorship.

TIME-SAVING TIP

Use a good organizational system for your computer files so you can easily borrow verbiage from things you wrote before (for example, for a grant proposal, an email to a colleague, or an award submission) from one area and paste it into content for a publication. Often, what we write without publication in mind can later serve as the foundation of a draft we tweak for publication.

- ❏ Use an interview format for a piece in which someone interviews you about your work. This way you merely answer questions and don't have to worry about the hook, flow, etc.

❏ Conversely, you can interview someone else about her work you admire. This way you merely have to draft interview questions and pull them together with an intro, conclusion, and transitions.

❏ If you're artistic and techy, you can get key points across in an infographic in place of a traditional article. Many online news sources, in particular, give infographics the same treatment as a full-length article.

❏ Write a chapter in a book, rather than an entire book (when the book is published, you'll still be a published author, can likely set up a www. Amazon.com author page, etc.). See the "Book Chapters" section of this chapter for details.

❏ Submit your work for others to write about it. For example, the NMC Horizon Report series used to compile education experts' input every year, and other reports can do the same. The next chapter covers how to pitch a story idea to journalists who can cover your work.

❏ Opt to write a short book rather than a full-length book. ASCD's Arias series of short books (equivalent to about 2 chapters in length, or 10,000 words) are with a notable publisher in the industry and receive much exposure. Visit www.ascd.org/Publications/Books/Proposal-Guidelines-for-Book-Authors.aspx and scroll down to the "Arias" section for details.

❏ Write the foreword for someone else's book you respect. Forewords give you the chance to frame and add to conversation.

❏ Create a blog (see the "Blogging" section of this chapter) and invite others, such as your colleagues or students, to write for it. You can curate material and facilitate posts that focus on a set or changing theme.

❏ Lead a full book project as an editor (this would put your name on the book's cover, allow you to set up an author page on each site where the book is sold, etc.). A great place to start is the IGI Global online proposal form (www. igi-global.com/publish/submit-a-proposal). This would involve reading and editing the submissions. You could opt to edit the book with a colleague to save time, though your reading could double as research for other projects.

❏ Write book reviews. It's hard to be at a loss for what to say when you are relaying your reaction to something. See the "Book Review" section of this chapter for details.

❏ Record yourself as you talk about your topic. Most smart phones and newer laptops have an audio recording feature. You can then replay and transcribe your words (or use transcription software, which can help even when you have to clean up its mistakes). This gives you a foundation you can edit to produce a polished draft.

❏ Dig up your old college essays and other papers. If these were unpublished and share something important, you can polish them up and submit them for publication. Most of your writing will have already been done for you by your past self.

❏ If you have your PhD and thus already wrote a dissertation, consider turning your dissertation into a monograph (specialist book). This way you won't have to start from scratch in writing a book. See Routledge, Taylor & Francis Group (2017) for guidance determining if publishers would consider your work to be commercially viable as a book.

If writing just doesn't flow naturally for you, know that if you apply the time it will get easier. Maya Angelou said, "What I try to do is write ... it might be just the most boring and awful stuff. But I try .... And then it's as if the muse is convinced that I'm serious and says, 'Okay. Okay. I'll come'" (Heffron, 2011, p. 219). Jodi Picoult also said, "I may write garbage, but you can always edit garbage. You can't edit a blank page" (Kramer & Silver, 2006, p. 1).

Don't be too critical of your first draft; just get it onto your paper or screen. The next step – editing that draft – will likely be a much easier process than the initial draft proved.

LIST OF WRITING OPPORTUNITIES (JOURNALS, MAGAZINES, NEWSLETTERS, BLOGS, REFERENCE TOOLS, AND NEWSPAPERS)

LIST OF WRITING OPPORTUNITIES

This book lists 239 short-form writing opportunities (such as journal papers, magazine articles, newsletter and e-newsletter pieces, blog posts, short answer and reference sites, and newspaper op-eds and articles) for you in an electronic file that makes it easy to find and pursue writing opportunities. You can sort the file by publication type and visit each website with a simple click. The list contains details like publication category and manipulation-friendly fields you can use to track your submissions. A separate list will feature book publishers (covered in the next chapter). See the "eResources" section near the start of this book for details on accessing and using this "List of Writing Opportunities".

SHORT ANSWER AND REFERENCE SITES

You can get published by submitting short answers, such as in ASCD's *Educational Leadership* magazine (for the "Tell Me About It" column) or Comparative and International Education Society's (CIES's) *CIES Perspectives* (for the "Dialogue and Debate" column). Open this book's "List of Writing Opportunities" eResource (described earlier). Sort the file by "Category" (by clicking the arrow atop that column) to find the writing opportunities listed as "Short Answer" in this column.

Another way to contribute snippets of text is to contribute to online reference tools used frequently by educators and others. Particularly when it comes to informing non-experts about your topic, it's important to reach out to people through the tools they use. For example, consider how contributing your expertise to the following resources will reach different populations:

- A parent or student could avoid a misunderstanding when referencing Wikipedia (https://en.wikipedia.org).
- A reporter could describe your topic in accurate terms after using the Glossary of Education Reform for Journalists, Parents, and Community Members (http://edglossary.org).
- An educator or researcher new to your topic could sidestep a common misconception when referencing the ERIC Thesaurus (http://eric.ed.gov/?ti=all).

You can lend your expertise to improving the above resources and more. Open this book's "List of Writing Opportunities" eResource (described earlier) and find listings with "Reference" in the "Category" column.

Wikipedia

A reference site deserving special attention is one to which educators often turn up their noses: Wikipedia. Yet this collaboratively-maintained online encyclopedia ranks the sixth most widely used website in the world, and users view 10 billion pages within merely the English version of the site every month (Simonite, 2013). Even if you deride the site for its susceptibility to inaccuracies, the site is used profusely. Why not help remove inaccuracies and improve users' understanding of concepts? Educators and non-educators alike visit the site for an initial, basic understanding of what terms mean (for example, "What is project-based learning? What is problem-based learning? How do these differ?"), and some use it to take their understanding deeper.

You can add your voice to existing Wikipedia articles (even a sentence or two added to an existing piece can make important points and prevent misunderstandings), and even create new articles for concepts not yet covered there. Though you must stick to the community's policies discouraging self-promotion, you may still add references to your pertinent work (like cite and add a link to your journal paper) and ensure any page concerning you (common for authors) is accurate.

Your voice is also needed to broaden the perspectives that shape users' understanding of our field. Men comprise 90% of those running Wikipedia, and founder

Jimmy Whales says editor diversity is the biggest issue facing Wikipedia (Simonite, 2013). This impacts the content read during those 10 billion monthly page views. For example, Wagner, Garcia, Jadidi, and Strohmaier (2015) found the lack of diversity in the Wikipedia editor community introduces gender bias into Wikipedia content. Imagine obscurities such as these shaping such a large number of users' understanding of concepts related to our students and their futures. Expanding the number and heterogeneity of education experts contributing to Wikipedia can help.

Quora

You can also post answers in online communities like Quora (www.quora.com), covered in the "Guide to Hunting and Harvesting" eResource covered in "Chapter 13. Multiply Your Impact". Search for questions related to your area of expertise and answer all related questions (not just one). For example, my answers relating to teacher burnout (one of my areas of expertise) rendered 2,422 views in one year (with each post averaging 269 views per year). This average is relatively small (compared to posts on popular topics like dogs). However, answers addressing topics within your expertise are read by those who follow and care about those specific topics. Think of the impact your words could have on those readers and the students they serve.

BLOGGING

The youngest recipient ever of the Nobel Prize, Malala Yousafzai, is known for her crusade for universal education and for being shot in the face by the Taliban at age 15 in response to her activism. What some do not know is that Yousafzai started blogging for the British Broadcasting Corporation (BBC) at age eleven. When you blog to share your ideas, the process can also sharpen those ideas and propel your passion.

Blogs offer freedom to share unconventional perspectives and provide great writing practice. Blogging can "hone your writing skills, pushing you to write in a more accessible style and to distill a paper or thought process into a brief, readable blog post" (Author Services, 2017).

Blogging can help you land a book deal, and not just by improving your craft through practice. "Publishers look favorably on blogging: It clearly demonstrates that a scholar is actively engaging with a research community and is interested in promoting their work. It's a marketing tool publishers cannot ignore" (Anyangwe, 2011).

Blogging can also lead to landing a column, speaking engagement, or other opportunity. Ray Salazar (2013) attributes his education blog (www.chicagonow.com/white-rhino) as the impetus that opened doors for him on National Public Radio (NPR)…and let us not forget Yousafzai's blogging en route to her Nobel Prize.

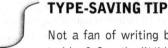

TYPE-SAVING TIP

Not a fan of writing but still want to blog? See the "Video Blogging" section of "Chapter 9. Speaking on Air and Recordings".

You can create your own blog, contribute to someone else's, or both. For example, the column I write for the *Psychology Today* blog gets far more hits than my website's blog, but I write pieces for the latter when they're better suited to the site's specific audience. I can also write a piece for my blog and then cross-post it on my *Psychology Today* blog, as well, as long as I add the line "Reprinted with permission from [initial source]" to the bottom (note your blogs might have different policies for cross-posts).

When you control the rights to your blog posts, you can always allow others to publish them for added readership. Consider Amy Illingworth (2017), a director at Sweetwater Union High School District who writes a blog at www.reflectionsonleadershipandlearning.wordpress.com. One of the editors at the School Superintendents Association (AASA) read Illingworth's work and asked her to turn the blog into a column for AASA's *School Administrator* magazine, where her words now receive added exposure.

While many education blogs are hardly read, other education bloggers gain large followings (Audrey Waters of Hack Education is one example) that lead to speaking engagements, book deals, and more. Education blogs with high readership tend to fit in at least one of the categories in Table 4.1.

Of course, success can be measured in different ways. You might want to blog simply as a creative outlet, or to help you reflect on your practice, or to support just a handful of practitioners you coach, or to infuse more diversity into the blogger pool, or to deliver occasional content to those who follow your work. If you deem blogging worthwhile, you can work toward your own definition of success.

Your Own Blog

If you are setting up your own website (see the "Website" section of "Chapter 2. Image"), that is one place to host your blog. Many web hosting platforms (for example, SquareSpace) allow you to also embed a form where visitors can opt to subscribe to your blog. You can then set up a free MailChimp (www.MailChimp. com) account that automatically emails (in e-newsletter form) your blog to anyone who subscribes, without you having to do anything beyond the usual way you

Table 4.1 Education Blogs with High Readership

Trait Encouraging High Readership	Example
Written by someone already highly influential or famous in the field	Yousafzai's current blog concerning education for girls at https://blog.malala.org
Received high recognition	Won "Best Blog" in Education Writers Association's National Awards for Education Reporting
Offers high value	Readers think, "Finally, this blogger tells me the specifics of how to give my slower learners added support while pushing gifted learners at the same time."
Refreshingly honest, brave, or enlightening	Readers think, "Finally, this blogger is saying what no one else has the guts to say!"
Is unique in some way	The posts provide something new (rather than regurgitating the same content seen frequently on the web)

would post your blog. Automatically alerting subscribers to new posts increases your blog's chances of being read.

Some services (often free) host blogging sites specifically for educators. Examples include Edublogs (www.edublogs.org) and Glogster EDU (edu.glogster.com). Other services (sometimes free) host blogging sites for anyone, and education experts frequently utilize these. Examples include Blogger (www.blogger.com), Tumblr (www.tumblr.com), and WordPress (www.wordpress.com). You might instead use LinkedIn's "article" feature in a blogging manner. Explore different options to find the setup you prefer.

RESOURCE TIP

Edublogs offers a free, self-paced course that walks you through the process of setting up a blog, posting, and more (teacherchallenge.edublogs.org/personal-blogging).

Other Blogs

Many blogs feature posts from multiple authors, and you can contribute to these (usually without the pressure of providing more). Teach 100 offers a daily ranking of educational blogs (https://teach.com/teach100) to peruse. Also, you can open this book's "List of Writing Opportunities" eResource (described earlier) and sort the file by "Category" to find publications categorized as "Blog/Site". Consider contributing to one of these.

If you struggle to get a piece accepted, don't lose heart. Commercial blogs are often particularly eager for contributors who work within the education field. If there is a product (edtech tool, curriculum series, etc.) you use or have studied, consider contacting the company to see if you can write about it for them. You can also pursue being featured (such as quoted or interviewed) on someone else's blog.

Successful Blogging

In addition to recommendations in the previous chapter, there are some additional things to keep in mind when you're writing a blog post or other online content:

- ❏ **Lean on the short side**, even if this means limiting what you communicate. Your reader is likely to be like other internet users, who tend to scan written work rather than read it in depth, so keep blog posts succinct; the best blogs are generally 1,000 words or fewer (Routledge, 2017). "Given individuals' decreasing attention spans, [a blog post] should be relatively short and easily digestible, so that someone can read it in just a few minutes" (Stewart, 2016, p. 78).

    One of the great things about online content is that it's easy to put links within your writing that lead to more information for those who want it. For example, if you mention "There are also strategies principals can use" in an article for teachers, you can make that statement double as a link leading to an article detailing those strategies, rather than go off on a tangent within your post.
- ❏ **Include an image.** Online content with relevant images receives 94% more views (Hall, 2015). Images also help readers understand what your post will address, thus helping you communicate your message.

    Some writers even start with an image before they write. Heather McGowen, one of LinkedIn's 2017 Top Voices in Education, says, "I always start with a picture. If I cannot articulate my idea in a single visual frame, I am not ready to write about it because the idea is not yet clear enough" (Anders, 2017, p. 2).

❑ **Brace yourself for feedback.** Since online content often has comment fields where readers can easily respond immediately to your work, you'll hear from more readers than you will when your writing is only printed. Other readers will see these comments, as well, which can result in comment-area dialogue.

Some education writers enjoy this dynamic, as it facilitates discussion. However, it can also be time consuming. If you find these comment sections taking away from the primary ways in which you help kids (like teaching or researching), consider turning the reader comments feature off, which you can typically do if you manage the blog.

HEARTACHE-SAVING TIP

When readers have a way to voice their reactions to your work, such as through letters to the editor, they can be harsh...but the immediacy and potential anonymity of online comment fields can open the door to particularly toxic criticism (racist and sexist comments, ignorant myth-spreading, political ravings, etc.). This is especially true if your work reaches national and international audiences outside the field of education.

There's no magic tonic to make your online articles and blog posts hostility-proof, but it can save you some heartache to anticipate possible aggression. This will prevent you from being blindsided, help you to not take comments personally (you are doing good work; your merit is not tied to the popularity of your article), and prepare you to respond appropriately (support your case with evidence rather than throw insults). If you have the option to turn off the comment field, consider doing so.

❑ **Don't let your title be a snooze-fest.** Rather, be concise and intriguing. While how to do this was covered in "Chapter 3. Writing Anything", it needs to be stressed again here. Readers who find journal papers and other forms of scholarly writing likely ran searches for something very particular and will base their interest in your work on whether it meets what they're looking for, whereas readers of online content are more evasive. Blog posts and online articles need titles that demand to be noticed.

> ## SCRAPPY TIP
>
> In December, note how sites and e-newsletters tout their "Top 10 Articles of the Year", "Must-Read Education Stories from 2018", "Most Emailed List", etc. These lists tend to be based on how many people visited the piece online or clicked a share option to spread it to others (easy to determine with web analytics). Reading these lists of titles can offer a sense of what grabbed readers' attention and can help you spice up your own titles and the angles of your content. Remember: more readers can mean more people helped by your expertise.
>
> For example, the most talked about pieces of Xavier Pavie and Karl Kapp, two of LinkedIn's 2017 Top Voices in Education, were titled "Why Are Innovative Individuals so Loathsome?" (in its English translation) and "Is eLearning Really Dead? Is Instructional Design Dying with It?" (Anders, 2017). This insight could inspire you to try a thought-provoking question as a title.

NEWSPAPER

Open this book's "List of Writing Opportunities" eResource (described earlier) and find listings with "Newspaper/Outlet" in the "Category" column (some categorized as "Blog/Site", "Magazine", or "Newsletter/eNewsletter" may also be open to commentaries). In addition to following the strategies in "Chapter 3. Writing Anything", a writer should follow some additional guidelines for newspapers (covered below).

Newspaper Op-Eds and Commentaries

Most newspapers and news sites have their own in-house journalists, but education experts frequently write opinion pieces for these news outlets. Newspaper websites often post guidelines for op-ed or commentary submissions, like *Education Week* does at www.edweek.org/go/comm-submit.

An op-ed was originally "a page of special features usually opposite the editorial page of a newspaper; also, a feature on such a page" (Merriam-Webster, 2018, p. 1), but the term has evolved to mean a commentary (and is sometimes *called* a commentary) in which an author outside of the publication's editorial board argues one viewpoint on an issue that is currently debated and of high interest.

Since op-ed topics are hotly debated, more people are likely to disagree with an op-ed than they would with an informational piece in which shared facts have an obvious, single implication. As you determine how to share your stance, remember that backing up your statements with evidence from respectable sources will be especially important. If you write a nationally-published op-ed, "be fully aware that your words, regardless of the evidence that you provide to back up your assertions, will be twisted, manipulated, taken out of context, and used against you by those that disagree with your position on issues" (Gasman, 2016, p. 120).

Make your stance obvious from the first paragraph. University of San Francisco Provost Donald Heller (2016) advises education op-ed writers to take a clear position on an issue (rather than arguing all sides), spend the bulk of the article arguing their point, and end with one or two paragraphs that summarize the piece and the issue's importance. For general interest publications, Heller stresses the need to use basic language, noting newspapers are generally written for a high school reading level or below.

If you bring up the opposing side, it should be because it's an elephant in the room readers are likely to be thinking of anyway, and it should be only to immediately slam it down with your counterargument. For example:

> In a survey of 1,000 school teachers, 76% of teachers reported most of their students' parents are uninvolved, and 47% of teachers regarded low parent involvement as a source of frustration (Reid, 2014). Some people conclude parents don't want to be involved in their children's educations. However, in a study of 803 parents of kids aged 3–18, 47% of parents reported wishing they could be involved in their child's education (NBC News Education Nation, 2015). The real reasons many parents appear uninvolved...

This way you've briefly acknowledged what readers are likely thinking, but only to knock it down. If you never address a misconception readers are likely to have, they'll read your article thinking, "This op-ed stands on thin ice, because it never addressed a 'fact' [actually a myth] I know that undermines this whole argument."

RESOURCE TIP

The OpEdProject (www.theoped project.org) arms women with connections and training to increase the diversity of voices in major commentary forums such as op-eds.

I especially encourage women to write op-eds, as so few currently do. "Nearly 80 percent of the op-eds published in the nation's leading newspapers are written by men, but that number appears to roughly reflect the gender breakdown of submissions" (Lepore, 2013, p. 4). In other words, 80% of submissions are by men. Society has traditionally discouraged women from stepping into conflict-rich environments, so we women need to conscientiously push past any hesitation we have to step into the op-ed fray. Otherwise our voices are not heard in this arena. We have too many important ideas to let that happen.

Newspaper Articles

Most newspapers and news sites rely entirely or predominantly on in-house journalists (and the journalists of partnered news outlets) for their articles. When outside authors *are* considered, follow the specific guidelines on a news source's website. When you ultimately write your article, lead with your core message ("don't bury the lead", as reporters say) and include details only after making your key talking points.

Pitch

Writing for a newspaper often involves submitting a pitch: a succinct description of a piece you'd like the publication to run. Like the pitch discussed in "Chapter 1: Introduction", you'll want to whittle your idea down to a compelling core, but here you must also convince someone to publish your message.

You can follow the news site's pitch guidelines, but you can also interact with reporters on social media, comment on their stories where they appear online, and reach out directly to reporters who cover topics related to yours.

Recommendations for a compelling pitch include:

- Be timely and insert yourself into the news of the day.
- Offer something unique: new information or a new perspective on an existing topic.
- Familiarize yourself with the news outlet and pitch something appropriate for it.

See the "News Media and Television" section of "Chapter 9. Speaking on Air and Recordings" for guidance and a sample pitch.

SCRAPPY TIP

Education Week opinion editor Elizabeth Rich told me the newspaper strives for diverse voices yet doesn't get enough pitches from the center of the United States and would like more. She even uses a map to track coverage. If you don't live in a coastal U.S. state, you might have an advantage when pitching your Commentary.

You might intend to write the commentary or article you pitch, but you can also pitch ideas to a journalist who will incorporate them into a piece *she* writes. If you're covered by a news outlet that partners with other news outlets that also run its stories, your exposure increases dramatically. For example, The Hechinger Report and Associated Press articles are duplicated by CNN, NPR, *The New York Times*, *The Washington Post*, and many others.

MAGAZINES, NEWSLETTERS, WEBSITES, AND OTHER ARTICLE VENUES

Magazines, newsletters, websites, and other article venues offer a chance to share your work in a less formal, highly accessible, and widely read environment. Compared to journal papers, book chapters, and books, articles are relatively short and faster to produce. Though editors are typically involved, formal peer review is generally not. This speeds up production time and allows you to quickly get your words into readers' minds.

Strategies covered in "Chapter 3. Writing Anything" can be applied to an article (remember your audience, be clear, etc.). However, there are some additional considerations for an article (below), which should be read before pursuing this short-form writing project.

Options

Open this book's "List of Writing Opportunities" eResource (described earlier) and find listings categorized as "Blog/Site", "List (Magazines)", "Magazine", and "Newsletter/eNewsletter". Most of these are read by educators or target other stakeholders like parents.

For mainstream mags, don't miss the List of Magazines by Circulation maintained with current, reputable sources at https://en.wikipedia.org/wiki/List_of_magazines_by_circulation. If you have a message for grandparents on how their involvement benefits students, it pays to know that *AARP The Magazine* and *AARP Bulletin* dominate with 24 million U.S. readers apiece (compare this to popular magazines like *Architectural Digest*, *Condé Nast Traveler*, *House Beautiful*, and *Fast Company*, which each have around 800,000 readers). U.K. circulations are smaller but can still reach hundreds of thousands of readers. Though the circulation list includes magazines that aren't education-specific, mainstream mags offer the chance to cater our messages to other stakeholders helping students (while still reaching those educators who read mainstream publications).

Submission

Find and follow the publication's submission guidelines. Some publications have processes similar to journals, where you submit a complete article to be considered for publication. Others (particularly prominent outlets) want you to pitch a possible article to them. In these cases, leverage guidance from the "News Media and Television" section of "Chapter 9. Speaking on Air and Recordings".

SCRAPPY TIP

Once I was guest moderator of an Edutopia (@Edutopia) Twitter chat, and the Edutopia team and I were simultaneously chatting via video conference to tackle the chat as a group. Samer Rabadi, Edutopia's Online Community Manager, remarked on which contributors (just regular educators who chose to join the chat) made comments so insightful that Edutopia should invite them to write some articles for the site.

Edutopia, part of the George Lucas Educational Foundation, has a large audience (just one of their social media platforms – Twitter – has 1.03 million followers) and is a highly respected resource in the field. Contributing to Edutopia is a great opportunity to reach educators and thus widen your impact on kids, and participating in a Twitter chat (something anyone can do) can lead to that chance, just as it can from chats facilitated by other organizations.

Content

"Chapter 3. Writing Anything" advised you to read your chosen publication's current articles to note published pieces' topics, voice, tone, style, format, and more. For article venues, you have the added chance to consider its top read articles. Many publications announce "this month's top articles" in emails to subscribers, or at least list the year's most popular pieces. Pay attention to what readers are most interested in, or why top titles might have drawn in readers.

Add links (leading from a term to more information on it, or leading to a resource readers can use) to online content. Many sites are happy to also include a link to your blog or website, which can earn you followers positioned to read your future work.

WHITEPAPERS AND REPORTS

In the education field, a whitepaper or report is generally a neatly-packaged, expert, in-depth account of a topic, paired with recommendations for improvements in the given area. Whitepapers and reports can be catalysts in the field. For example, the national report *A Nation at Risk*, commissioned by the Reagan administration in 1982, is credited with launching our modern era of U.S. education reform (Coggins, 2017) and shifting political conversations away from equity to economic competitiveness (Waisanen, 2018).

Kat Stein (2016), Executive Director of Communications at University of Pennsylvania's Graduate School of Education, writes, "Academics in my own organization have begun to realize that…presenting findings via a graphically designed report can increase its impact greatly. Rather than being slick and commercial, it is perceived as professional and more credible" (p. 115). Just Google "education report" or "education white paper" for examples. Notice these vary from short, like Illuminate Education's *Building a Blueprint Around Formative Assessment* (www.illuminateed.com/resources/library), to long, like the U.S. Department of Education's *The Condition of Education* (https://nces.ed.gov/pubs2017/2017144.pdf). For design tips, see "10 Page-Turning White Paper Examples and Design Tips" by Sara McGuire (https://goo.gl/gnfp2J).

JOURNALS

Most of what you learned in "Chapter 3. Writing Anything" can be applied to a journal or research paper (remember your audience, be clear, etc.). However, there are some additional considerations for a paper (below), which should be read before pursuing this very formal writing project.

If you are new to writing papers for academic journals or chapters for academic tomes, and particularly if you are new to scholarly writing in general, understand how different this outlet is from more mainstream publications. There are very stringent formats, rules, and expectations for scholarly writing. This section will help you find success in the journal arena, even if this is your first foray.

Read Top Papers

Before writing your paper, read journal papers that have won Outstanding Publication types of awards (these are often published and available on the award-giver's website) or are in top-rated education journals (covered later). This practice will give you a sense of what successful academic papers look like, how their sections are meant to work, and how an effective paper is crafted. Having this context will make other journal writing guidance easier to understand and apply.

> ## SCRAPPY TIP
>
> An earlier tip involved reviewing lists like "Top 10 Articles of the Year" for a sense of what grabbed readers' attention. Some journals offer similar lists (Google "AERA Announces Most Read Education Research Articles of 2017" for an example). These can help you identify which titles and abstracts readers find most appealing. Use what you find to improve the appeal of your paper's title and abstract in order to improve your paper's reach.

Group Authorship

If authoring your piece with a group, aim for diversity. "Peer-reviewed publications with gender-heterogeneous authorship teams received 34% more citations than publications produced by gender-uniform authorship teams...Promoting diversity not only promotes representation and fairness but may lead to higher quality science" (Campbell, Mehtani, Dozier, & Rinehart, 2013). Through a study of 697 volunteers working in teams of two to five, the top three factors determining group success were the presence of women in the group, higher empathy scores (which women had), and the ability for group members to freely participate in discussions (which likely improved with greater empathy) (Alda, 2017). This finding persisted even when the group's communication took place online. In a study of over 2.5 million scientific papers, Freeman and Huang (2014) found that greater ethnic diversity in co-author groups was associated with publication in higher impact journals and received more citations than others; "These findings suggest that diversity ... leads to greater contributions ... as measured by impact factors and citations" (p. 2).

Though the success of a journal paper isn't determined entirely by citations, the degree to which your paper is shared is just one of diverse authorship's perks. Co-authoring a paper with people of different backgrounds involves bringing a wider range of perspectives and ideas likely to improve your project's quality and enhance your understanding of your topic.

Picking Your Journal

Aim to submit to well-read journals. I once saw a man receive the Outstanding Paper Award from the California Educational Research Association. He thanked his mentor for telling him to "publish in journals people actually read" and believed his findings spread because of this.

Since your goal is to help students, you'll want your paper to land in a journal with a good reputation and wide circulation. Reference the education journal rankings at a site like SCImago Journal and Country Rank (www.scimagojr. com/journalrank.php, with the subject category set to "Education") for help. For more journal ranking sources and an exploration of metrics used, see Walters (2017).

RESOURCE TIP

If you paste your paper's title and abstract into Elsevier's Journal Finder tool (https:// journalfinder.elsevier.com), it will show you which journals are well suited to publishing that specific paper.

The right audience is more important than a big audience. If your paper lands in a well-read journal on brain science yet your research is more pertinent to special education fitness curriculum, your paper's impact could be minimal. There are so many journals in the field of education that you can strike a balance of relevant *and* read.

That said, if you do publish in an obscure journal there is much you can do to promote it (see "Chapter 13. Multiply Your Impact"), particularly if you published open access (meaning people can read – and thus share and cite – your work without paying a fee). Share your promotion efforts with the journal editors, as your work to share your paper also helps to elevate the journal.

Adhere strictly to your chosen journal's submission guidelines. Note that simultaneous submissions (sending your paper to more than one journal at a time) are usually prohibited.

Style and Format

Read and reference a guide on how to write an effective journal paper. A single section in this book cannot encompass everything you should know, whereas a series of chapters or a guide can walk you through how to appropriately craft every portion of the paper (from its abstract and keywords, all the way down through its conclusion).

See the "Resource Tip" text box on the next page for academic writing guides. Since the information in such guides can be overwhelming, read the guide as you work on each stage and section of an actual paper (rather than reading the entire book or handout series first and then writing the paper afterwards).

RESOURCE TIP

For free, searchable academic writing assistance, I recommend:

- Elsevier Researcher Academy (https://researcher-racademy.elsevier.com), which has learning videos to help you through different stages and types of academic writing (and earns you certificates of completion).
- Purdue Online Writing Lab (https://owl.english.purdue.edu/owl), which has guides for the academic writing process (located under General Writing) and for APA and other citation styles (located under Research and Citation Resources).
- U.S. Department of Education's *Going Public: Writing About Research in Everyday Language* (https://files.eric.ed.gov/fulltext/ED545224.pdf), which includes a glossary pairing research terms with revised usage, so you can make complex concepts simpler without losing accuracy.

Regularly reference a guide on the writing citation style you'll be expected to use (for example, the manual found at www.apastyle.org). That "style" relates not just to citations but also to format and content. In the U.S. we standardly use American Psychological Association (APA) style, though when I've written for international publications I've been asked to follow other styles, such as Modern Language Association (MLA) or Chicago Manual of Style. Each journal has a required style. See the "Resource Tip" text box for style guides.

Always use the most up-to-date version of a style (unless otherwise directed), as formats evolve over time. For example, APA style is in version six as I write this, which is slightly different from APA version five.

Title

Craft an effective title. "Editors hate titles that make no sense or fail to represent the subject matter adequately" (Borja, 2014, p. 14). Consider what your target reader will search for when trying to find a paper like yours. Aim for being concise while still communicating what the paper will cover. Elsevier publisher

Jennifer Franklin told me twenty words maximum is a good guideline for journal article titles. Avoid abbreviations, jargon, and location unless central to the study (such as in "How Educators Collaborated Across the Berlin Wall").

In his research on journal paper titles, Madan (2015) found the following:

- **Recommendations from findings:** Titles that described the study's results or described the research question were met with increased citations. Question-worded titles were more likely to engage readers and increase memorability. Titles that are catchy – such as by suggesting innovation or being intriguing – can attract readers, but only if the titles are also informative. Titles should be clear, informative, concise, and accurate.
- **Mixed findings:** Some studies found shorter titles rendered higher citation rates, while other studies found longer titles to be cited more often. Some studies found titles with colons rendered higher citation rates, while other studies found colon-featuring titles to be cited less often.

Once you've drafted a title, search for words you can remove without hurting the title's meaning. For example, consider the following title:

- A Quantitative Study on How Concentrated Poverty Influences the Field of Education as Examined in Randomized Experiments in Michigan's Urban Schools

Your methods ("quantitative study" and "randomized experiments") and location ("Michigan's") can be easily shared in your abstract and introduction. Anyone who finds your paper in a journal or database is already working with content in "the field of education" and doesn't need a reminder in your title. You likely don't need the phrase "concentrated poverty" when "poverty" communicates the general idea. "How" is just clutter. These omissions change our title to:

- Poverty Influences the Field as Examined in Urban Schools

However, the above title doesn't tell us much and is confusing. What does the author mean by "influences the field"? The title's impersonal nature makes the topic seem unimportant, and its generality cuts its chances of being found and read by those who would care about its specific content. Consider this change:

- Poverty Hinders Urban Students' Determination to Graduate

See how different the above title is from the version before, and also from its original draft, and how much more compelling and revealing it now is. The new title is worded as a statement, but you could also phrase it as a question (Does

Poverty Hinder Urban Students' Determination to Graduate?) or a shocking finding (Poor Urban Students Are 50% Less Determined to Graduate). Note you can always add a colon followed by more details, but your core title should be strong enough to woo readers on its own.

Abstract

A defining component of journal papers, conference papers, and research papers is the abstract. The abstract is a 150–250-word summary that precedes your paper's introduction and is typically displayed like teaser text in online databases that house your paper.

Potential readers will use your title and abstract to determine whether or not to keep reading the rest of your paper. Your abstract will need to communicate that such a read is worthwhile. To increase your abstract's effectiveness:

- ❏ Include your purpose, methods, findings, and implications (as your citation style defines these terms, and in the same order they appear in your paper) ...but don't let the novelty and "cool" factor of your ideas get lost in rhetoric. Remember what you've learned in this book about your core message and be sure that message is obvious in your abstract.
- ❏ When sharing your paper's ideas in your abstract, it is best to choose up to five on which to focus. Otherwise it is hard to communicate points well, and you end up listing concepts without capturing the nature of your paper.
- ❏ Maximize what your sentences say by trimming excess words and being very clear. For example, rather than say, "The study findings are known to have limited generalizability in some demographical contexts," say something like, "The study findings do not apply to non-urban schools."
  Remember: potential readers are hoping to learn about your topic and don't necessarily know the topic jargon or research jargon you might frequently use. Such jargon may sometimes be unavoidable in the body of the paper, but it must be avoided entirely in the title and abstract.

Reading the abstracts of other papers (like those you find at https://eric.ed.gov) can help you understand what works (which abstracts give you a good sense of the papers and make you want to read more?) and what doesn't work (which abstracts fail to follow the best practices listed above?). Imagine someone is reading your abstract through the same critical lens and adjust your words as necessary.

Review and Rejection

Question. What do Ernst, Fermi, Gell-Mann, Higgs, Krebs, Mullis, Shechtman, and Yalow all have in common?

Answer.   Their papers all won the Nobel Prize ... (wait for it) ... after previously being rejected for publication.

"The average acceptance rate for journals is 50%" (Wilson, 2012, p. 12). There is no correlation between a journal's rejection rate and its impact factor (a ratio of citations and citable items from the journal), so even journals with low impact factors can reject over 90% of papers (Matthews, 2016).

Paper review is a subjective process, and rejection does not mean you or your ideas are unworthy. The "After Receiving Verdict" section of "Chapter 3. Writing Anything" covers the process of receiving and responding to feedback that is typical for journal submissions, as well as ways in which rejection can strengthen your work.

RESOURCE TIP

While an impact factor (IF) concerns journals, an *h*-index quantifies the output of individual authors. See what your *h*-index is at SCOPUS (www.scopus.com). Elsevier publisher Jennifer Franklin told me it's really hard to get a high *h*-index; for example, an *h*-index of nine requires you to have authored at least nine papers that have each been cited at least nine times.

SHORT-FORM EDITOR

Journals, magazines, newsletters, and more regularly need new editors. If you sign up to receive education organizations' free e-newsletters, you'll be alerted to these opportunities. You can also visit publication websites (see those in the "List of Writing Opportunities" eResource) and speak with publication staff to learn of editor prospects.

Publisher support of editors varies, depending on the publication. For example, editing a short newsletter might be on a voluntary basis, whereas editing a major journal could involve financial compensation, training, and staff.

All publishers want good editors. Their wish list of qualifications you should meet will often include:

- Writing published in publications similar to the one for which you want to be an editor.
- Editor or reviewer experience.

- Strong reputation (when people in the field hear your name, they know it to mean a leading expert on the publication's topic).
- Can help the publication with its individual needs (by improvising if resources are limited, managing growth if subscriptions are booming, etc.).
- Able to see the big picture ("Does this collection of papers due justice to this issue's theme?") as well as details ("That introduction is a grammatical mess").
- Strong communicator and decision-maker.

Honing your traits to meet the above qualifications will increase your chances of securing an editor position.

YOUR TURN

"Chapter 3. Writing Anything" provided guidance to write well. This chapter provided added tips, as well as multiple opportunities to share your expertise through short-form writing. Select a publication (use the "List of Writing Opportunities" eResource for suggestions) to which you will submit a written piece. Then complete Exercise 4.1 to plan your submission. Reference sections in this chapter and the previous chapter as you complete the exercise.

EXERCISE 4.1: SHORT-FORM WRITING PLAN

1. What will you be writing?
   - ❏ Blog Post
   - ❏ Op-Ed/Commentary
   - ❏ Article
   - ❏ Whitepaper or Report
   - ❏ Academic/Journal Paper
   - ❏ Other:

2. To which publication will you submit your piece?

3. Read the publication's submission guidelines. What is the specified word count, formatting, title length, etc.?

4. Note any details that will influence what you write.
   - ❏ Time of year:
   - ❏ Publication theme:
   - ❏ Current newsworthy events:

5. Who is your audience made up of? This can be one main audience or a few key groups.

6. What does your audience need from you?

---

7. What are your key purposes in writing this piece?

8. What new understanding will your audience gain from your piece?

9. What will your audience be able to do after reading your piece?

10. Describe what your style will be (humorous, casual, formal, etc.).

11. What will your piece's title be?

12. What magic will you use to make concepts resonate? Remember Table 3.2.

13. Create a template and use it to outline your piece. Then add to each line item, gradually turning your template into a complete draft.

14. Proof and revise your piece as necessary. Ensure your piece meets submission requirements and criteria described in this chapter and the previous chapter (communicates your core message, is very clear, doesn't overload your reader, etc.).

15. How will you introduce or pitch your piece in your cover letter or email?

REFERENCES

Alda, A. (2017). *If I understood you, would I have this look on my face?: My adventures in the art and science of relating and communicating.* New York, NY: Random House.

Anders, G. (2017, December 12). *LinkedIn top voices 2017: Education.* Retrieved from www.linkedin.com/pulse/linkedin-top-voices-2017-education-george-anders

Anyangwe, E. (2011, August 23). How to get ahead in academic publishing: Q&A best bits. *The Guardian.* Retrieved from www.theguardian.com/higher-education-network/blog/2011/aug/23/academic-publishing-summary

Author Services. (2017). Blogging: How to make it work. Retrieved from http://authorservices.taylorandfrancis.com/blogging

Borja, A. (2014, June 24). 11 steps to structuring a science paper editors will take seriously: A seasoned editor gives advice to get your work published in an international journal. *Elsevier.* Retrieved from www.elsevier.com/connect/11-steps-to-structuring-a-science-paper-editors-will-take-seriously

Campbell, L. G., Mehtani, S., Dozier, M. E., & Rinehart, J. (2013). Gender-heterogeneous working groups produce higher quality science. *PLoS ONE, 8*(10), e79147. doi:10.1371/journal.pone.0079147

Coggins, C. (2017). *How to be heard: 10 lessons teachers need to advocate for their students and profession.* San Francisco, CA: Jossey-Bass.

Freeman, R. B., & Huang, W. (2014). Collaborating with people like me: Ethnic co-authorship within the US (N0. W19905). *National Bureau of Economic Research.* Retrieved from www.nber.org/papers/w19905.pdf

Gasman, M. (2016). *Academics going public: How to write and speak beyond academe.* New York, NY: Routledge, Taylor & Francis.

Hall, D. (2015, April 6). Content with relevant images gets 94% more views. *Social Media Today.* Retrieved from www.socialmediatoday.com/marketing/2015-04-06/content-relevant-images-gets-94-more-views-infographic

Heffron, J. (2011). *The writer's idea book 10th anniversary edition: How to develop great ideas for fiction, nonfiction, poetry, and screenplays.* Ontario, Canada: Writer's Digest Books.

Heller, D. E. (2016). Writing opinion articles. In M. Gasman (Ed.), *Academics going public: How to write and speak beyond academe,* (pp. 21–37). New York, NY: Routledge, Taylor & Francis.

Illingworth, Amy [@AmyLIllingworth]. (2017, November 4). *I was honored to be asked to turn one of my recent blogs into a column for the @AASAHQ Administrator journal: http://my.aasa.org/AASA/Resources/SAMag/2017/Nov17/colIllingworth.aspx* [Twitter moment]. Retrieved from https://twitter.com/amylillingworth

Kramer, M. J., & Silver, M. (2006, November 22). Jodi Picoult: You can't edit a blank page. *NPR Books.* Retrieved from www.npr.org/templates/story/story.php?storyId=6524058

Lepore, J. (2013, September 3). The new economy of letters. *The Chronical of Higher Education.* Retrieved from www.chronicle.com/article/The-New-Economy-of-Letters/141291

Lynch, M. (2016, September 23). Should writing for the public count toward tenure? *The Edvocate.* Retrieved from www.theedadvocate.org/writing-public-count-toward-tenure

Madan, C. R. (2015). Every scientist is a memory researcher: Suggestions for making research more memorable. *F1000Research 2015, 4*(19). doi:10.12688/f1000research.6053.1

Matthews, D. (2016, January 28). High rejection rates by journals 'pointless': Analysis suggests higher selectivity fails to increase journals' impact factors. *Times Higher Education.* Retrieved from www.timeshighereducation.com/news/high-rejection-rates-by-journals-pointless

Merriam-Webster (2018). Dictionary: Op-ed. Retrieved from www.merriam-webster.com/dictionary/op-ed

NBC News Education Nation. (2015). Parent toolkit: State of parenting: A snapshot of today's families: A national survey of parents for NBC News. Retrieved from www.parenttoolkit.com/files/ParentingPoll_PrintedReport.pdf

Reid, K. S. (2012, May 2). Survey: Most teachers want involved parents but don't have them. *Education Week.* Retrieved from http://blogs.edweek.org/edweek/parentsandthepublic/2014/05/survey_finds_most_teachers_want_parents_in_their_classrooms.html?cmp=ENL-EU-NEWS3

Routledge. (2017). *Promoting your book*. Retrieved from www.routledge.com/resources/authors/promoting-your-book.

Routledge, Taylor & Francis Group. (2017). *Author directions: Navigating your success from PhD to book: 5 key tips for turning your PhD into a successful monograph*. Boca Raton, FL: CRC Press.

Salazar, R. (2013, May 17). *Top 10 reasons teachers should blog*. Retrieved from www.chicagonow.com/white-rhino/2013/05/top-10-reasons-teachers-should-blog

Simonite, T. (2013, October 22). The decline of Wikipedia. *MIT Technology Review*. Retrieved from www.technologyreview.com/s/520446/the-decline-of-wikipedia

Stein, K. (2016). How to write an influential press release. In M. Gasman (Ed.), *Academics going public: How to write and speak beyond academe*, (pp. 105–117). New York, NY: Routledge, Taylor & Francis.

Stewart, D. (2016). Crafting an online scholarly identity. In M. Gasman (Ed.), *Academics going public: How to write and speak beyond academe*, (pp. 71-–85). New York, NY: Routledge, Taylor & Francis.

Wagner, C., Garcia, D., Jadidi, M., & Strohmaier, M. (2015). *It's a man's Wikipedia? Assessing gender inequality in an online encyclopedia*. arXiv:1501.06307v2 [cs.CY]

Waisanen, D. (2018). *Education as a civic marketplace: The political rhetoric of Arne Duncan*. Paper presented at the 2018 Annual Meeting of the American Educational Research Association, New York, NY.

Wilson, J. (Ed.). (2012). Peer review: The nuts and bolts. *Standing up for Science 3*. Retrieved from http://senseaboutscience.org/activities/peer-review-the-nuts-and-bolts

Chapter 5

Writing Books

Theodor Geisel believed the *Dick and Jane* early reading books actually turned kids off reading because they were so boring. Instead of writing a paper on the books' failings, which might have reached a handful of scholars, he simply wrote a better book, which nearly everyone we know has read: *The Cat in the Hat*, under the pen name Dr. Seuss. Geisel said, "I have great pride in taking *Dick and Jane* out of most school libraries. That is my greatest satisfaction" (Conradt, 2018, p. 3). The monumental and sustained success of *The Cat in the Hat* – far exceeding that of *Dick and Jane* – suggests Geisel made an important contribution to turning children into readers.

Is there a topic you see being mishandled by current field literature, or a crucial book that doesn't yet exist? Are you someone who could write a book that has a positive impact on students and our field? If so, write one.

A book's length allows you to dive deeper into topics, explain them more thoroughly, and share more knowledge than shorter formats allow. This gives authors an opportunity to better educate readers in ways that can better help students.

Contrary to popular opinion, you don't need to "know people" in high places to land a book deal. I set out to publish my first book without any special introductions or contacts. I simply noted which publisher's books I most respected, looked up its author submission guidelines online, and mailed in my chapters and proposals. This approach worked for me, and it can work for you too (though this chapter includes a Scrappy Fast Track anyway to increase your odds).

If you do know an editor, definitely approach him about your submission plans, but don't fret if you don't know anyone on the inside. Even after my first book was published and I had an editor, my proposals and manuscripts still have to pass peer review, the publisher's marketing team, and its editorial board. No matter your veteran status in publishing, the most important determinants in your publication are your book proposal and manuscript quality.

This chapter will help you craft a good book, and it will also help you get published. Don't miss the Scrappy Fast Track. It contains a formula I've shared with friends, who used it to immediately achieve book publishing success (far faster than they thought possible) with prominent publishers. If you craft a well-written book that amply meets education readers' needs, you can be a published book author too.

HOW THIS CHAPTER WORKS
(You Need Chapter 3)

"Chapter 3. Writing Anything" provided you with the fundamental guidelines that apply to all writing opportunities described in this book. The writing guidelines provided in this chapter are supplemental and are meant to be considered *with* the guidelines in "Chapter 3. Writing Anything".

LIST OF BOOK PUBLISHERS

LIST OF BOOK PUBLISHERS

This book lists 90 book publishers for you in an electronic file that makes it easy to find and pursue education book authoring opportunities. You can sort the list by publisher type and visit each website with a simple click. The list contains details like publisher websites, categories, and manipulation-friendly fields you can use to track your manuscript and proposal submissions. See the "eResources" section near the start of this book for details on accessing and using this "List of Book Publishers".

BOOK CHAPTERS

You might opt to write a chapter in a book, rather than an entire book. I recommend doing this even if you ultimately want to write a full-length book, as the "published author" status and perks that come with writing a book chapter will also help your full-length book proposal to be well received.

These opportunities are listed as "Book Chapter" in the "Category" column of the "List of Writing Opportunities" eResource (discussed in "Chapter 4. Writing

Short-Form"). One example of these prospects is IGI Global's "Call for Chapter" site (www.igi-global.com/publish/call-for-papers/?dt=book-chapters), where you can find a topic that matches yours and submit a chapter for consideration. Most book chapter opportunities involve scholarly writing and are equivalent in style and length to a journal paper. Thus the "Journals" section of the previous chapter can help you craft these.

However, authors are sometimes invited to write single chapters that are gathered as a collection in a less formal practitioner book. Consulting "Chapter 10. Connecting" and putting the word out that you want to author books and chapters can expose you to these opportunities.

Writing a single chapter establishes you as an author, even if you still haven't written a full-length book. When the book is published, you'll officially be a published author and can likely set up a www.Amazon.com author page, etc. The "Exposure for Your Books" section of "Chapter 13. Multiply Your Impact" also applies to your book chapter.

WRITING BOOKS

If you search Amazon.com, the world's biggest online bookseller (Rushton, 2017; Williams, 2018), its Education and Teaching category offers 1.1 million books. There is clearly a demand for books in our field. Do you want to add your voice to those shaping readers' understanding of what's best for kids? I know I do.

As the "Scrappy Fast Track" in "Chapter 3. Writing Anything" shows, publishing is not the unattainable pipe dream many assume. I meet many education experts who aspire to this goal. Being a strong writer is immensely helpful in this endeavor, but those who aren't can grow (pursuing and perfecting short-form writing will help), co-author, or pay for editorial services in order to overcome this hurdle.

Your message could be well suited to a book if:

- your message isn't well communicated by available books (you say something no one else is saying, or say something in a way no one else is saying it), and
- there is a strong *need* for your book (it can help readers help students).

Note I say "need" rather than "demand", as sometimes stakeholders don't know they need a book until one is written and brought to their attention.

Most of what you learned in "Chapter 3. Writing Anything" can be applied to a book. However, there are some additional considerations for this long-form project (below), which should be read before writing a book.

Picking a Publisher

It's a good idea to determine your most desired publisher before writing your book (or at least very early in the book writing process, such as after you've crafted a few sections to better understand what kind of book you'll write). Though this decision may change as you develop your initial chapters, identifying a likely publisher is necessary in order to write a book proposal you are likely to use when your chapters are ready for submission.

See the "List of Book Publishers" eResource mentioned earlier for publishers that produce quality books for our field. When finding a publisher that's right for you, it can also help to:

❏ Pick up your favorite books in your area of specialization and see who published them.

❏ Visit the publishers section of a large education conference like the American Educational Research Association (AERA) Annual Meeting. This allows you to roam from one publishing house to the next while viewing their latest offerings, chatting with their editors and marketing leads, and sometimes meeting recent authors.

❏ Present at conferences your desired editors likely attend. "Editors on the lookout for manuscripts become fixtures at academic conferences, and monitor the voices behind conference papers" (Alexander, 2011, p. 1). When I taught a course on this book's topic at a conference, an editor of a prestigious university press reached out to me and asked if I would be interested in turning the class into a book (I already hoped to publish this book with my current

TRADITIONAL PUBLISHING VS. SELF-PUBLISHING

Some authors opt to self-publish their books, which means they get their books printed and sold without the involvement of a traditional publishing house. Though self-publishing provides the author with a greater share of book proceeds, a traditional publisher:

- uses processes (like peer review, editor feedback, and copyediting) that improve the quality of your work;
- lends credibility to your work (this helps others accept your ideas);
- uses its own channels to sell your book (this reaches readers you wouldn't reach on your own); and
- can open doors to sharing opportunities, such as a radio interview in which you discuss your book (this helps your wisdom reach more people).

For these reasons I have always used the traditional publishing route and recommend this route to others.

publisher, but if not, I would have pursued the other editor's offer). If I had never taught that course, that editor would likely never have heard of my work or reached out to me.

❑ Consider which publishers sponsor your favorite events and endeavors related to your topic. Knowing Routledge/Taylor and Francis (the publisher of this book) is often the main sponsor of the AERA Annual Meeting and the BERA Annual Conference – an act that reflects its commitment to supporting research and the field – is one of the many reasons it appeals to me.

❑ Talk to authors you know about their book publishing experiences. If they have editors who could be appropriate matches for your work, ask if an introduction is possible. Editors are more likely to view your project through the lens of possibility if someone they respect has introduced you to them, as opposed to your submission arriving as a stranger's project.

❑ Look for a publishing house that subjects all potential projects to a rigorous peer review process. While this might sound counterproductive, this criterion will help you weed out publishing houses with weaker reputations and will also expose you to quality feedback that will improve your work. The field's acceptance of what you write will be strongly influenced by the reputation of your publisher. As author Martin McQuillan, PhD, wisely noted, "In general, the more peer review that your manuscript is subject to, the better it will be. You should immediately be suspicious of a publisher with no peer review process" (Murray, 2014, p. 3).

Submission Process (Know Before You Write)

The publisher's book submission guidelines will tell you how many chapters you'll need to provide up front for an editor's consideration and – if he is interested in your project – to be peer reviewed (a process defined in "Chapter 11. Serving"). Most publishers will want to see only *some* finished chapters (usually the introductory chapter and one or two others that need not be consecutive), as well as a book proposal (which typically describes all chapters) before making a decision to publish your book.

Can you imagine laboring over an entire book, only to discover at submission time that you only needed to submit one chapter? I can, because I completed my first two books (a related set) in their entirety before submitting them, simply because I was ignorant concerning how publishers worked. The good news is that the more complete your entire book is, the better you're able to describe all chapters in the book proposal.

A happy medium is to work on the book until you have a good sense of its direction and can finalize the one to three chapters your publisher will request. While the editor is considering your project, and then while the book is being peer reviewed (which can take months), and then while your editor takes a successful submission before his marketing team and editorial board for its final approval… you can be plugging away at finishing the book in the meantime. Even if your book is ultimately rejected, your chapters and proposal will be more refined the next time you submit.

Writing the Book Proposal

Remember "Find Your Message", "Craft Your Pitch", "Craft Talking Points", and "Consider Packaging" from "Chapter 1. Introduction"? Those lessons apply well to a book proposal: to write a good proposal, you need to first identify the core message and purpose of your book, know how to best pitch it, and consider the big picture of how you'll package concepts (for example, *Teach Like a Pirate* by Dave Burgess approaches student engagement differently than *Hacking Engagement* by James Alan Sturtevant).

SCRAPPY TIP

When you list already-published books that are similar to your proposed book, put these in a table where each book has its own row. Then create a column to the right where, for every one of these books, you explain what that book doesn't do or provide that your book will. This way those reading your book proposal will not wonder if one of these books already has your project covered.

I also recommend starting to write a book proposal at the onset (or very early in) the book writing process. Beginning the proposal this early in the game will help you solidify what audience you're writing for, what your purpose is, what hole in the market you are filling, etc. For example, a common proposal requirement is to list similar books and describe how your book will differ from these. Can you imagine writing a book without doing this first, only to discover afterwards that someone else has already written and published the book you thought was so original? Answering a book proposal's questions (as best you can) prior to writing will help you avoid missteps and focus your writing.

Reference the proposal requirements (often in an "Author Guidelines" section) on your publisher's website to use the template or specifications provided. The book proposal is typically a list of questions you answer about your intended book. It's OK to go back and forth between crafting the proposal and crafting your book, as your intentions might change as the manuscript develops.

Of course, you'll thoroughly perfect the book proposal once your initial book chapters are finalized for submission to a publisher. See Routledge, Taylor & Francis Group (2017) at www.crcpress.com/rsc/downloads/r3-lr_GVCMG1712_Book_Proposal_SS.pdf for a free, online guide that will help you perfect your proposal.

> **SCRAPPY TIP**
>
> If you know a well-known expert in the field who would be willing to write a foreword for your book, mention this in your book proposal. This will enhance your credibility in the editors' and reviewers' eyes.

Writing the Book

Just as "Chapter 3. Writing Anything" covers the need to create a template ahead of time, you'll want to create a template for your book. Using a program like Microsoft Word, create an outline (such as listing topics that will become chapters and sections within chapters) based on what you planned in the book proposal. You can then gradually turn that outline into your book as you flesh out each chapter.

Add the title, preface, introduction, author bio, and back cover content at this stage (pasting and reworking content from your book proposal will help). Look at a book like this for a sense of what goes into these parts. I also love to do a front cover mockup (it's never used – as professional artists do the cover art – but this helps remind me of the book's intended nature).

For articles and other short-form writing you'll dream up packaging (ways to explain concepts) and magic (such as stories that hook the reader) before you outline. For a book you'll craft these throughout each chapter, especially as you introduce or explain new concepts. Table 3.2's magic examples in "Chapter 3. Writing Anything" can help. As you work, try to keep each chapter roughly the same length, and rearrange content as necessary to ensure concepts are categorized logically and follow a smooth flow.

It's common for publishers to want a reference list at the end of every chapter (rather than all references at the book's end). This allows your publisher to sell individual chapters through academic outlets as an additional source of revenue and reaches readers who won't buy the whole book.

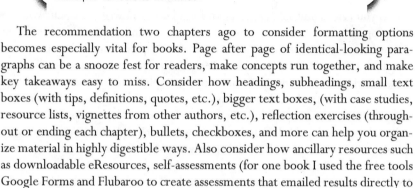

SCRAPPY TIP

Education field publishers like a book to serve multiple functions. This increases revenue but also furthers the book's impact. Consider how your book can be read by a single individual, or by a group as part of a book study, or as an accompaniment to professional development (which can incorporate within-book exercises), or by students in college courses. Write your book (and its proposal) with multiple functions in mind.

The recommendation two chapters ago to consider formatting options becomes especially vital for books. Page after page of identical-looking paragraphs can be a snooze fest for readers, make concepts run together, and make key takeaways easy to miss. Consider how headings, subheadings, small text boxes (with tips, definitions, quotes, etc.), bigger text boxes, (with case studies, resource lists, vignettes from other authors, etc.), reflection exercises (throughout or ending each chapter), bullets, checkboxes, and more can help you organize material in highly digestible ways. Also consider how ancillary resources such as downloadable eResources, self-assessments (for one book I used the free tools Google Forms and Flubaroo to create assessments that emailed results directly to the taker upon completion), courses, and other tools can support readers.

Strategies in the previous two chapters will help with the rest of your writing endeavor. Revisiting education books you like will give you countless samples of ways to convey ideas.

Contract

"Chapter 3. Writing Anything" covers the need to adhere strictly to submission guidelines as you write. For a book, this involves the added need to regularly reference your book proposal and contract with your publisher. What did these say about your intended audience, special features, word count, etc.? You don't want to complete your book, only to realize it doesn't fulfill the promise you made to your publisher. If you haven't yet secured a publisher, refer to the notes you made in the previous "Writing the Book Proposal" section concerning the intended nature of your book.

Keywords

In addition to your manuscript, your publisher will likely collect keywords and abstracts or descriptions on each chapter you've written. This information will become metadata, which helps online search tools locate your work for appropriate users. This Search Engine Optimization (SEO) means your work is more likely to show up (and show up high on the list) when someone Googles it.

Embed keywords within each abstract or chapter description, and also within the captions of images and tables. To help metadata increase your work's discoverability, describe content accurately and concisely, carefully consider which words and phrases potential readers would search for, avoid repetition of keywords (opt for synonyms instead), and place these keywords near the beginning of your abstract (Routledge, 2017). When search engines encounter each abstract, they will determine whether to "recommend" your work based on whether you used the keywords the searcher used and whether these words appeared near the start of your abstract.

BOOK EDITOR

Just as you can submit a book proposal for a book you write yourself, you can also propose a book you edit yourself, which contains chapters from different authors. Some of the best books in our field offer chapters from different experts. Marybeth Gasman's (2016) *Academics Going Public: How to Write and Speak Beyond Academe*, which I cite throughout this book, exemplifies such a collection.

Editors of collected works typically contribute the preface, introduction, and a single chapter, so you still have the chance to write. Though options abound, one academic book publisher that has expansive reach and allows you to get very specific with your topic is IGI Global (www.igi-global.com/publish/submit-a-proposal). Submitting a proposal for a book you plan to edit is similar to proposing a book you plan to write in its entirely. The tips provided earlier in this chapter regarding the submission process and writing the book proposal can be applied to book editor projects, as well.

BOOK REVIEWS

You are likely reading books for your own professional development anyway, so why not review them? Rita Platt (elementary school principal and graduate course instructor) writes book reviews for MiddleWeb (www.middleweb.com). In doing so she helps reader-educators, and a bonus is how this increases her exposure, which compliments her work as an educational consultant.

If you plan to read a book anyway, committing to reviewing can earn you a free copy and cause you to learn the content more deeply as you craft your response. If you want to review practitioner-targeted books, check publication pages (the front of the magazine where editorial details are listed in tiny print, or at the end of the book review section) for details on becoming a book reviewer, search publication emails and websites for review guidelines, or contact a publication's book review editor to express your interest, succinctly convey your area of expertise, and attach your CV and (if available) a previously published book review. MiddleWeb exemplifies practitioner-friendly venues that offer clear guidelines for potential reviewers. For other sites on the "List of Writing Opportunities" eResource, like edCircuit (www.edcircuit.com), you'll know they accept book reviews because you'll see reviews on their sites.

Book reviews aren't only for practitioner audiences. Journals publish reviews of scholarly texts (books, essays, etc.), and they often actively recruit reviewers. If you want to review books for a journal, check journal pages (in the front and back, as well as the pages housing its current book reviews) for details on book review submission, search journal emails and websites for invitations to review, or contact a journal's book review editor to express your interest in the same manner described above. *Coaching: An International Journal of Theory, Research and Practice* (www.tandfonline.com/doi/full/10.1080/17521882.2017.1281983) exemplifies journals that offer clear guidelines for potential reviewers.

YOUR TURN

"Chapter 3. Writing Anything" provided guidance to write well. This chapter provided added tips, as well as multiple opportunities to share your expertise through a book. Select a publisher (use the "List of Book Publishers" eResource for suggestions) to which you will submit chapters. Then complete Exercise 5.1 to plan your submission. Reference sections in this chapter and "Chapter 3. Writing Anything" as you complete the exercise.

EXERCISE 5.1: BOOK WRITING PLAN

1. What kind of book will you be writing?
   - ❏ Practitioner-Friendly
   - ❏ Academic (e.g., monograph)
   - ❏ Other:
2. To which publication will you submit your manuscript?
3. Read the publication's submission guidelines. What is the specified chapter number, formatting, title length, etc.?
4. Who is your audience made up of? This can be one main audience or a few key groups.
5. What does your audience need from you?
6. What are your key purposes in writing this book?
7. What new understanding will your audience gain from your book?
8. What will your audience be able to do after reading your book?
9. Complete as much of a publisher's book proposal template as you can. What additional details did you establish (similar books already out, your core message, etc.)?
10. Describe what your style will be (humorous, casual, formal, etc.).
11. What will your book's title be?

12. **What magic will you use to make some concepts resonate?** Remember Table 3.2.

13. **Create a template and use it to outline your book.** Then add to each chapter, gradually turning your template into a complete draft. When your publisher's required number of chapters are complete, apply the next two steps to those chapters.

14. **Proof and revise your chapters as necessary.** Ensure your chapters meet submission requirements and criteria described in this chapter and "Chapter 3. Writing Anything" (communicates your core message, is very clear, doesn't overload your reader, etc.).

15. **Return to your book proposal.** Complete and rework your book proposal until it reflects your finished chapters and the book they will occupy. You might make changes to your chapters based on your proposal answers, as well.

16. **Submit your work.** Follow the publisher's submission guidelines carefully. Simultaneous submissions (submitting to more than one publisher simultaneously) are discouraged and some publishers prohibit them.

REFERENCES

Alexander, P. H. (2011, October 17). The less-obvious elements of an effective book proposal. *The Chronical of Higher Education*. Retrieved from www.chronicle.com/article/The-Less-Obvious-Elements-of/129361

Conradt, S. (2018, March 2). The stories behind 10 Dr. Seuss books. *Mental Floss*. Retrieved from http://mentalfloss.com/article/28843/stories-behind-10-dr-seuss-books

Gasman, M. (2016). *Academics going public: How to write and speak beyond academe.* New York, NY: Routledge, Taylor & Francis.

Murray, D. E. (2014, March 6). 10 point guide to dodging publishing pitfalls: Veteran academic authors share their hard-won tips. *Times Higher Education*. Retrieved from www.timeshighereducation.com/features/10-point-guide-to-dodging-publishing-pitfalls/2011808.article

Routledge. (2017). *Promoting your book.* Retrieved from www.routledge.com/resources/authors/promoting-your-book.

Routledge, Taylor & Francis Group. (2017). *Author directions: Navigating your success in book proposals: Key tips on how to write a successful book proposal.* Boca Raton, FL: CRC Press.

Rushton, K. (2017, September 1). Cut your prices to 99p like we do to sell more books, Amazon tells publishers as furious row erupts. *Daily Mail*. Retrieved from www.dailymail.co.uk/news/article-4845838/Cut-prices-99p-like-Amazon-tells-shops.html

Williams, M. (2018, January 5). Retail apocalypse or retail evolution? Publishers need to help Barnes & Noble evolve — or join it in extinction. *The New Publishing Standard*. Retrieved from www.thenewpublishingstandard.com/retail-apocalypse-or-retail-evolution-publishers-need-to-help-barnes-noble-evolve-or-join-it-in-extinction

Part III

Speaking

Chapter 6

Speaking Anywhere

I'm going to tell you something you might not want to hear: You need to speak (in the formal presentation sense). Even if you are only interested in writing, speaking is necessary for your written work to proliferate. For example, when it comes to spreading your wisdom, let's suppose you are only interested in writing books. In that case, speaking engagements would:

- expose you and your work to a wider audience;
- lead to keynotes that can culminate in book signings;
- increase your credibility; and
- expose you to new people (which brings more opportunities for writing and more).

...All of which would mean more book sales, which means more students impacted by your work.

Speaking allows your expertise to help more people and – through them – help more students. Conferences, TED Talks, media interviews, podcasts...there are many venues through which you can talk about your work. If travel is a problem, you can even present at online conferences from the comfort of your home. While speaking opportunities allow you to share, these occasions also offer chances to connect with other change-makers and form relationships that open even more doors for sharing your expertise with the world.

HOW THIS CHAPTER WORKS
(You Need It for the Next Three Chapters)

As with the earlier "Writing Anything" chapter, this chapter's title "Speaking Anywhere" is hyperbolic: it means this chapter will provide you with the fundamental guidelines that apply to all speaking opportunities described in this book. The subsequent chapters in this "Speaking" part of the book will offer slide guidelines, as well as additional guidelines specific only to certain types of speaking (such as how to plan a TED Talk), but this chapter will give you the basics you need for speaking at varied venues to better our field. Though this chapter is broken into subsections ("Before Presenting Anything", "While Presenting Anything", etc.), it is most beneficial to read the entire chapter before your next writing project and then return to it throughout your writing endeavors.

This chapter and the next contain no exercises. Instead, "Chapter 8. Speaking at Conferences and Other Events" and "Chapter 9. Speaking on Air and Recordings" feature exercises where you can apply what you learn in this chapter and the next, combined with what you learn in those chapters. Those chapters will also lead you to choose events to present at, which you'll want to have in mind as you consider your audience, purpose, and other aspects introduced in this chapter.

SCRAPPY FAST TRACK

If you want to skyrocket quickly to speaking to thousands (for example, if you have no notable speaking experience but are anxious to do keynotes or give a TED Talk), I recommend you use the information in the "Speaking" chapters of this book (including their eResources to find opportunities) to take this route:

Step 1. Apply to speak at many online conferences. As this chapter explains, online conferences are an easy way for beginners to gain speaking experience and obtain recordings of their sessions (required when applying to give a TED Talk).

Step 2. Perfect your slide designs and delivery (covered in the next chapter) and present for at least five live conferences or other events. At home you can videotape and then watch yourself deliver many speeches to speed up your progress. Also work on your branding (covered in "Chapter 2. Image") so the specific expertise you offer is clear. If you produced a resource that captures this expertise (such as a book, journal article, free online content, popular Twitter chat you host, etc.) highlight this in your communications, since people selecting speakers like to know they can say things like, "The author of ... " when announcing and introducing you.

Step 3. Apply to give a TED Talk. If you are familiar with TED Talks and their awesome reputation, you might be taken aback by the notion you should apply to give one if you aren't yet an icon in our industry. In this book I encourage you to be scrappy and aim high. Doing a TED Talk — something that carries much clout — will open countless doors for you. So why not try to give one? As this book covers, there are many TED and TEDx opportunities just waiting for you to apply. When you do, use your online conference recording links whenever an application requests a live recording (unless you have live recordings that show you presenting).

Step 4. Make your TED or TEDx experience obvious to anyone visiting your social media sites, reading your email signature, visiting your website, or reading your CV or bio. If you have another uber-impressive accomplishment, like a bestselling book or appearance as an education expert on *BBC World News*, that can be used instead (or in addition).

Step 5. Follow the tips in the "Conference Keynote" section to start booking keynotes. There are additional scrappy tips in that section.

BEFORE SPEAKING ANYWHERE

Have you ever dressed inappropriately? Maybe you wore a sweater and wool pants without checking the weather forecast, only to spend the day sweltering under a surprisingly sunny sky. Or maybe you wore your rattiest jeans to meet your new partner, only to learn you'd also be meeting her family that day. Not determining the conditions and purpose of a situation can lead to discomfort, embarrassment, and a missed opportunity.

The same is true of speaking. Considering your audience, circumstances, and submission norms up-front will help you select words and shape your presentation so it best meets your audience's and venue's needs, as well as your own.

Determine Circumstances

Considering the circumstances of your speaking venue will help you know the speaking waters you're about to sail so you can plan accordingly. Is the purpose of the event to get practitioners and researchers to collaborate? Is the conference theme "Embracing Diversity"? Venue aspects such as these will shape what you present, as well as what you propose to present. Identify any venue aspects your presentation should reflect.

Consider Your Audience

Revisit Table 3.1 from "Chapter 3. Writing Anything" to consider aspects of your likely audience. If you have a highly mixed audience, try to determine main groups, and plan to relate your recommendations and examples to them all or else cater to each at different times (based on what will be most effective in each case).

Determine Purpose

Now that you know your audience, determine your purpose in presenting something. Detailing your purpose will help you plan a presentation that provides the listeners with what they need to act upon what they learn. This action will typically be tied to a problem you illuminate, such as a problem the audience struggles to solve. This purpose will line you up to...

Finesse Your Title

The title and description must capture viewers' attention, make them want to watch your presentation, and capture the nature of the presentation. Concepts you learned in the "Before Writing Anything: Draft a Title" section of "Chapter 3. Writing Anything" also apply here.

An unexpected title is far more gripping that the usual blah, blah, blah you often hear in our industry. For example, I attended a presentation by Kandice Sumner at the 2018 New Teacher Center Symposium on race. Sumner could have titled her session "The Role That Race Plays in the Institutions That Guide Our Daily Lives" (a line from the session's description). But... *yawn*. That title would have communicated, "This session will have boring bulleted slides and boring delivery, because its title is so bland." ... Whereas Sumner's presentation was anything but bland.

Instead, Sumner wisely titled her session "Race and Other 4-Letter Words". Boom! That title gets attendees' attention. It stands out. It says, "I'm a different kind of session. I won't mince words – I'll shoot straight for what needs to be said."

Note Sumner is able to be efficient with her word use because this title builds on what people already know. Remember the "Consider Packaging: Description" section in "Chapter 1. Introduction" about tapping into people's preexisting knowledge (example: a pomelo is like a supersized grapefruit). People have an immediate association with the term "4-Letter Words". That association carries a strong, negative emotion with it (you might utter a 4-letter word when you stub your toe or catch your partner cheating on you). By tapping into people's preexisting association, Sumner's title stirs up all that emotion and meaning with a single term. Emotion is memorable and draws people in, as it did for Sumner's standing-room-only presentation. Berger (2013) found concepts are more likely to spread (meaning people will tell others about them) when they provoke arousal emotions like awe, amusement, excitement, anxiety, or anger. See the "Acceptance" section of "Chapter 8. Speaking at Conferences and Other Events" for more tips.

Finesse Your Description

Like the title, your description must capture viewers' attention, make them want to attend your presentation, and capture the nature of the presentation. In addition, you must communicate how the session will transform attendees in a valuable way (such as through action-oriented objectives). See the "Acceptance" section of "Chapter 8. Speaking at Conferences and Other Events" for more guidance.

Determine Solutions to Share

Plan to share solutions, not just problems. This can mean listeners learn how to apply (or about) specific strategies to combat the problem, what causes the problem, leading theories on solutions, recommendations for future research, or what stakeholders should not do.

For example, your presentation on "The Roots of Absenteeism" might begin with stories and statistics that further the audience's understanding of how problematic chronic student absenteeism is. However, your audience should not leave your presentation merely understanding that absenteeism is a problem that must be overcome. Rather, your audience should leave your presentation knowing specific strategies to combat absenteeism, or leading theories regarding solutions, or different approaches school districts and academy trusts have used to solve the problem, or recommendations for future research that can inform solutions, or other ways in which your audience can act.

Plan to Prime the Audience

Priming is an aspect of behavioral economics, which is essentially how our brains strive to make decisions efficiently. Priming involves exposing people to something to trigger specific thoughts and attitudes. For example, people voted significantly more in favor of increased school funding when their voting booths were located in schools, because the schools primed the voters to think and care about schools (Kahneman, 2011).

Plan to ground the audience in the core of your topic from the beginning of your presentation to prime them to care. No matter your topic, the most important person it likely boils down to is the student. Too often we launch into tips, statistics, or research methods without ever acknowledging the very personal story (and value) behind what we have to share. See the "Story" example in Table 6.1 for a story I tell of Gail Thompson to ground the audience in the reason behind everything I'm about to say in a presentation: the student.

Consider how you might prime your audience to care about the topic you're about to share. This likely means connecting them with your topic's impact on students. While sharing big picture statistics is valuable, remember what you learned in "Chapter 3. Writing Anything" about why charities mail us photos of individual children. Hearing one child's story is far more compelling, memorable, and action-inspiring than learning of the plight of a single child. A highly personal story draws the viewer in and makes her care.

Choose real stories (don't make them up) to ground your audience in the topic you are introducing. Your own first-hand experiences can be especially powerful, as long as they are clearly tied to your message and your presentation's purpose but telling stories you learned from others can also work well. Your colleagues, teachers, and books like the teacher versions of *Chicken Soup for the Soul* can offer stories and inspiration.

Consider Packaging

Consider concepts to package the lessons you give listeners. See the "Consider Packaging" section of "Chapter 1. Introduction" for details and inspiration.

Dream up Magic

After you have key audience "take aways" in mind and have considered packaging, do not start outlining just yet. Once you outline your delivery, you end up with a clear game plan. However, it can then be hard to insert some magic into such a finished product. Spend time devising ways to include magic, as defined in "Chapter 3. Writing Anything".

Magic "wow" moments help audience members connect to your content and are typically the most memorable parts of your presentation. They help your audience care about what you say and increase your presentation's impact. If you determine some of these magic moments up front, you can then produce an outline that incorporates them.

Table 6.1 Ways to Insert Magic into Your Speaking

Magic/Hook	Example
Activity *More activity examples are provided in the "Specific Slide Types" section of "Chapter 7. Preparing Slides for Anywhere"*	When I delivered a keynote on ways to avoid burnout, there were 1,200 teacher attendees and thus not much room to maneuver. However, audience involvement is always possible. In introducing a segment on the necessity of collaboration, I had all audience members stand and face their chairs. I then gave them this series of directions: "As long as it won't physically hurt you, please lift your chair off the ground." Attendees lifted their chairs with ease. "Please put it down but keep standing." "If you are someone who struggles with getting everything done that you want to get done, put one hand behind your back and keep it there." "If there is anything (when it comes to teaching) that a colleague at your school is better at than you, put your other hand behind your back and keep it there." "If some days, you're just tired, or feel overworked, lift one leg off the floor and leave it there." "Now, lift your chair." At this point the audience laughed as some struggled to lift chairs with only one of four limbs free. As I invited them to sit again, I asked, "Was it easier to lift before, when we had the use of numerous limbs instead of just one?" The audience called out, "Yes!" I then said, "Somebody tell me, what does this exercise teach us about collaboration?" The responses (such as, "The help of many makes a job easier") provided a perfect introduction to my segment on collaboration, as audience members were fully aware of how important collaboration would be to their jobs as teachers.
Analogy, Metaphor, or Simile	Anyone who watched TV in 1987 likely remembers the Partnership for a Drug-Free America commercial displaying a close-up of an egg dropped into a frying pan. This is accompanied by a voice-over saying, "This is drugs. This is your brain on drugs. Any questions?" (Rossen, 2017, p. 2). Everyone has a brain, which makes the metaphor personal for all viewers. Whether someone uses drugs or not, and whether someone approves of the ad or not, seeing one's brain being fried is a visceral experience that is hard to forget. The metaphor says so much, yet in so few words. Analogies and similes can also strengthen a delivery.

(Continued)

Table 6.1 Continued

Magic/Hook	Example
Contrast	When I gave a Talk at TEDxTUM (TEDx, 2016) on the need to make data "over-the-counter" so it is easy to use, I told three stories in succession. First, I told how Dr. John Snow ended a cholera outbreak by successfully mapping where deaths occurred (deaths congregated around a water pump until its handle was removed). Next, I told how Florence Nightingale used polar area diagrams to convince Britain to fund better health care conditions during the Crimean War, attributed to dropping allied troops' death rate from 42% down to 2%. My third story, however, provided contrast. I told of how the Challenger Space Shuttle exploded, killing all crew members, yet many data visualization experts believe the tragedy would have been avoided if the graphs prior to launch were better designed.
	In all three instances, I showed the data visualizations used, and in the case of the Challenger I show how simple improvements to a graph would have made the explosion's culprit (cold launch temperature) immediately apparent and would have likely changed the launch decision. Contrasting how good data visualization saved lives with how poor data visualization likely lost lives demonstrated the importance of the topic and the importance of the research-based recommendations I was about to share.
Demonstration	To teach a class the meaning of *cultural literacy*, Eng (2017) started calling on students to answer sports questions. He asked things like, "What's the team's overall field goal percentage?" and used terms like "jumper" and "offensive rebounds" (p. 31). He then asked the class if anyone there didn't follow sports, to which 25% raised their hands, and asked if they understood the conversation, which they did not. Eng asked, "But how can that be? We *were* speaking English, no?" (p. 31).
	Eng had provided the audience with an experience that enabled them to understand how a lack of familiarity with cultural content prevents one from understanding and assimilating in the culture. This demonstration launched the class into discussing a topic that was now more personal and tangible.

(*Continued*)

Table 6.1 Continued

Magic/Hook	Example
Example	Alan Alda (2017) of the Center for Communicating Science described how difficult he found it to explain the complex physics concept of particles, then shared how physicist Brian Greene did so expertly: "If you cut a loaf of bread in half, and then take one of the halves and cut that in half, and keep doing that, eventually you'll get down to the smallest bit possible. That's a particle." (p. 64). Centering this example on bread, which everyone is familiar with, makes even an intimidating concept like physics relatable. The example would also lend itself well to prop use during a presentation.
Fable or Parable	Coggins (2017) told of how Larry Cuban used the parable of the blind men and the elephant to introduce a lesson on education policy: A group of blind men seek to learn about an elephant, but each one touches a different part. One feels the smooth, hard ivory tusk; another a pliable, wrinkly knee; a third man feels the heat and moisture at the end of the trunk; and yet another feels the big wall of the belly. When they describe what they feel, it is clear that they are having completely different experiences. There is no question that each of them is feeling what a real elephant feels like, but their own realities make it hard for them to understand the others' experience of the same elephant. I've never found a better analogy to explain education policy and the complexity of getting the different parts of the system to speak to one another. (p. 22) The parable allows us to understand – in a way a mere statement like this wouldn't achieve on its own – how people's own realities are concrete and difficult to augment.
Grouping	When most people present on how to improve teachers' data use, they focus solely on how to improve the data user (such as through teacher training) or the climate surrounding teachers (such as through school leadership). The tool teachers use to view data is rarely addressed, and attendees could thus have a preconceived notion that the tool has little bearing on data use.

Table 6.1 Continued

Magic/Hook	Example
	To avoid this attitude (which could reduce audience attention to what I say about electronic data systems), I start one segment of my presentation by dividing the audience into two teams (an aisle down the middle makes this easy). I tell attendees to imagine their teams are going to race each other on the race track.
	I tell them, "You all take the same driving classes and thus receive the same training. You all have identical driving coaches and pit crews and thus have the same leadership and support. You start your engines. The gun fires and you start to drive. This team is driving a Lamborghini [slide shows gorgeous sports car], and this other team is driving my first car ever [slide shows 1973 Volkswagen Bus]. Who wins?"
	Laughter and shouts about the winning Lamborghini follow. "But they received the same great training," I say. "But they have the same leadership and support," I continue. The audience shouts that it doesn't matter. "So, you're saying the car makes a difference? In other words, the *tool* you use – regardless of how great your training or support is – makes a *massive* difference." Now I'm ready to talk about needed improvements and components to the data systems teachers use to work with data, and my audience is now ready to understand.
Humor	At the start of my AERA PD course on how to best share one's education research, I stood behind the lectern and read (in monotone) an unattractive slide crammed with confusing research jargon. My audience started giggling as they gradually caught on: I was demonstrating the bad speaking style seen too often in conference sessions. By the time I said, "Just kidding," attendees were amused, relieved I wouldn't be teaching that way, and thinking about the impact of the course's topic.
Modeling	Kelly Knoche promotes teacher well-being through The Teaching Well. When delivering an Illuminate Education Equity Symposium session on trauma, she explained Dan Siegel's Hand Model of the Brain. Knoche could have simply held up her own hand in this model of how the brain stem (palm), limbic area (thumb, folded in),

(*Continued*)

Table 6.1 Continued

Magic/Hook	Example
	and cortex (fingers folding over thumb, operating as a higher part of the brain) function together, and what happens to these brain areas when we experience trauma (fingers flying back up). Knoche did use her own hand as a model, but she had all audience members raise their own hands and move their fingers as she did while following along with the explanation. This made the content more concrete. We remained seated, yet we were physically (and thus more mentally) engaged. Concepts are more understandable and memorable when they are concrete (such as based on easy-to-visualize images) (Heath & Heath, 2008).
Mystery	In studying the best ways to teach course curriculum, Cialdini (2005) found the most frequent approach (describing phenomena) to be the least effective, asking students questions about the phenomena to be better, but generating mystery stories for students to solve (through an understanding of the phenomena) to be best because this spurs listeners to explain processes themselves. This approach can be successfully adapted for other presentations, as well.
	For example, education experts often present findings derived from their research studies or from their classroom observations and experiences. Rather than begin such a presentation with the findings, or by a mere statement of the problem, you can introduce the problem as a mystery. What was happening that you couldn't initially understand? What solutions did you try that failed? Put the audience in your shoes to discover the solution "with" you, having their own guesses and theories along the way. This is an effective way to invest attendees in your topic while also communicating its nature.
	Another way to use mystery is to embed lessons (related to your message) along the path to the solution. When I present to parents of gifted children, I need to convey lessons on nurturing their children's creativity, growth mindset, grit, determination, and more. I tell the story of Jack Andraka and his teenage journey to cure pancreatic cancer after the death of a loved one. As the audience experiences the mystery of a quest to cure cancer,

(*Continued*)

Table 6.1 Continued

Magic/Hook	Example
	I highlight aspects of Jack's journey that involved creativity, growth mindset, determination, etc. and his parents' involvement in nurturing such traits. The audience gets to experience how these traits advance Jack in unlocking various pieces of the pancreatic cancer puzzle. The audience remains hooked, anxious to learn how the mystery is solved, as they learn about nurturing their kids.
Personal Anecdote	Alda (2017) also described how the inventors of the world's thinnest glass needed a way to make their findings resonate with listeners. They needed a better entry point than the speakers would have jumping straight into the findings of their paper: *Direct Imaging of a Two-Dimensional Silica Glass on Graphene* (Huang, 2012).
	The nanoscientists learned that telling the story behind their discovery – which happened by accident when an air leak produced what they first mistook for muck – introduced a very human element that made people excited and want to know more (Alda, 2017). A personal anecdote can make content that is complicated and dry more interesting and accessible.
Props	Props can become gimmicky if they don't add much to what you're saying, but when used effectively they can help viewers remember and connect to your words. Heath and Heath (2008) tell of how UNICEF's director used to speak with rulers of developing countries about dehydration (the leading killer of the nations' young children) and the best method for saving kids from such deaths: Oral Rehydration Therapy (ORT) to replenish fluids and electrolytes. UNICEF's director would take a packet of salt and sugar (the ORT ingredients) from his pocket and say, "Do you know that this costs less than a cup of tea and it can save hundreds of thousands of children's lives in your country?" (p. 125). Consider how much more effective that statement – paired with the simple prop – was than relying on mere words. If a prop will help you bring your presentation's content to life, consider how you might use it onstage.

(*Continued*)

Table 6.1 Continued

Magic/Hook	Example
Quiz	If you're giving a talk on Angela Duckworth's (2016) research on grit, why not start by giving the crowd the Grit Scale quiz (www.angeladuckworth.com/grit-scale) to assess their own grit? This would connect the topic to attendees' own lives. Throughout the rest of your talk, your listeners would be able to apply your teachings to their own experiences, making the content more understandable and memorable.
Spontaneity	In an education summit talk, Terrell Strayhorn (2016), Director of the Center for Higher Education Enterprise, stated his main thesis and three coordinating points, and then ran from the lectern, jumped atop a table, and explained how stakeholders need to work "across the aisle" to address higher education's Black male crisis. Strayhorn found his spontaneity to be an effective speaking tactic that kept the speech alive and made his aisle concept visible.
Story	When I delivered a keynote on the importance of recognizing all gifted learners, I displayed a photo of a young Black girl named Gail. I detailed Gail's struggles in life (on welfare, abusive and neglectful home life, siblings lost to crime and violence) and in school (labeled a behavior problem, held back in first grade, struggling academically, told she was stupid).
	Then I displayed a photo of a professional Black woman delivering a speech on stage. The photo bore the name Gail Thompson, PhD. I shared this woman is a tireless advocate for students, was an endowed professor, writes books that help educators change students' lives, and has won more awards than I can list (when I delivered this same keynote to teachers in the Democratic Republic of the Congo, I also included slides of Dr. Thompson serving in the Peace Corp in the Congo).
	I then displayed the young and grown photos of Gail side-by-side and asked my audience, "How did *this* Gail grow up to be *this* Gail? Who made the difference in this child's life?" Many attendees called out, "A teacher!" I displayed a third photo of Gail's 6th grade teacher. I tell the audience, "This teacher recognized that Gail... was... " With my arms extended to the audience, I let the crowd complete my sentence with "Gifted!"

(*Continued*)

Table 6.1 Continued

Magic/Hook	Example
	The crowd had just seen how a gifted student can be overlooked, and also how a life (and the world!) can be changed when a teacher recognizes and supports a student's giftedness. I then showed statistics reflecting these facts, which would not have resonated as strongly without Gail's story. When I went on to share strategies for engaging gifted students, the audience was invested in the need for such strategies to reach *all* gifted students.
	Stories disarm audiences, who are so caught up in the drama they lack the cognitive resources to resist what you're saying (Berger, 2013). Stories also make concepts more memorable (Heath & Heath, 2018). Just be sure your message is so essential to the story that it can't be retold without carrying your message with it.
Surprising Statistic or Fascinating Fact	When I present on the best ways to display data for educators, attendees often enter my presentation without much passion for the topic. Sure, we should display data in helpful ways, but they often care more about training teachers to simply get better at data use.
	At some point in my presentation, I thus share data on how many educators understand the data they use. At randomly selected (average) schools, educators understand only 11% of the data they view, even though most believe they understand the data. I then show data on schools selected as national exemplars, where teachers are well-trained in data use, have onsite data coaches, and have strong data leadership and cultures. At those "top" schools, educators understand 48% of data they view.
	These statistics shock attendees and let them know that strong professional development and leadership are not enough to prevent misuse of data. Attendees are left thinking, "Then what can we do to solve this?". My presentation offers a solution the audience will then appreciate.
	See the "Slide Images" section of the next chapter for help visualizing data. Most attendees are easily overwhelmed by too many numbers, charts, or graphs. Statistics should be selected carefully based on what will best propel your message.

(*Continued*)

Table 6.1 Continued

Magic/Hook	Example
Video	Presenters sometimes show video clips to demonstrate a process they just introduced (for example, teachers using webcams to scan assessments), show how students respond to a lesson (after obtaining parents' permission to show the students), or capture feedback from educators or study participants. The key is to introduce a concept and show a quick clip, rather than letting a video take your place as the main presenter.
Visualization (Imagine)	In a keynote I delivered titled First Aid for Teacher Burnout, I opened with a visualization. I asked attendees to imagine they were going on a trip to somewhere they've always wanted to go.
	As slides illustrated each stage, I had them picture boarding the plane and sitting beside a child. I asked them to imagine their chairs were their seats on the plane (I sat on a chair onstage), and to buckle up (I mimed this) as the flight attendant explained emergency procedures. I described the plane taking off, and said, "You're expecting this great trip. This is something you've always wanted to do. But the clouds get denser. The wind picks up. Pretty soon, turbulence sets in. Give yourselves some turbulence." Audience members and I shook around in our seats. I continued, increasingly frantic, "You're tossing and turning. This plane is going *down.* Your oxygen mask drops. So does the mask for the child beside you." I rose to my feet and called out, "*Whose mask should you put on first?*"
	The audience cried "My own!" I said, "Yes! As the flight attendant *always* tells us, you need to put your own mask on first. Why?" I then heard lots of shouts along the lines of "Because otherwise we won't be around to help the kid!" I then ask what this has to do with teaching, at which point my whole audience knows. When I deliver the rest of my keynote on ways teachers can better care for themselves to fight burnout, my audience is keenly aware of why this is necessary for themselves but also for the students (whom teachers must be present and uncompromised in order to help).

(*Continued*)

Table 6.1 Continued

Magic/Hook	Example
Visualization (Recall)	At the 2017 Rocket Ready Day, Michael Morrison began the event by having attendees close their eyes and remember their most influential teacher. After a moment Morrison asked the audience to open eyes and share what it was about the remembered teachers that made them so impactful. The qualities people shared – helping students find their voices, engaging students in meaningful lessons, making students believe they mattered – provided the perfect introduction to a day about empowering students to develop their own world problem solutions.
Voices of Those Involved	Sharing the voices of students or educators (such as through a video clip embedded in your slide) can drive home a message. Viewers can perceive presenters as having ulterior motives. They might think we primarily want our study to be well received, or we want to sell books and more speaking engagements... and thus might exaggerate the merits of whatever we're recommending. Students and non-presenting educators are perceived as trustworthy in that they have nothing to gain by simply sharing their experience for someone else's presentation, and they're intimately involved in the topic. This gives these voices a different kind of credibility that helps an audience embrace what's being shared. If you display a clip of a minor, get her parent's written permission first.
Volunteers	Asking for volunteers to join you in an activity related to your topic can be very powerful. Attendees tend to connect with what you're doing when they feel "one of their own" is actively involved. Volunteers also add an element of unpredictability that is exciting. Near the start of a session I attended on race and bias, the presenter, Kandice Sumner, conducted a Privilege Walk (search for "Privilege Walk" on YouTube to see one for yourself, noting versions vary). Sumner invited seven volunteers to line up at the front of the room. After ensuring participants were comfortable with what would transpire and establishing ground rules, like the need for attendees to remain silent and not judge participants, Sumner read a script for volunteers to follow. Directions included

(*Continued*)

Table 6.1 Continued

Magic/Hook	Example
	things like, "If you have a parent who graduated from college, take one step forward," and "If you speak English as a second language, take two steps backward."
	Watching the line of volunteers separate, with distance immediately and steadily growing between volunteers based on innate traits like skin color, was profound (and arguably would have been even more stark if volunteers weren't all educators enjoying financial stability, college and graduate level degrees, and other perks to which marginalized groups have less access). The exercise helped all attendees sense (albeit not feel to the extent that those experiencing bias in real life feel) how marginalized groups face more life obstacles than others. The room was silent and somber at the end of the exercise, forming the perfect moment for Sumner to facilitate discussion on race and bias.

These memorable moments most commonly happen at the start of your speech, but they also occur at other points (such as through a demonstration of a concept). Like their written counterparts, magic elements of a presentation can take a variety of forms. See Table 6.1 for examples of these and more. Use the examples as inspiration for your own presentation.

You'll notice in Table 6.1 that magic often takes the form of stories. Embedding stories throughout your speech is a great way to hold the audience's attention and make your message memorable. It is far easier for people to remember stories than facts, because the human brain processes experiences we hear about in practically the same way it processes experiences that really happen to us (Gillett, 2014). Since your story will stick with people long after your speech, so will your message (as long as it is captured clearly by the story).

Most of the magic examples in "Chapter 3. Writing Anything" can also be adapted well for public speaking. You might also revisit the "Consider Packaging" section of "Chapter 1. Introduction" for inspiration; clever packaging of the lessons you present can certainly inject magic into your speech.

You will likely devise additional magic moments during and after outlining your presentation. Throughout the process, stay focused on your audience's needs and the best ways to meet those needs, whether this means adding, removing, or changing the magic moments that will complement your delivery.

Plan to Address Inequity

The next chapter will cover recommendations like showing diversity in your slides and avoiding images that propagate stereotypes, but the words you speak should do something more. Unless you are giving a very short speech (such as a TED Talk), there will be room in your presentation to address the equity aspects that impact your topic. Rarely will there be a topic in our field that doesn't merit addressing how some student populations are underrepresented or underserved, paired with strategies to combat disparity.

For example, I'm often invited to give keynotes on the topic of engaging and challenging gifted students. The organizers and audience are expecting me to launch right into engagement strategies. However, I don't go there until I've addressed the fact that in the U.S., a Black student is half as likely to be labeled "gifted" by his school than a White student when they have *identical achievement scores*. In other words, Black students are just as frequently gifted as White students, yet their giftedness is frequently overlooked by their schools. I share similar statistics involving overlooked English language learners, Hispanic students, and girls, with an even bleaker outlook for poor kids, followed by strategies for identifying all gifted learners (for example, universal assessment for giftedness, rather than only testing some students based on teacher or parent recommendation) to avoid the exclusion some groups face. If I did not first address this disparity and share strategies for overcoming the inequity, then when I talked about engaging and challenging gifted students I would only be helping my audience engage and challenge *some* gifted students, without even knowing they were excluding many others.

In our mission to help *all* students with our work, we have a moral responsibility to address the many times bias and disparity impact our field and our students. No matter your topic, I challenge you to find where equity intersects it. If you don't, you will lose credibility with those in the audience aware of the inequity (who then have to watch you ignore an elephant in the room) and you will miss the chance to inform those in the audience unaware of the inequity. If you struggle in this endeavor, attend sessions related to gender, LGBT+, and racial/ethnic struggles at your next education conference, read related articles, and share your topic with friends whose demographics differ from yours.

Plan to Repeat Main Ideas

Since this repetition will be reflected in your slides, this topic is covered in the "Specific Slide Types: Repetition of Main Ideas" section of "Chapter 7. Preparing Slides for Anywhere".

Plan to Actively Engage the Audience

Since it's helpful to create slides that assist activities, this topic is covered in the "Specific Slide Types: Activity" section of "Chapter 7. Preparing Slides for Anywhere".

Create a Template

The first time you plan a speech, you will likely want to write your outline on a single page. However, in time you might want to outline directly with slides (like I do), using the "Slide Sorter" view in PowerPoint to move slides around, adding slides with a simple word or two to finish later, etc. Both approaches let you play with a framework ahead of time before you delve into each slide's perfection.

If you do want to pull some slides together at this point as a template (such as creating a title slide and some basic section slides), go ahead. The "Technology" section of "Chapter 7. Preparing Slides for Anywhere" will help you.

Outline

See the "Specific Slide Types" section of "Chapter 7. Preparing Slides for Anywhere" to help plan which slides you'll include. If you will speak for more than 15 minutes, it is a good idea to "chunk" your presentation into subtopic segments.

As you outline, regularly reflect on concepts covered earlier in this chapter. When you finish outlining, skim this chapter again to be sure you hit all concepts. For example, does your outline reflect a presentation that will share solutions and meet the audience's needs? If your presentation description claimed attendees will walk away from your session knowing how to plan an equity-sensitive master schedule, does your plan provide attendees with the resources and knowledge they will need to accomplish that task? Adjust your outline as necessary, and feel free to deviate from it if you notice flaws while perfecting your actual slides and content.

Prepare Content

You may plan your content (examples you'll use, stories you'll tell, which bits of magic you'll use where, etc.) in a number of ways, so pick what works best for you. Just as I outline directly with slides, I also plan my content directly in Microsoft PowerPoint (adding simple headings to slides as placeholders and using the "Notes" section to record ideas on what to say). Some people like to write out all speaking notes in a single document before tackling slides. Others like to add phrases to their outline to remember ideas they plan to share. Don't worry about doing this perfectly, as you'll have plenty of time to play, rearrange, and change your approach as you prepare your slides.

At this stage you'll accomplish two main things:

❏ **Prepare compelling and effective slides**. There is a *lot* to know about this task. Read "Chapter 7. Preparing Slides for Anywhere", which covers this extensively.

139

❑ **Prepare an effective handout**. Post it online for attendees to access electronically and consider also physically distributing printed copies. Your handout can be a sheet or packet of paper – whatever length is necessary to provide all the web addresses and summaries you want your audience to have. I try to include information my audience might otherwise be scrambling to write down during the session, so I can say, "Don't worry about catching any of these resource names – they're all included on your handout, and your electronic handout will allow you to simply click web links to visit them."

Your handout should mesh with your brand (covered in "Chapter 2. Image") and be visually appealing and current. Use headings and boxes as necessary to separate types of information and make things easy to find. These visual markers also help when you direct your audience to areas of the handout throughout your presentation.

SAMPLE HANDOUT

See the "eResources" section near the start of this book for details on accessing a handout I've used in the past. Note my handout looks nothing like a copy of my slides.

If you follow this book's strategies, particularly from "Chapter 7. Preparing Slides for Anywhere", your slides will be a collection of images, isolated words, and short phrases that won't make much sense without your explanation. Your handout should package key information you shared in a way that's easy to understand.

As you work, reflect on what was already shared in this chapter. Most of all, don't forget to use magic (discussed earlier) to make your core message and key points accessible, informative, engaging, and memorable to attendees.

Practice

Once your slides are relatively complete you are ready to practice. Stand up, face a mirror (or videotape yourself to view afterwards – most current laptops have webcams that can work for this), speak loudly, and time yourself.

Don't follow a script of pre-written sentences, which would result in a robotic, boring delivery. Rather, remember enough to recall the concept you're supposed to be talking about with each new slide. Then just talk about each of those concepts, from your heart and with passion.

Pay attention to anything that feels "off" in your content, such as:

❑ abrupt transitions;
❑ boring patches;

- ❏ timid speech (mitigated speech or excessive upspeak, which makes statements sound like questions);
- ❏ concepts requiring better explanation or illustration;
- ❏ lack of magic (see Table 6.1) to make concepts come alive;
- ❏ lack of meaningful activities allowing audience to connect to materials;
- ❏ overkill (it's better to be selective about what you communicate than it is to force-feed audience brains);
- ❏ slides not pulling their weight;
- ❏ leaving listeners without a way to act on what they learned.

Adjust your slides as necessary and keep practicing. Read the rest of this chapter so you can practice applying the speaking strategies covered next.

WHILE SPEAKING ANYWHERE

Event Day

1. Before the day of the conference, learn what you should bring with you. A screen, projector, and microphone are usually provided for you. But:
   - You are typically expected to bring your own laptop and power chord.
   - If you use a Mac, bring a "dongle" (adapter). This is sometimes needed for a Mac to connect to some projector hookups yet is rarely provided for you.
   - If you will be introduced by someone prior to taking the stage (common for keynotes or panelists), bring a print-out of your bio to hand to this person, even if you've emailed it to event organizers ahead of time. I always bring a sheet with my bio written at different lengths (long, medium, and short versions) so the introducer isn't forced to modify one she deems too long or short.

     Before this practice, I was frequently introduced incorrectly (to a surprising – and even comical – extent); imagined achievements were erroneously attributed to me, outdated information was provided, my most relevant and recent experience was omitted, and names of my institutions were botched. The worst way I've ever started a keynote (in the wake of an inaccurate intro) was when I felt a moral obligation to say, "Actually, I only have one PhD, not two" (to a chorus of disappointed sighs in the audience). Ugh! Handing the introducer your bio saves you from this awkward experience.

   Other items to ask about are:

   - a clicker (to move through slides without having to touch your laptop); I always bring my own clicker because its familiarity makes me more comfortable;

- handouts (how many should you bring, or will the organizers copy these for you?).

If you are new to presenting or tech-intimidated, you can ask for the name and cell number of whoever will be on hand to offer technical help setting up. If you can't get it before the day of the event, ask again when checking in at the registration desk.

I always ask if a portable, wireless microphone can be provided (rather than secured to a lectern) so I can move around the room. Wireless microphones typically have to be hooked to your clothing, so avoid streamlined dresses with no attachment-friendly spots like waistbands, belts, or pockets.

2. Arrive to your assigned presentation room at least 20 minutes early and set up your slides so they appear on the screen (click through several slides to be sure all is well). Use PowerPoint's "presenter view" so your laptop screen shows you the current slide you're on, but also gives you a peek at the next slide coming up.

3. Arrange your laptop and microphone so you will have as much movement potential as possible. This way you can "work the room" and circulate as a good teacher does rather than hide behind the lectern.

4. Set out your business cards, pen and paper or device (whatever makes it easiest for you to record important information people share with you), handouts, and any books you recommend. Author Gail Thompson taught me the importance of holding up books when you mention them. This isn't about book sales; it's about connecting people with information that can help them help kids.

5. Take a photo to use on social media. A photo of your opening slide on the screen, with the podium to the side, can serve as a clear image. About 15 minutes before your session begins, tweet this with your session details using the conference hashtag (#). For example:

   What 2 practices can render 90% parental involvement in your school? Join us 2:00 PM today #CERA2018 in "Mark Twain" ballroom to talk solutions!

   This often brings in additional attendees who are watching the event's Twitter feed.

   You can also post that photo after your session (covered later). If you take a photo of the audience minutes before you begin and announce you'll Tweet the photo, some attendees like to find their photo on social media after your session ends.

6. Power pose for one to two minutes. Stand up straight, pull your shoulders back and down, and lift your chin slightly. If no one is around (like in an empty conference room or a bathroom stall), raise your arms in a victory V or plant your hands on your hips like a superhero, and widen your stance (basically open up your body).

Amy Cuddy (of Harvard Business School and viral TED Talk on body language), Wilmuth, and Carney (2012) found that adopting an expansive (high-power) pose prior to delivering a speech resulted in reduced stress and significantly improved performance. Adjust your posture until you sense it embodies confidence. It can help to also visualize success, such as the crowd applauding as you finish.

SCRAPPY TIP

If you feel nervous, tell yourself you're just excited. Brooks (2014) found that when people experiencing pre-performance anxiety told themselves "I am excited!" they consistently outperformed those who told themselves they were experiencing other emotions, like calm. The fact that nervousness and excitement are so similar (rapid heartbeat, stomach butterflies, etc.) makes this emotional reappraisal easy and successful, whereas you can't fool yourself into believing you're calm.

Simon Sinek (2014), whose TED Talks are the third most-watched of all time, uses this tip. Excitement gives speakers a big advantage, even over speakers who are calm. As politician consultant and Harvard University lecturer Marjorie Lee North (2017) notes, "Some nerves are good. The adrenaline rush that makes you sweat also makes you more alert and ready to give your best performance" (p. 1). Few people want an unexcited presenter. So, use that nervousness to your advantage and *get excited*!

7. Consider interacting with the audience before your start time. Walk among the seats or greet folks as they arrive. Introduce yourself; find out attendees' names, where they're from, and what they do. Ask how they're enjoying the conference or event, etc. People's cognitive systems use familiarity to judge if something is safe, which makes people prone to think they like someone simply because they have met the person (Markman, 2008); this will help your presentation be well received. These interactions are also chances to establish commonality. People are more likely to agree with speakers they perceive as being similar to them (Alda, 2017).

Forgo pre-talk interaction, however, if it will throw you off your game. For example, if you have trouble squashing nervousness (such as swapping it with excitement) and need to simply breathe deeply and visualize success before taking the stage, go ahead and take that time for yourself.

8. Deliver your killer presentation using the strategies in this book. The next section will cover the presenting phase in depth.

When You're Up (Speaking Strategies)

At a family reunion, the relatives might enjoy a game of touch football. If one of these family members is a professional football player, he will be acutely aware of the others' poor playing practices. But when Brother Lee runs in the wrong direction and Cousin Emmy catches the ball with her face, this pro player might just laugh or feel sympathy. After all, none of the other relatives should be expected to be football pros. It's not their professional field.

When I attend education-related conferences and events, my experience as a teacher means I view the events' speakers through my teacher's lens. When I do this, I see a lot of teaching blunders equivalent to the football mishaps of Cousin Emmy and Brother Lee. The difference here is that those speaking at these events *are* experts in the field. They should understand the fundamentals of good teaching, and thus it's fair to expect them to teach their content well.

Regardless of the speaking venue, when you share your education expertise with others *you are teaching*. It's important you use effective speaking and teaching strategies in order for your time with your audience to mean something for the field. If you put the crowd to sleep with a dry lecture, lose some attendees with jargon, fail to evoke emotion for the student-impact of findings, or deliver something forgettable, you waste or reduce your chance to impact lives.

In a seminal study at the University of Minnesota, Nichols and Stevens (1957) found the average person remembered only 50% of what she heard immediately after hearing it, regardless of how vigilantly she listened, and this retention dropped to as low as 33% within eight hours and to 25% after two months passed. Sullivan and Thompson (2013) also found it typical that after an oral presentation only 10 minutes long, only 50% of listeners (all adults) could describe its content just moments after the talk, and only 25% of listeners could recall the subject matter 48 hours later. Aside from forgetting learned concepts, there is also the question of how much attendees will understand and learn in the first place.

Your job as a speaker is to sidestep these pitfalls as effectively as possible: to make your presentation riveting, clear, relevant, eye-opening, memorable, and packed full of potential to augment or change your listeners in some way that will help them help students even more.

Nobody is perfect. I might inadvertently use "um" in my opening statement or fail to anticipate the number of questions (thus running short on time). But we should all *plan* to use effective speaking and teaching strategies when we present.

Subsequent chapters will cover a variety of speaking opportunities, and many of them offer a surprisingly high level of comfort (such as speaking at online conferences). However, if you follow this chapter's guidelines and perfect your craft, you will likely catch the speaking bug and deliver captivating presentations for some time to come. People will leave your presentations caring about your topic, understanding what you shared, and ready to do something worthwhile with this new knowledge. Guidelines include:

❏ **Summon your inner teacher.** What you tell attendees doesn't matter; what attendees actually *learn* from you is what matters. If you just spray out information like a firehose without regard for how attendees connect with the concepts and add them securely to their mental repertoire, you'll give a pointless presentation.

Think of everything you know about good teaching. While some strategies will need tweaking for different audiences, most of what you know will work well with any presentation. For example:

- Just as it's great to meet students at the door of your classroom, it helps to meet and chat with attendees as they arrive, before your presentation begins.
- When teachers circulate throughout the classroom, it keeps students on task, helps hold their attention, and helps teacher/student connection. Circulating among your audience during appropriate times (like when the same slide will be in place for a while, or to make yourself easily accessible during an audience activity) is also helpful.
- A teacher's humor and gripping stories entertain students and keep them riveted in the classroom. Adult attendees are just as intrigued when a speaker leverages humor, storytelling, and other strategies to entertain and hold an audience.
- Students quickly tune out when they sense a teacher doesn't care. Things like a weak lesson, lackluster slides, or showing up late are telltale signs of an indifferent teacher. Your audience will feel disconnected if you don't care enough to plan an extraordinary session.
- A good teacher doesn't let a single or handful of students prevent others from finishing a lesson. If too many questions threaten to prevent you from delivering the content you've promised to deliver, say, "This is the last question we'll have time for, but I'll be happy to answer any remaining questions immediately following this presentation" or "So we're able to hear from all of you, please limit your questions and comments to two sentences maximum; thank you."

More examples abound. Reflect on what you know about good teaching, and leverage it as suited to your audience and purpose.

❏ **Be very clear.** Your message from "Chapter 1. Introduction" needs to stand out clearly in your presentation. Whereas writing allows us to file our message

145

down to a pitch or carefully selected statements, a live moment – complete with excitement or jitters – can cause key points to get buried in excess babble. Fortunately, in live moments we can leverage dramatic pauses, verbal emphasis, and strong gestures (like one hand chopping into the other hand's palm with each new word) for the main words we want listeners to remember.

In speeches we also have the visually glorious assistance of slides. If you show a single slide displaying nothing but the words "YOU can stop the preschool to prison pipeline" during your stories on how kids from key ethnic and racial groups were funneled into incarceration as adults, it is likely few attendees will forget the checklist you distributed of specific things they can do to end the racial homogeneity of our prison systems.

The other hallmarks of clarity still pertain to speaking, just as they do for writing. Use packaging, straightforward sentences, substitutes for jargon (and if you absolutely must use one piece of jargon, be sure to explain it clearly), and establish context (when you say "schools", what type of schools do you mean?). When presenting for international audiences, clarify words that mean different things in different countries or regions. See the "Terminology" section of the Preface for examples of these.

❏ **Do not focus on sounding smart.** You are smart. Trust me. No one reads a book with the word "Research" in the title unless she is smart. Focus on helping all audience members understand your content, which means avoiding jargon and elaborate phrasing. When your sentences are difficult for the listener to process, they fight the listener's *cognitive ease*, which means she is less likely to trust you or believe what you are saying (Kahneman, 2011).

DEFINITION OF JARGON

Jargon describes terminology used by a specific group of people (such as terms and phrases professionals use when they "talk shop" that people outside their profession wouldn't fully understand).

Problems with Jargon

When you use jargon in a presentation:

- Some people don't understand the jargon, resulting in confusion.
- Some people kind of understand the jargon but might have different interpretations as to its meaning.
- Some people understand the jargon but are not as comfortable using it as the speaker is.

In the above cases, the speaker risks confusing or intimidating listeners. Intimidated listeners can experience an emotional filter that causes them to worry they don't understand what is being said. This fear can actually *prevent* listeners from understanding what is being said. Plus, no one likes feeling dumb or excluded.

When and How to Use Jargon

Jargon is helpful as a shorthand when communicating with a small number of people you know well enough to be sure they know this shorthand as well as you do. For example, when I was a junior high school teacher talking to my principal, I would refer to the "RFEPed students" (four syllables) rather than the "students redesignated as Fluent English Proficient" (15 syllables), because this was an oft-used truncation on our campus and I knew my principal knew the term well.

As soon as someone is in the room who you do not know well, as is typically the case with public speaking, jargon has no place. If you *must* use jargon in a presentation, define it clearly and in an accessible, inviting way.

❑ **Don't overload your audience.** It's tempting to tell the audience every detail and every example concerning your topic. However, an audience is more likely to digest, maintain interest in, and remember what you say if you stick to the most important information, allow time to pause, and don't overload your audience.

Some presentations allow for plenty of detail (for example, a half-day professional development class), while most (for example, a 45-minute conference session) force you to severely prioritize what you say so that what you *do* say gets across.

When stopping short of overload, you can always point attendees to resources for more information when they're ready. Handouts (whether online, for which you give the audience a web link, or printed so attendees can take them home) are great for this. If you use your time to get the audience to care about your topic and to understand its fundamental truths, they can use provided resources as a next step. If you want to personally walk your crowd through that next step, you can provide links to resource sheets, articles, or videos in which you personally provide more details and guidance.

SCRAPPY TIP

Establish and maintain commonality. People are more likely to accept the message of speakers they perceive as being similar to them (Alda, 2017).

If you're a researcher and author speaking to kindergarten teachers but spent most of your career as a kindergarten teacher, you'd better make that last fact clear. You can further a sense of unity with your speaking style. Imagine you are like your listeners (empathy will help you find commonalities) and speak to them in that way.

Also, if people like you initially, they are more likely to like everything about you (such as what you have to share). This is known as the *halo effect*, where people tend to like (or dislike) everything about someone (Kahneman, 2011). Thus, establish commonality early.

❏ **Control your nonverbal signals.** Seminal Research conducted at the University of California, Los Angeles (UCLA) (see Mehrabian & Ferris, 1967; & Mehrabian & Wiener, 1967) revealed 38% of communication comes from the tone of our voices and 55% comes from our body language, whereas only 7% of communication comes from the words we say. Though those findings are often too-liberally applied to all instances of information exchange, a series of subsequent works confirmed that much of a presenter's communication relates to how she delivers a message, outside of the message itself.

I learned most of the following tips working with the fabulous speaking coach Danny Slomoff of Slomoff Consulting Group:
- Maintain good posture and don't make angles with your body, such as tilting your hips to one side. Poor posture looks weak. Slomoff says, "While you stand straight, your chest has to be relaxed. A stiff chest makes you rigid. A soft relaxed chest conveys confidence."
- Use gestures that describe your sentences to the audience, rather than unrelated gestures like fidgeting or hand-wringing. Slomoff says, "Descriptive gestures are always perceived as projecting presence."
- Establish eye contact with one audience member at a time (giving each a sentence) rather than sweeping your gaze over the audience. Vary who these people are. Slomoff says, "Great communicators don't talk to floors, walls, or ceilings. To project presence, they go through the eyes to their listener's mind. They make mind contact."

- Match your expression to your words. Slomoff says, "Presence requires emotional congruence. That means whatever you compose you want to match your facial expression and tone to your words. You can't have a blank expression on your face while saying 'I'm so excited to be here.' You can't have a smile when you're giving strong feedback."

The people-pleaser in me makes me want to smile when I'm on stage, but this is inappropriate when I'm talking about people dying (something I do as I introduce how education data impacts lives). At other moments, however, a smile puts the audience at ease and promotes trust. Just be sure your demeanor matches what you're talking about.

❏ **Don't read your slides.** Sweller's (1988) work on cognitive load theory established that when someone reads text on a slide and hears it (from the presenter) at the same time, this overloads the brain and reduces cognition. This finding was reiterated by researchers like Mayer (2014). Hopefully you kept your slides text-sparse anyway, as recommended earlier in this chapter.

❏ **Move.** Covering more territory is a sign of power, keeps your audience alert (following movement is an innate component to our survival), and allows you to move closer to different attendees at different times to further draw them in. Work the stage. If it won't mess up a film crew, hop down from the stage and get out into the audience, as well. Use strong gestures, and physically point to places you want your audience to look.

❏ **Embrace emotions.** I open my speeches on gifted education by telling of a student who endured great hardships (in and out of school) and almost slipped through the cracks but was empowered by a teacher who recognized her giftedness. As I reach the point in this story where the child becomes an educator, changing the lives of countless other children and forging a legacy as a change-maker, I cannot hold back my tears or keep my voice from cracking. I am too moved by this story, as are many of my audience members.

Don't be afraid to let your feelings show. As long as your mood fits your message, your feelings can help carry your audience with you and embrace the weight of your message.

If your audience feels emotion during your talk, as well, your words will be more memorable. Events like the birth of a child, a college graduation, and a marriage proposal are easily remembered because they were full of joy. Getting grounded as a teenager, getting turned down for a date, or getting into a car accident are also easily remembered because they were full of sadness or fear. No matter the feeling, experiencing a strong emotion as something happens causes people to remember that something better.

When appropriate, try to move your audience. If you make them laugh or make them cry, you will likely make them remember.

❏ **Use an appropriate and consistent style.** Do you want to sound like you're speaking to the reader in a familiar, casual way? Do you want to be humorous? Do you want to be blunt or formal? The answer to questions like these is a very personal one. Think hard about what you want your voice to sound like and use a style that will fit your nature and your purpose.

❏ **Alter and control your voice.** Monotone tells the audience to tune out. Even if every sentence is said passionately, this continuity gets stale and makes it harder for listeners to navigate your meaning. Speak your sentences in the way the content requires. Speak slower than you might impulsively speak, and pause after you want a particular sentence to sink in. Listen to TED Talks or podcasts and note how the speaker's voice works for or against your engagement and understanding.

❏ **Speak confidently.** Tina Fey (2011) wrote, "Speak in statements instead of apologetic questions. No one wants to go to a doctor who says, 'I'm going to be your surgeon? I'm here to talk to you about your procedure? I was first in my class at Johns Hopkins?'" (p. 77). Your attendees will quickly lose confidence in what you're saying if they suspect *you* don't have confidence in what you're saying.

Search www.TED.com for Julian Treasure's TED Talk titled "How to Speak so That People Want to Listen". Starting halfway through, Treasure delivers excellent examples of how you can manipulate your register, pace, pitch, and more to speak powerfully.

There is controversy concerning the common suggestion to avoid upspeak (which makes statements sound like questions, with rising intonation). Uptalk is generally associated with a lack of confidence yet is more common in women's speech and is a strategy woman have historically employed in light of society's double standard concerning assertiveness (thus a strong argument is that the problem lies with audience bias, rather than upspeak). I see that problem as having more to do with society's common penalization of woman for being assertive (see Sandberg, 2013).

I thus encourage speakers to sound confident and caution anyone against using excessive uptalk. Women concerned about the upspeak they might employ can make their expertise especially clear at the onset of a speaking engagement, as context impacts uptalk's reception. Listeners are less likely to interpret upspeak as a sign of incompetence or insecurity if they perceive the speaker as an expert (Tomlinson Jr. & Fox Tree, 2011).

❏ **Remain flexible.** Despite your best plans, you might discover that the first of a set of audience exercises goes poorly, or your humor might fall flat. To improve the situation, you can do the next exercises in a different way or omit the jokes for that particular crowd. Change things up in ways that won't cause your presentation to fall apart (for example, you can skip some slides, but you can't redesign individual slides on the fly).

Remember Martin Luther King's "I Have a Dream" speech? That famous "I have a dream" line wasn't even written into the speech King had planned; rather, 11 minutes into the speech, a gospel singer named Mahalia Jackson shouted, "Tell 'em about the dream, Martin!" (Grant, 2016, p. 100) from behind King, compelling him to spontaneously add the entire "I have a dream" section of his speech. Unlike King, you probably have an audience smaller than 250,000 in person and millions watching from home, and the stakes might not be of civil rights movement magnitude. Surely you can wing it, too, to tweak your presentation as necessary based on how your audience is responding.

RESOURCE TIP

Consider joining Toastmasters (www.toastmasters.org), which helps members to improve speaking and leadership skills.

❏ **Actively engage the audience.** Though you already planned for this in the "Before Speaking Anywhere" section of this chapter, remain aware of this need during your presentation. This will allow you to spot opportunities to engage, and to intervene if your audience's energy drops (such as by saying, "Raise your hand if…" to wake up attendees).
❏ **Recap.** See the "Specific Slide Types: Repetition of Main Ideas" section of "Chapter 7. Preparing Slides for Anywhere" for tips on this type of repetition.
❏ **Thank your audience.** Those present gave their time and attention to you (precious commodities for the busy folks who work in our field). A simple, "Thank you for participating here today, and for all you do for kids," communicates gratitude and lets your audience know the session has ended.

In the movie *The Guilt Trip*, Seth Rogan presents a cleaning solution to an audience of buyers in a way one might expect: sharing facts and listing the solution's attributes. Rogan then realizes attendees are checking their cell phones, sending emails, or otherwise tuned out. Rather than continuing to plod through his list of scientific facts and selling points, Rogan shifts gears. He asks the moderator about her home life and cleaning needs. Rogan then notes how safe his product is for her family, pours his cleaning product into a glass, and drinks the entire glass of cleaning solution. Even though the scene is fictional, the reasons why Rogan ultimately caused the audience to invest in his solution are real. Rogan's enhanced approach involved learning the audience's needs, remaining flexible, connecting with the audience, matching his message to the audience, and other strategies from this chapter (such as using a prop and surprising the audience). When you apply this chapter's tips as best suited to your own message, you can – like Rogan's character – win over the crowd, get listeners to care about what you're saying, and spur them to action.

Fielding Questions

Question asking is typically a sign that listeners are engaged. With these tips, your answers can further the impact of your presentation:

❏ **Somewhere near the beginning of your presentation**, establish whether attendees should ask questions throughout your session or save them for a "Q&A" period at the end. Some presenters provide notecards for the audience to submit questions, which can be reviewed during a bathroom break or by a colleague (who can condense wording and combine similar questions) and answered later. Whatever your approach, be sure your audience knows about it.

❏ If time is limited, **ask attendees to limit each question** to one sentence if you have any of these circumstances, which are prone to long-winded Q&A:

  • Fifty or more attendees (large audiences mean more potential questions).
  • Attendees known for their inquisitiveness (examples: Mensans love to question, and young children often raise their hands simply to get involved).
  • Attendees who love to hear themselves talk (some high-level leaders fit this mold when their questions include unnecessary tangents).
  • Your stance is highly controversial (example: if you present "Students Should Not Enter School until Age 10", expect many folks to challenge what you say).

❏ **Don't make a questioner look bad.** Attendees deserve respect for their time and investment, and questioners deserve added appreciation for their vulnerability and contribution to dialogue. Try to be grateful for the question ("Thank you for bringing that up, as it's a common question" or "I think others are probably wondering that, too"). Even the worst questions can be approached in a positive fashion. See Table 6.2 for examples.

❏ **If you don't know an answer, don't try to fake it.** You would risk giving your audience misinformation, and that could hurt them and their students. Rather, it is perfectly acceptable to say:

  • "I don't specialize in that [related] topic, so I wouldn't feel right about answering that question, but if you were to contact [organizations], I'm sure they could give you that information."

Table 6.2 Ways to Respond to Unideal Questions

Question Type	Response Examples
The question concerns something you will address later (this is especially common in long training sessions).	• "I love that you're wondering about that, because we'll cover it extensively after the next bathroom break." • "That provides a perfect transition into this next section of the training..."
The question is misguided.	• "I've been reading that a lot lately, too, since a lot of sources are saying that. However, the true situation..." • "I can see why you'd think that, because common sense tells us that [support of question]. However, due to..."
The question is defeatist or insulting.	• "I know firsthand how frustrating that is, when you're giving a student your all and she still isn't progressing. It can be tempting to think, 'She just can't do it!' but research shows us that mentality makes matters far worse because..." • "I'm sorry you feel I'm anti-teacher. I taught children for 16 years, and I believe teachers to be our most honorable and influential stakeholder. When I say teachers are misusing data, I don't mean this as an attack on teachers. Rather..."
The question is confusing.	• "I want to be sure I'm understanding you so I can give you the best answer. Are you saying... " • "I can think of two ways to interpret that question, and both of them can be helpful for the audience, so I'll answer in terms of both [A] and [B]."

- "You know, I'd never thought about that direction. I'll do some research to find a definitive answer and will post it on my website [provided to audience] by the week's end."
- "I'd need to review those examples in depth to give you an accurate answer. If you please email me [provided to audience] or talk to me after this session, we can arrange for that."
- ❑ **When presenting online**, there is typically a chat field where attendees can ask questions throughout your presentation. Some presenters are able to monitor this feed as they speak, and to immediately integrate answers as they present. I've tried this but find it difficult to do. There is unexplained silence as I read the questions, I lose my train of thought, and the

answers are out of place with my current comments. Thus, I tell attendees early on to use the field, but that I'll answer questions there at the end of the presentation.

For online conferences, there is usually at least one other person contributing to the session, either as a co-presenter or a facilitator. The latter is often a tech-savvy volunteer who logs on early with you, makes sure your audio and visuals work, and remains virtually present to support you. I ask this person to monitor the chat field for me. Advantages include:

- If a question is one that everyone is likely having and their understanding hinges on me answering it immediately (such as a clarifying question), this person can interrupt me with that single question.
- If this person is also an expert on my topic, she can answer many of the questions.
- This person can assemble all unanswered questions, combining similar questions and condensing wording as necessary, to audibly ask them at the end of the session. This also gives the questions a voice all attendees can hear.

AFTER SPEAKING ANYWHERE

Congratulations, you did it! You got up there and shared important information that can help students everywhere. As you enjoy the presentation after-glow, complete just a few more tasks to make a positive difference in future sharing.

Tweet, Post, and More

I post the photo I took (item #5 in the earlier "Event Day" section) on social media, using the event's hashtag, and sharing something positive about the event. For example, "Loved working with the brilliant, enthusiastic teachers at #ISTE18! #edtech" "Chapter 13. Multiply Your Impact" has some additional tips to make the most of your appearance.

Consider Feedback

Now it's time to reflect on how things went. Some judge whether or not they did a good job by criteria such as:

- Did I avoid freezing up and embarrassing myself?
- Did I come across as competent?
- Did I get through everything I planned to say?

These are OK considerations for your first time on stage (Hey, you got through it! That is definitely something of which to be proud!). However, there are more accurate markers of success you should strive to consider if you want to assess and perfect your delivery. Reflect on your presentation and ask:

❑ Was my audience telling me non-verbally that they were following my message (nodding their heads, leaning in, maintaining eye contact and looking at places I pointed to, using facial expressions that matched what I was saying) rather than disengaged (using electronic devices for purposes unrelated to the presentation, spacing out, looking confused, having off-topic conversations, etc.)?

❑ During activities, did attendees understand what to do? Did they seem engaged and energized?

❑ Did attendees ask questions that indicated an interest in applying what they were learning (rather than questions indicating frustrated confusion, or no questions at all)?

❑ After the presentation, did I get a vigorous (rather than cursory) applause?

❑ Did some attendees approach me afterwards to express their gratitude, share how the topic relates to their work, or ask deeper questions?

If a feedback form, conference app, or online form was used to collect attendee comments, ask conference organizers if they can send you input related to your session. Consider feedback with an open mind and use it to improve your next presentation.

Even if some input is harsh, don't judge yourself too harshly: You got up there! You shared information that can make a difference for students. When you consider feedback, know that every presentation you give will likely be better than the one before it. What you are doing is noble and needed in our field, so keep at it.

Others' Sessions

Anytime you're at a conference (such as one at which you're speaking), attend other people's sessions. You can learn what these presenters are teaching, but you can also learn from *how* they're teaching. Take note of:

- what they do that doesn't work (resolve to not do this in your future presentations);
- what they do that does work (consider incorporating similar elements into your future presentations).

You can learn something from every presentation you attend to help you better deliver your message in the future.

Courtesy for Organizers

Always thank event organizers. This step is especially important if you were invited to speak or were one of the event's main speakers.

Event organizers work hard and juggle a large number of balls in the air to make an event come together. Just as you appreciate an audience member thanking you for your session, it is courteous to thank event organizers for pulling together a great event and for giving you the chance to share your message.

I aim to thank organizers in person as I leave, but only if they are easily available (an organizer quarreling with the caterer over who is supposed to handle the buffet cleanup will hardly appreciate being pulled away for some small talk). I also send an email afterwards in which I thank anyone who played a role in arranging for me to speak or assisted me at the event.

REFERENCES

Alda, A. (2017). *If I understood you, would I have this look on my face?: My adventures in the art and science of relating and communicating.* New York, NY: Random House.

Berger, J. (2013). *Contagious: Why things catch on.* New York, NY: Simon & Schuster.

Brooks, A. W. (2014, June). Get excited: Reappraising pre-performance anxiety as excitement. *Journal of Experimental Psychology: General, 143*(3), 1144–1158.

Cialdini, R. B. (2005). What's the best secret device for engaging student interest? The answer is in the title. *Journal of Social and Clinical Psychology, 24*(1), 22–29.

Coggins, C. (2017). *How to be heard: 10 lessons teachers need to advocate for their students and profession.* San Francisco, CA: Jossey-Bass.

Cuddy, A. J. C., Wilmuth, C. A., & Carney, D. R. (2012, September). The benefit of power posing before a high-stakes social evaluation. Harvard Business School Working Paper, No. 13–027.

Duckworth, A. (2016). *Grit: The power of passion and perseverance.* New York, NY: Simon & Schuster.

Eng, N. (2017). *Teaching college: The ultimate guide to lecturing, presenting, and engaging students.* New York, NY: Author.

Fey, T. (2011). *Bossypants.* New York, NY: Reagan Arthur Books.

Gillett, R. (2014, September 18). Why we're more likely to remember content with images and video (infographic). *Fast Company.* Retrieved from www.fastcompany.com/3035856/why-were-more-likely-to-remember-content-with-images-and-video-infogr

Grant, A. (2016). *Originals: How non-conformists move the world.* New York, NY: Penguin Books.

Heath, C., & Heath, D. (2008). *Made to stick: Why some ideas survive and others die.* New York, NY: Random House.

Huang, P. Y., Kurasch, S., Srivastava, A., Skakalova, V., Kotakoski, J., Krasheninnikov, A. V., Hovden, R., Mao, Q., Meyer, J. C., Smet, J., Muller, D. A., & Kaiser, U. (2012). Direct imaging of a two-dimensional silica glass on graphene. *Nano Letters*, *12*(2), 1081–1086. doi:10.1021/nl204423x

Kahneman, D. (2011). *Thinking, fast and slow*. New York, NY: Farrar, Straus and Giroux.

Markman, A. (2008, November 20). To know me is to like me I: Mere exposure. *Psychology Today*. Retrieved from www.psychologytoday.com/blog/ulterior-motives/200811/know-me-is-me-i-mere-exposure

Mayer, R. E. (2014). Cognitive theory of multimedia learning. In R. E. Mayer (Ed.), Cambridge handbooks in psychology. *The Cambridge handbook of multimedia learning* (pp. 43–71). Cambridge, NY: Cambridge University Press.

Mehrabian, A., & Ferris, S.R. (1967). Inference of attitudes from nonverbal communication in two channels. *Journal of Consulting Psychology*, *31*(3), 48–258.

Mehrabian, A., & Wiener, M. (1967). Decoding of inconsistent communications. *Journal of Personality and Social Psychology*, *6*(1967), 109–114.

Nichols, R. G., & Stevens, L.A. (1957, September). Listening to people. *Harvard Business Review*. Retrieved from https://hbr.org/1957/09/listening-to-people

North, M. L. (2017). 10 tips for improving your public speaking skills. *Harvard University Blog*. Retrieved from www.extension.harvard.edu/professional-development/blog/10-tips-improving-your-public-speaking-skills

Sandberg, S. (2013). *Lean in: Women, work, and the will to lead*. New York, NY: Alfred A. Knopf.

Strayhorn, T. L. (2016). Big ideas in academic public speaking. In M. Gasman (Ed.), *Academics going public: How to write and speak beyond academe*, (pp. 39–53). New York, NY: Routledge, Taylor & Francis.

Sullivan, B., & Thompson, H. (2013). Now hear this! Most people stink at listening [excerpt]. *Scientific American*. Retrieved from www.scientificamerican.com/article/plateau-effect-digital-gadget-distraction-attention

Sweller, J., Cognitive load during problem solving: Effects on learning. *Cognitive Science*, *12*(1988), 257–285.

Tomlinson Jr., J. M., & Fox Tree, J. E. (2011, April). Listeners' comprehension of uptalk in spontaneous speech. *Cognition*, *119*(1), 58–69. doi:10.1016/j.cognition.2010.12.005

Chapter 7

Preparing Slides for Anywhere

Which of the slides shown as Figures 7.1 and 7.2 makes you want to learn more? Either slide could be used for the same talking points. However, visual slides are more intriguing and effective (Carmichael, Reid, & Karpicke, 2018; Madan, 2015).

Sadly, the boring, word-heavy slide in Figure 7.1 is the type seen more commonly at education conferences . . . and we're supposed to know about good teaching strategies! Imagine the irony of someone lecturing about good teaching strategies while using poor teaching strategies. This contradiction happens too often.

Some amazing speeches (such as some TED Talks viewed by over 10 million people) are slide-less. However, those speeches generally leave the audience with a feeling or a new, strong-yet-singular understanding. In the education field, you are trying to relay more information than that. To make all that information easy to understand and easy to remember, you'll need visuals.

HOW THIS CHAPTER WORKS

(You Need Chapter 6)

"Chapter 6. Speaking Anywhere" provided you with the fundamental guidelines that apply to all speaking opportunities described in this book. The slide guidelines provided in this chapter are supplemental and are meant to be considered *with* the speaking guidelines in "Chapter 6. Speaking Anywhere".

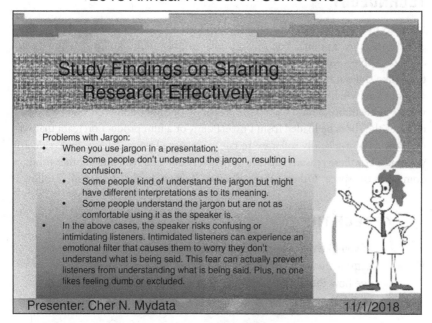

Figure 7.1 Bad Slide Example

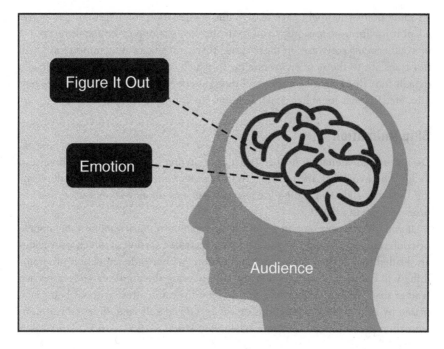

Figure 7.2 Good Slide Example

TECHNOLOGY

Learn to use a presentation program like Microsoft PowerPoint (products.office.com/en-us/powerpoint). You might prefer another tool, like Prezi (www.prezi.com) or Apple's Keynote (www.apple.com/keynote), but be aware of any limitations (like slides not functioning if you cannot access the internet) before doing so.

Since you will likely give this same presentation (or large portions of it) at other venues in the future, you'll want to be prepared for online conference software that requires the slides be loaded from PowerPoint, or a film production team that will use PowerPoint-friendly software to cut to images of your slides in their video of your talk. For these reasons I always use PowerPoint and will until another product dominates the space. Other ways to sidestep "technology behaving badly" follow.

TECH TIP

If you like the look of Prezi but choose to use PowerPoint, search www.YouTube.com for "Zoom for PowerPoint" to see how the Zoom Summary feature can make Prezi-like slides in PowerPoint.

Forgo Obscure Fonts

At some point you might have to give this presentation (or a version of it as you adapt it for future occasions) from someone else's laptop or online using course or conferencing software. In those cases, there is a chance uncommon fonts will not translate to the new environment, in which case your text will appear in a default font that might be larger and thus get cut off, or be smaller and less legible, etc. Popular fonts like Arial, Courier New, or Verdana are safer bets.

Skip Animation

Do not use an animation feature (such as arranging for text to appear beside an image when you click the mouse). Get the exact same effect by simply duplicating the same slide and adding the changes (such as the newly appearing text) to otherwise-identical slides.

If you give this presentation (or a future adaptation of it) online using course or conferencing software or you present a recorded session in which your slides are loaded by a technician in post-production, within-slide animation programming will commonly not function. By simply using the duplicate-slide approach (rather than the animation tool), you can get the same effect without being surprised by not-working animations or having to redo all your slides to suit non-animation presentation conditions when they arise.

Avoid the Web

Avoid internet reliance whenever possible. Even if conference organizers promise you'll have web access, things can go wrong. Attendees' use of multiple mobile devices (tweeting via phone, checking email via laptop, etc.) during conferences can easily overload even convention centers' bandwidth capabilities, causing your internet access to be blocked or ruinously slowed. You might successfully check your access when you arrive, but then be thrown out of the web in your mid-presentation demonstration.

SCRAPPY TIP

To forgo the web during a presentation, I plan ahead. If I have a video I want to play, I embed it in my slide rather than plan to play it online. If I have a series of online steps I want to share, I add a "screen capture image" to each slide so it looks like I'm following the steps online when I am actually clicking through slides (this also allows me to add a red-line circle around each place to click, making it easier for attendees to follow along). This way I don't have to chance misfortune.

Slide Design

If you have no slides, people might be wowed by your eloquent turn of phrase but they won't remember your content. Even if you do have slides, they will only help your message if they are well crafted. To create good slides, stick to the following guidelines.

Adhere to Event Requirements

IMAGE COPYRIGHT

See the "Slide Images" section later in this chapter for help determining which images you can legally use.

The organization hosting your presentation will likely have some guidelines to which you must adhere. You might have discovered these when you first applied to speak (for example, the length of the time slot or the theme strand) or after acceptance (for example, the audience to which your session is assigned, or a specific slide with which all presenters must start). Review such guidelines before, during, and after you build your content and slides. Make sure your planned speech will adhere to the event organizers' wishes.

Be Design-Savvy and Current

Google *amazing PowerPoint designs* or study some other examples. Notice the aspects that make designs effective and timely (dark gray text rather than a thick bubble-like font that screams "1980s", plenty of open/white space rather than cartooned clipart from early word processing projects, etc.). Note which aspects allow the different slide types (cover slide, section slide, content slide, etc.) to look cohesive.

Find some slide styles you feel confident replicating. Determine which of these will best match your brand, the content you will typically present, and the venues at which you hope to present. Learning to use PowerPoint's drawing tools will expand your slide design abilities and thus your options.

Don't Put a Cap on Your Slides

The common yet misguided recommendation to limit your number of slides to whatever number a particular source establishes as "the rule" is a mistake (Kaushik, 2017). Instead, limit your slides to whatever number will best communicate your messages.

Avoid Visual Clutter

Let a word or phrase breathe with plenty of white space around it. This "white space" can also be part of an image. For example, if your photo of an airplane fills your entire slide and a swath of white clouds comprises the bottom part of the image, you could add a highly-legible phrase across the white clouds.

Rely on Images More Than Sentences

Several studies have shown that including images in presentations increases viewers' recollection and positive attitudes concerning the material displayed (Abela, 2008; Madan, 2015). In a Purdue University study in which 110 undergraduate students viewed videos (including mine), Carmichael, Reid, and Karpicke (2018) found the versions of presentations containing graphics resulted in improved judgement of learning, engagement with the speaker, interest in the speaker, and enhanced student memory. In a Stanford University study, Kessel (2008) found visualizing information can enhance cognition, schematize and reduce complexity, assist problem solving, enhance memory, and facilitate discovery, but only if the visualizations are applied effectively. That last caveat is covered in the next section ("Slides Images").

Rather than include a slide with words you read or paraphrase for the audience, instead try a slide with one of these:

- an image with no words;
- an image with a single word or phrase that captures the idea;
- an image with no more than three distinct words or phrases;
- one or two images (each with or without a word pairing) juxtaposed.

162

Unless sharing a direct quote (such as when you display a student's exact words), avoid complete sentences entirely. Sadly, slides at education-related events are often laden with text, devoid of images, or accompanied by irrelevant images that don't drive home intended meaning.

TIME-SAVING TIP

I tend to stick with the same design style for all my presentations (even when they're on different topics). It's very common for me to grab slides from multiple presentations (the content slides from one presentation, the activity-introducing slides from another presentation that can be adapted, etc.) for a new presentation, and this way I don't have to adjust the style of some slides to make the new presentation cohesive.

Make Text Easy to Read

Using no smaller than font size 32 is a good rule of thumb. Keeping your slides text-sparse (recommended in the previous bullet) will make this easy. Also avoid fonts that are hard to read, such as those that look like cursive or calligraphy.

Proof and Edit Meticulously

Use your presentation software's spell check and grammar check tools. Proof your slides for errors, clarity, and recommendations given in this chapter and others.

Turn any presentation requirements into a checklist (I add a to-be-checked box next to each required item) and ensure you've met every demand. Step into your audience's shoes and consider whether the "big picture" comes across and the flow works.

SLIDE IMAGES

Using powerful images in powerful ways can catapult your message into viewer's minds, hearts, and memories. There are exceptions to the following guidelines but break them only when it improves your delivery to do so (for example, if four compelling images, when juxtaposed on a slide, hammer home your message in a way a single image can't).

Amp up Scale

Let the image take up the whole slide rather than place a small image somewhere on the slide. Eliminate borders between the image's edges and the slide's edge's.

Consider cropping photos to make them more compelling. For example, someone throwing a ball zooms the viewer into the moment of action better that a view of a park with a ball-thrower in the distance.

Let Single Images Shine

Use one powerful image rather than many smaller images. Remember the 1987 anti-drug commercial described in the previous chapter, in which an egg was dropped in a frying pan to the words, "This is drugs. This is your brain on drugs. Any questions?" A decade later, Entertainment Weekly named that simple commercial the 8th Best Commercial of All Time (EW Staff, 1997). That image made a much stronger impression than a list of facts would have; people who read or heard facts might be able to recall one or two of the facts later, but no one would likely forget the image of an egg being fried, even years after seeing it.

Juxtaposing two or three strong images also works well. A single, important word on a slide can also be effective. Search "Elon Musk Debuts the Tesla Powerwall" on www.YouTube.com and notice how well Musk's slides complement his presentation.

Give Images Consistency

Use a similar style for images. For example, stick to all black and white photos, or all photos with sepia tones, or all photos zoomed in close, or data visualizations in which you stuck to the same style and color palette, or illustrations done in the same style (such as by the same artist or from the same image set). See the "Images: Stock Photos and Illustrations" section of "Chapter 2. Image" for help finding and selecting images.

SCRAPPY TIP

Using photographs rather than illustrations (knowing you can still include data visualizations and other graphics to complement the photographs) tends to make it easier to stick with the same image style. Photos from many different photographers can still look like a unified collection, whereas it is harder for a single illustrator's offerings to meet all your needs. Even if a single set of illustrations works well for one presentation, you will likely reuse portions of this presentation in the future, and it is easier to add a new photo than it is to find a new (yet style-matching) illustration.

Don't Include Irrelevant Images

A cartooned character sitting at his desk beside your list of bullet points will confuse viewers and look silly. Irrelevant information can overload an audience's ability to process communicated information, and this visual clutter detracts from communication due to people's limited processing capacity (Abela, 2008).

Show Diversity

It is common to see only White people in every slide. Yikes! Our towns, countries, and world contain people of all colors and backgrounds, and our images should reflect this.

Don't Propagate Stereotypes

All the principals in your slides should not be men, all the students in your slides about expulsions should not be of color, etc. Though it's disheartening to consider common stereotypes, it's important to reflect on them enough to be sure our presentations don't support them. Your slides can reject stereotypes by either (a) avoiding stereotypical representations altogether (such as showing a girl conducting a science experiment rather than a boy if you'll only be covering science in a single image) or (b) representing people of a variety of backgrounds so that your slide collection, as a whole, does not present a one-sided view (such as showing both girls and boys enjoying science). The next section will help you find images that defy stereotypes.

Stock Images

You can buy stock images, but there are many sites where you can get images for free. For example:

- The British Library (www.flickr.com/photos/britishlibrary)
- DesignersPics (www.designerspics.com)
- Getty Images "Lean In Collection" (www.gettyimages.com/collections/leanin)
- New Old Stock (http://nos.twnsnd.co)
- Pixabay (www.pixabay.com)
- StockSnap (https://stocksnap.io)
- Videvo (www.videvo.net)
- Visual Thinkery (www.visualthinkery.com)
- Women of Color in Tech (www.flickr.com/photos/wocintechchat)
- The Public Domain Project (www.pond5.com)

165

When picking images, be wary of those that won't make you appear current. For example, you don't want to pick clip art that looks like it came from a 1990s slide presentation. If you are techy, you might use image manipulation software like Adobe Photoshop to alter ready-made images (such as to erase backgrounds or add shadows) to make disparate images look like they belong together as a set.

USE IMAGES WITHOUT VIOLATING COPYRIGHT

Copyright laws differ from country to country, with some treaties offering some foreign protections. Learn more about copyright at www.copyright.gov (U.S.), www.gov.uk/copyright (U.K.), or other country's copyright site. The following summarizes current U.S. protections:

Use an image easily if...

- You created your own image (i.e., drew or photographed it) and conceptualized it.
- You purchased the image along with its publication rights.
- The image was created before 1923.

Use an image but credit its source if...

- The image was created between 1922 and 1964 (unless its owner filed a renewal with the Copyright Office specifically during the image's 28th year, which is unlikely).
- The image's owner gave you written permission to use the image in the way you use it.
- The image is in the public domain (i.e., its owner released rights to it); this is something that would be specifically stipulated.
- The image is copyrighted, but its author added a creative commons license that allows it to be used in the way you use it (e.g., not modifying the image).

Even if none of the above conditions applies, you might still be able to use an image as Fair Use (Section 107 of the Copyright Act) if...

- You use the image for reporting, teaching, scholarship, research or other activities that qualify as fair use *and* you will not profit from the image's use (e.g., you aren't using the image for commercial purposes).

There are additional considerations for Fair Use, which is a subjective determination. To determine if your use of an image qualifies as Fair Use, reference the Copyright Office's description of Fair Use at www.copyright.gov/fair-use/more-info.html or the Fair Use Checklist by Kenneth Crews and Dwayne Butler at www.copyright.columbia.edu/basics/fair-use/fair-use-checklist.html for assistance.

For the Artsy and Techy

Consider drawing your own graphics. If you struggle with technology or don't have a natural affinity for design, you might not attempt this one, but if you are able to make quality images quickly and easily, this ability ultimately saves you time and enhances your presentations.

Microsoft PowerPoint and Word have relatively easy to use "draw" tools (you can typically click "Insert" and select "Shape", then double click any shape you create to further customize it with the "Shape Format" tools) to create graphics (like diagrams and data displays) specific to what you're trying to communicate. Knowing how to create your own graphics lets you illustrate concepts with exactly what you want and makes it easy to change or add images without the collection of images seeming disjointed.

Visualizing Data

In a paper from Harvard University and Massachusetts Institute of Technology (MIT), Conner-Simons (2015) found visual representations of data – such as pictograms and infographics that simplify complex topics – dramatically improved viewers' ability to recall information viewed, as graphics provide additional associations for users that help them retain and recall information presented.

TECH TIP

Microsoft Excel's graphing tools, Microsoft Word's draw tools, and Microsoft PowerPoint's "Shape" and "SmartArt" tools can produce far more advanced data displays than people often know. Infographic makers like www.canva.com, www.visme.co, www.piktochart.com, and www.venngage.com can also help you build professional-looking displays.

167

SCRAPPY TIP

Signing up for e-newsletters from a data visualization or infographic site (like www.venngage.com) can provide a steady stream of ideas for illustrating information.

Visualization allows for much of people's understanding of data to be managed within the visual cortex, which is extremely fast and efficient, whereas the processing of non-visual data displays is handled primarily by the cerebral cortex, which is much slower and not as efficient (Few, 2014). In other words, well-executed data visualizations allow viewers to understand your data faster and more easily.

See the slides shown in Figures 7.3 and 7.4, which convey the exact same information in different ways. Notice how Figure 7.4 is more inviting and clear.

To avoid miscommunicating values or confusing your viewers, you'll want to also follow research-based data design advice. Follow the OTCD Standards at www. JennyRankin.com/s/OTCDStandards.pdf (particularly the Packaging/Display standards) to produce data displays others will interpret easily and accurately.

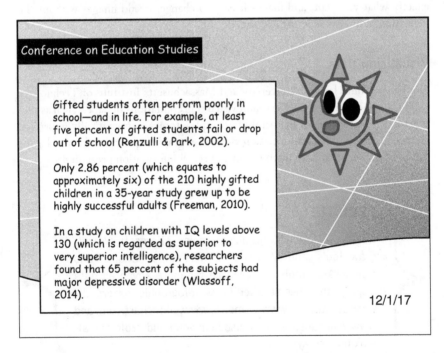

Figure 7.3 Bad Slide Example

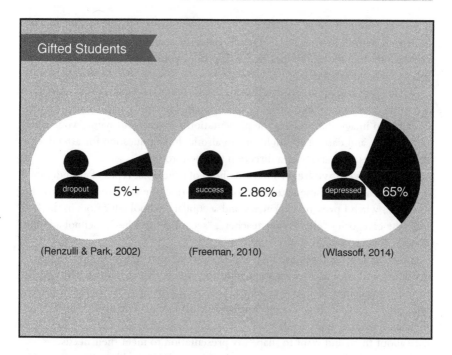

Figure 7.4 Good Slide Example

BAD SLIDE VS. GOOD SLIDE

Download the "Bad Slide vs. Good Slide" eResource (see the "eResources" section near the start of this book for details) to see a bad slide (sharing data horribly) vs. a good slide (that displays key data gradually and effectively). The bad slide and the good slide share the exact same data, but in two very different ways.

EXERCISE 7.1: SLIDE REDESIGN

Rework an old or new slide in a way that will be more compelling, communicative, and memorable for viewers. Use what you just read in this chapter, as well as the "Images" section of "Chapter 2. Image" for guidance.

SPECIFIC SLIDE TYPES

Consider including the following slide types in the order they are explained. If your presentation is less than one hour or is in a non-traditional format, you will likely skip some of these. For example, an 18-minute TED Talk would be over-burdened with slides devoted to agenda, objectives, and other training-appropri-ate aspects. Include slide types that will propel your message and help viewers follow what you're sharing.

Title. This first slide, displayed as attendees enter the room, tells people they are in the right place and intrigues them to stick around. This slide commonly contains an image that reflects the presentation's focus, your name, your affilia-tion, event, and date. You might opt to also include a question for attendees to think about as they arrive or a direction for them to do.

Who do we have here? Find out ahead of time what types of attendees will be present and put these categories on a slide (include an "other" option). For example, when I present to primary and secondary school educators in the U.S. I use the categories "elementary teacher", "secondary teacher", "school adminis-trator", "district administrator", and "other".

I then have attendees raise their hands as I read each category so I know more about my audience and where each educator type is sitting. Now when I give an example pertaining to young children, I can face a group of elementary teachers who can relate to it. If no one fits one specific category, I will not waste time giv-ing examples that apply to that role. This quick exercise also tells my audience I care about them and want to shape my presentation to meet their needs.

Me. A slide that communicates your background simply, like with a timeline or a trio of images, can assure the audience you are qualified to present on your topic. Cater this to your topic. For example, only when I present on gifted education do I add my volunteer role with Mensa's Gifted Youth Program to my timeline.

Magic. Sometimes it's appropriate to place magic slides (those that accom-pany a Table 6.1–type stunt) right after your title, or to wait until after you've shared objectives. Its placement depends on the flow of your speech and is a subjective decision. In a presentation of 45 minutes or longer, I generally begin each segment (covered later) with its own bit of magic. This firms my hold on the audience's attention and leads people to care about and understand what I'm saying. This should be done in a time-efficient way. See Table 6.1 in "Chapter 6. Speaking Anywhere" for examples of presentation magic.

SCRAPPY TIP

Every time I reach a slide that introduces a new activ-ity or segment of my PowerPoint, I secretly peek at two times (like 12:15 / 12:30) that are displayed small and discretely at the bottom of the slide. These tell me if I'm running behind or ahead of schedule, so I can adjust my pace accordingly:

- **Current time.** Click "Insert" and "Date & Time" to add this to an existing text box (select "Update Automatically" when the option appears so the time will be current when it displays).
- **Time I should be reaching the slide.** Add this to an existing text box, and figure it out with this formula (adjusted after practice and to allow for questions at the end of the session):

> [slide number you're entering the times on] divided by [total number of slides] times [the total number of minutes allotted for presentation], then add those minutes to the presentation's start time (for example, if I end up with a total of "38" minutes from that formula, and my presentation starts at 8:00 AM, I put "8:38" on that particular slide).

Since both times (the one showing the time you should be on, next to the time it actually is) will display side-by-side, you'll be able to quickly judge if you're running ahead or behind. Just be sure you are clear on which clock is which.

Agenda. Share only the big topics (typically segments) of your presentation and include a "Questions" agenda item at the end. I tell attendees to feel free to interrupt the presentation if they have quick clarifying questions but note we will have time at the end for in-depth questions or comments. I also let them know there will be opportunities throughout the presentation when I will invite them to share.

Objectives. Summarize what attendees will know and be able to do at the end of your presentation.

Segment Title. "Chunk" your presentation into subtopics, much like you would designate chapters if writing a book. This will help frame your points for attendees so they can better follow you.

Content. Within each segment you will have multiple slides to support the bulk of your presentation.

Activity. I usually place one activity slide at the end of each segment. We work in the education field. Thus, we understand the importance of engagement and active participation. If you speak for 15 minutes or more, your audience will need a break from lecture format to engage with what they are learning. Brainstorm on how activities like those in the next text box can support attendees' application of the concepts you share.

WITHIN-PRESENTATION ACTIVITY IDEAS

Consider how you could complete these directions to engage your audience in activities

- "Turn to your neighbor and share..."
- "Get into groups of three or four and discuss..."
- "Notice the 'True' sign on your right side of the room, and the 'False' sign on your left side of the room. I'm going to read a few statements. After each statement, move to one side of the room based on whether you believe the statement is true or false. We'll then discuss the statement before moving on to the next."
- "I'm going to throw this stuffed animal, and if you catch it tell us... and then throw it to someone across the room."
- "Use your handout to..."
- "Write down the reason you..."
- "Notice the eight posters arranged around the room, each bearing a topic. Go to the one that pertains to you and discuss... with the group that gathers there."
- "Get up and collect a strategy from one person for every category on this slide."
- "Using the white board [this can be cheaply laminated card stock] and dry-erase marker you were given, list your answers in large letters. We will then walk around the room while holding up our boards. Every time you see an answer you like on someone else's board, add it to your board."
- "Form a group of four to six in which teachers, principals, and district administrators or executive principals are all represented. Then discuss how this summary of research pertains..."
- "Visit the posters around the room and add a sticky note to each on which you have written different..."
- "Grab a colored sticky note based on the color assigned to your role (e.g., blue for researchers) and add it to the "Yes" or "No" poster based on whether you agree with this statement..." You can instead use polling software like Poll Everywhere (www.polleverywhere.com) or OMBEA (www.ombea.com).
- "Each side of the room will be a different team as we..."
- "Grab the sticky note stuck to the bottom of your chair. Each one is different..."

The California STEAM Symposium (2017) noted in its call for submissions what other conference organizers also find: "Every year the highest-rated presentations are those that include interactive activities or exercises. Rather than exclusively lecture from the front of the room, presenters should incorporate hands-on demonstrations, collaborative worksheets, group discussions, or other engaging methods" (p. 1).

COUNTDOWN TIMER SLIDES

For activities that take one minute or more, I include a countdown timer on my slide. This helps the audience stay on task. Download the "Countdown Timer Slides" eResource (see the "eResources" section near the start of this book for details) for timers you can use in your own presentations. There are seven timers to choose from, counting down from one, two, three, four, five, ten, and fifteen minutes.

In addition to incorporating activities that give attendees opportunities to speak, move, and interact, engage attendees between these activities with quicker ways to contribute. Consider how you could complete these directions for your audience:

- "Raise your hand if…"
- "Stand up if…"
- "Turn to your neighbor and say…"
- "Shout out your biggest challenge concerning…"
- "Applaud if you think…"
- "Tell me…" Feel free to call on someone; if you greeted people as they arrived, you will even know some names.
- "Write down one quality that…"
- "Pick one of these three categories and think of ways it applies to your…"
- "If I throw this to you…"

Get creative and think of some new ways to involve your audience in quick spurts. Then incorporate those, as well as the longer activities provided earlier, into your speech.

Repetition of Main Ideas. Consider Martin Luther King's "I Have a Dream" speech, where King repeated "now is the time" and "I have a dream" (King, 1963, pp. 2–7) to inspire listeners to act for a better future. Consider Winston Churchill's "We Shall Fight Them on the Beaches" speech, where Churchill repeated the "We shall fight…" (Churchill, 1940, p. 6) clause seven times to stress Britain's united vision of working together no matter one's individual location.

In their seminal study, Nichols and Stevens (1957) found that after hearing someone speak, people tend to forget more of what they learned within the first eight hours that follow than they do in the next six months. Though you'll strive to not let them, audience members will naturally tune in and out of your presentation at times. They will have other thoughts ("What will I say to the person I'm meeting after this session?" "Who just texted me?" "I'm hungry") and miss some words you say. These challenges provide added incentive to recap what you have covered, especially if you can get attendees to apply the concepts to what they'll do in their own practice once they leave you.

Based on the purpose you established earlier in this chapter, you should know the primary goals your presentation is meant to achieve. When crafting and reviewing your content, be sure those few points are exceptionally clear and delivered throughout the presentation rather than only in a single statement. In the words of Winston Churchill, "If you have an important point to make, don't try to be subtle or clever. Use a pile driver. Hit the point once. Then come back and hit it again. Then hit it a third time – a tremendous whack" (Mayer, 2011, p. 200).

Alda (2017) wrote, "I try to explain difficult ideas three different ways. Some people can't understand something the first couple of ways I say it, but can if I say it another way. This lets them triangulate their way to understanding" (p. 98). Repetition also breeds a sense of familiarity in the audience, which leads to increased comfort and agreement with an idea (Badgett, 2016). This occurs as an aspect of priming, where seeing or hearing something multiple times makes the information easier to process, which contributes to the audience's cognitive ease, which fosters trust and agreement (Kahneman, 2011).

I sometimes recap throughout the presentation as I build on concepts ("Now that we've explored A and B, let's take a look at C."). I've also finished a presentation with a matching game where I showed a grid of nine images (that were used in the presentation to represent nine key concepts) and attendees filled in a blank grid on their handout with the topics covered. They could speak with other attendees to determine those they couldn't remember (which naturally triggered dialogue to help them recall concepts, as one attendee would summarize a concept for the other).

Many speakers seek to prevent immediate retention loss by prompting attendees to develop an action item – related to what they learned – that they will put into effect by the next day. Others encourage attendees to visit the links on the session's handout as soon as possible.

There are several ways in which you can repeat your message so it isn't missed. Consider Table 7.1's examples, which are built around a presentation where "teacher burnout hurts low income students" is the main speaking point. Consider how you could apply each strategy to your own main message:

Table 7.1 Repetition Strategies

Strategy	Example
Before your talk, search your presentation for unnecessary "side points" and remove them if they'll cut your audience's chances of understanding and remembering the main point you reiterate.	Maybe your points on how low-income students rate their experiences in school is informative but digresses from your main point. If so, eliminate it or use only the portion that helps illustrate your main point (such as how these students express feeling when teachers quit).
Explain what your main idea is before you get into detail.	You: "The main point of this session is that teacher burnout hurts low income students more than anyone else."
After providing details, have audience members discuss or share the implications of what you said.	You: "I've just shown you a lot of statistics. Why would this scenario be most devastating to students in high poverty areas?"
After each segment, engage your audience in a call and response that reiterates your main point. Attendees might need coaching the first time you call out (extend one open palm to them and cup the other hand to your ear in an exaggerated gesture that you want to hear from them), but if the call and response remains the same it will happen increasingly naturally.	You: "...and who does this hurt most?" Audience: "poor students!"
At the end of segments, particularly in a long training session, recap what you've said so far and then introduce the next segment.	Show a slide that stacks images of your two previous points (You: "We've looked at what teacher burnout is, and we visited stats indicating it hurts low income students the most...") and then add an image representing your next point (You: "Now let's look into exactly WHY it hurts low income students the most").

(Continued)

Table 7.1 Continued

Strategy	Example
Repeat (such as after each chapter-like segment of your speech) a visual that represents your main point.	If you showed a simple graph or image that shows poor kids are hurt more by teacher burnout than other kids, display it silently at the end of each segment and spend a moment considering how what you just said hurts these students.
Throughout your presentation, whenever it fits, use the same catchy phrase that summarizes your main point. After a few times you might even turn this into a call and response, where the audience completes your sentence.	You: "When teachers burn out, poor kids lose out." Read the "Consider Packaging" section of "Chapter 1. Introduction" to gain inspiration from former First Lady Michelle Obama.
At the end of your presentation, repeat your main point loud and clear. You can involve the audience in this.	You: "What do you think the main point of this presentation was?" Audience: "Teacher burnout is most devastating to poor kids." You: "Take a moment to discuss with one to two neighbors which talking points you'll share with colleagues regarding this main point and what you can do about it."

Unless you're giving an all-day training, incorporating all of the above strategies would be overkill. Just consider which fit best with your speech and will help make your main point(s) memorable, then use those strategies.

Conclusion. You might build a slide to wrap up key take-aways from your presentation, or you might simply wrap things up while the final slide (next) is displayed.

Contact and Questions. Reserve at least 5 minutes at the end of your presentation to hear and answer the audience's questions. During this time, display a slide that includes your name, email address, website, and most active social media site(s). This way people will have plenty of time to record the information.

If you run out of time, say something like, "I'll be just outside this room if anyone wants to meet me there to ask questions." You can then leave the slide up as you accept your applause and begin to pack up.

EXERCISE 7.2: NEW SLIDE

Pick a single slide type (as described in the last section) and create a new slide that captures what you've learned in this chapter. You might incorporate this slide into the next two chapters' exercises.

REFERENCES

Abela, A. (2008). *Advanced presentations by design*. San Francisco, CA: Pfeiffer.

Carmichael, M., Reid, A., & Karpicke, J. (2018, February). *Assessing the impact of educational video on student engagement, critical thinking, and learning: The current state of play*. SAGE Publishing. Retrieved from https://us.sagepub.com/sites/default/files/hevideolearning.pdf

Conner-Simons, A. (2015, November 5). *Making visualizations more memorable: Eye-tracking research reveals which types of visuals help people remember*. Retrieved from www.seas.harvard.edu/news/2015/11/making-visualizations-more-memorable?utm_content=buffer60053&utm_medium=social&utm_source=twitter.com&utm_campaign=buffer

EW Staff. (1997, March 28).). The 50 best commercials of all time. *Entertainment Weekly*. Retrieved from http://ew.com/article/1997/03/28/50-best-commercials-all-time

Few, S. (2014): Data visualization for human perception. In Soegaard, Mads & Dam, Rikke Friis (Eds.), *The encyclopedia of human-computer interaction*, 2nd Ed., 35. Aarhus, Denmark: The Interaction Design Foundation.

Kahneman, D. (2011). *Thinking, fast and slow*. New York, NY: Farrar, Straus and Giroux.

Kaushik, A. (2017). PowerPoint: 5 lessons to unsuck. *The Marketing < > Analytics Intersect Newsletter, 92*(2017).

Kessell, A. M. (2008). *Cognitive methods for information visualization: Linear and cyclical events (Doctoral dissertation, Stanford University, Stanford, California)*. Retrieved from ProQuest Dissertations and Theses. (3313597)

Madan, C. R. (2015). Every scientist is a memory researcher: Suggestions for making research more memorable. *F1000Research 2015, 4*(19). doi:10.12688/f1000research.6053.1

Chapter 8

Speaking at Conferences and Other Events

Think of something you did in the past that scared you – riding a roller coaster, skydiving, giving birth, asking someone out on a date – but that you ended up being glad you did. Those of you who still hate roller coasters and still feel the sting of rejection… quickly think of something else. There has to be something that added a valuable, proud memory to your life that would be missing if you hadn't pushed through that terrified feeling.

Bad public speaking can leave you feeling awful afterwards… but apply the strategies in this book to do an incredible job, and the thrill of having done it will leave you feeling proud, joyous, and wanting to brave that stage again. Even if you are visibly nervous the whole way through, a well-laid plan with well-crafted content (covered in the previous two chapters) will still impress your audience. You don't have to be perfect: just plan well, take that chance on stage, and celebrate afterwards.

HOW THIS CHAPTER WORKS

(You Need Chapter 6)

"Chapter 6. Speaking Anywhere" provided you with the fundamental guidelines that apply to all speaking opportunities described in this book. The speaking guidelines provided in this chapter are supplemental and are meant to be considered *with* the guidelines in "Chapter 6. Speaking Anywhere".

LIST OF CONFERENCES (INCLUDING SYMPOSIUMS, ONLINE CONFERENCES, RESEARCH MEETINGS, AND OTHER EVENTS)

LIST OF CONFERENCES

This book lists 179 speaking opportunities (including symposiums, online conferences, research meetings, and other events) for you in an electronic file that makes it easy to find and pursue speaking engagements. You can sort the file by event type, location, or month, and you can visit each website with a simple click. The list contains details like submission link, deadlines, conference type, location, event date, and manipulation-friendly fields you can use to track your submissions. This file also includes TED Talks covered in the next chapter (since Talks are events that are also broadcast). See the "eResources" section near the start of this book for details on accessing and using this "List of Conferences".

RESOURCE TIP

If you're not delivering a conference's keynote or featured session (which typically involves compensation), you might be concerned about hotel, airfare, and other travel expenses. Fortunately, many workplaces will consider funding your trip.

Learning Forward offers a Justify Your Attendance Kit for Learning Forward's Conference (https://goo.gl/qxSfn5). The kit's talking points and sample letter (requesting approval to attend) are designed for the Learning Forward Annual Conference but serve as excellent templates for convincing your employer to fund your attendance at other events, as well. Talking points include what you will learn from the event, how this will benefit students and your peers (offer to train colleagues when you return), and how you are being proactive (booking travel early and sharing a hotel room) (Learning Forward, 2017).

CONFERENCE SESSIONS

There are so many conferences dedicated to education that you could attend two per week if you were inclined to do so. Use the "List of Conferences" eResource (described earlier) to locate conferences appropriate for your expertise.

New events arise regularly, and there are many specialized conferences you might find on your own that match your specialties. If travel would be difficult for you, contact your local universities and other organizations (or search their webpages) to learn of events in your area. If money is an issue, find out (before applying to present) if conference organizers let presenters attend for free (not all do) or if travel grants are offered (common for large educational research associations).

> ### SCRAPPY TIP
>
> Some conferences require you to submit an unpublished paper when applying to speak. This paper is then peer reviewed and is often automatically published in the conference proceedings if you are accepted as a speaker. The Society for Information Technology & Teacher Education (SITE) International Conference is one example (you can even request to make this presentation online). This provides you with a peer reviewed publishing credit to add to the publications section of your CV, which can make a lack of journal publications less jarring.

Volunteer to be a session chair or discussant (like at AERA), where you get to introduce presenters and you often also get to sum up presentations at the end (adding your own impressions or pointing out recurring themes) and ask questions of presentation panel members. This is a great option if you aren't ready to give your own presentation or if you didn't get accepted to present but still want to participate.

Acceptance

For many presentations (such as for conference sessions), you will submit an application to speak. Submission requirements vary; you might have to submit a simple description, a formal abstract, or even a complete paper. Less common requests include links to previous speeches or a presentation outline.

TIME-SAVING TIP

When you apply to speak somewhere (entering session description and other information on an online form), always save the information you enter on a Word document on your computer, as well. I have a single "Conferences" folder on my computer that contains a separate folder (within it) for each conference to which I apply (for example: "AERA2017"). This way I can quickly find and then copy/paste my information to reuse it in the future. Also, since composition takes time, an online form can "time out" during the entry process (losing your information) before you finish your submission.

One or more people will review your application to determine if you can present. To increase your odds of acceptance:

❑ **Check to see if the event offers acceptance tips**, and ensure your entry adheres to those tips. For example, Student Affairs Administrators in Higher Education (NASPA) offers a tutorial for writing an effective NASPA presentation proposal (www.naspa.org/events/program-submission-guidelines), and AERA offers a webinar titled "Behind the Curtain: Inside Insights in Writing a High-Quality AERA Proposal" (www.aeramail.org/l.jsp?d=2853.409071.78.2aqJIEibh), as well as sample proposals.
❑ **Avoid long titles**. Aim for brevity rich with meaning and appeal.
❑ **Avoid confusing titles**. If only viewing your title, people should be able to guess what your presentation will cover.
❑ **Avoid dry titles and descriptions**. Planners and reviewers want to offer sessions that people will be excited to attend. An intriguing title will also mean more attendees, which means more students you can help through them.

SCRAPPY TIP

For huge conferences like AERA's (with more than 2,500 sessions) that alphabetically list the sessions for each time slot, start your title with "A". This will put your session at the top of the list where most people will see it. Otherwise, some attendees will see another session first that interests them and never read the rest of the long list to discover your session.

❏ **Determine what the conference acceptance criteria is.** Sometimes the rubric that peer reviewers use to score entries is shared with applicants. Before, during, and after you prepare your entry, consider how your description will meet all criteria.

❏ **If paper entry (common for education research conferences) guidelines say something about sections**, like, "Submissions will be reviewed on the following elements: purpose, theoretical framework, modes of inquiry, [etc.]," use those exact words (like "Purpose") as the subheadings in your paper so judges experience no confusion over whether you addressed a particular element they score.

❏ **If submitting an abstract (common for education research conferences)**, write with reviewers *and* attendees in mind. The abstracts of accepted work will likely appear in the event program, so they must ultimately hook conference-goers into attending your session.

❏ **If asked to submit learning outcomes (which are sometimes required)**, your goals should reflect a session that engages attendees and arms them for action. Thus, your goals should be light on passive-audience outcomes like "Attendees will understand..." and "Attendees will comprehend...", and heavy on action-oriented outcomes like "Participants will be coached in how to implement..." and "Participants will use provided resources to..." Also make objectives positive (for example, "achieve a productive and engaged classroom") rather than negative ("stop students from misbehaving").

❏ **Determine what the conference theme is** (if there is one). Be sure your session's title and description both relate to this theme (this differs from reiterating the theme). If there is no theme, instead reflect the hosting organization's mission and values.

❏ **Determine the appropriate strand for your presentation** (if the event categorizes presentations by strand). Strands are usually topics or target audiences stipulated in the conference program to help attendees who want to stick to a particular presentation type.

❏ **Be sure your session will appeal to at least one of the conference's key audiences.** Often this is an audience you must specify from a menu of options. Write your submission with this audience in mind.

❏ **If you have an accomplishment that is related to the session** and appropriate to include, see if you can mention it in the session's description without sounding egotistical. For example, if you work at a particularly prestigious university you might write, "The presenter will share content from the class she teaches on this topic at Harvard University." If you delivered a TED Talk, you might try, "The presenter will include segments from her TED Talk."

❏ **Write with enough clarity** that even people unfamiliar with your topic (as planners or reviewers might be) can easily understand your message and its appeal.

❑ **Don't be intimidated by research conference submission processes.** If you don't have a doctoral degree and have not conducted an official study, you can still typically present at an educational research conference. Well-written literature reviews and interpretations of another's data can make quality research papers and conference presentations. Rich data sources include the Civil Rights Data Collection (CRDC) (https://ocrdata.ed.gov), Pew Research Center (www.pewresearch.org), National Center Education Statistics (NCES) (www.nces.ed.gov), Statistics at DfE (www.gov.uk/government/organisations/department-for-education/about/statistics), and Gallup (www.gallup.com).

When applications to speak involve submitting an original research paper, as is common for education research conferences, these papers are often housed somewhere the public can access online. Reference these papers (especially if you are new to research, not sure what a "theoretical framework" write-up should look like, etc.) to get a feel for the type of work that is accepted.

SCRAPPY TIP

Many conferences use volunteers to "peer review" presentation applications and determine who gets to speak (they look for specific criteria and score accordingly). Around the time the conference is announced, the conference website or emails will call for people to apply to volunteer. Volunteers are often in short supply, whereas it is desirable to have many volunteers (meaning less work for each volunteer and increased fairness of determinations). It is thus relatively easy for professionals to be approved to serve on review panels.

Serving on a review panel will give you an inside peek into the review process, what organizers are looking for, common flaws in submissions, and more. This inside scoop can help you prepare a submission that is selected for this conference in the future, but also for others. Plus, you can include your service as an expert reviewer as an honor in the "Awards and Honors" section of your CV if that section is sparse.

Sometimes only one or two people determine your submission's score and acceptance. Thus, the selection process can be capricious (one year reviewers might dislike your entry, whereas the next year they love it). Keep this in mind

183

if you aren't accepted, and try again (at other venues, and for this same event in the future).

ONLINE CONFERENCES

Online conferences are great for all presenters, but if you are a beginner speaker I especially encourage you to present there. Open this book's "List of Conferences" eResource (described earlier) and sort the file by its "Location" column to find conferences listed as "Online".

Due to the internet and conferencing technology (which event organizers will help you use), online conferences:

- Allow you to speak from the comfort of your own home. No one can see you (as long as you keep your webcam display turned off, which is expected), so you can even be in your pajamas. The audience only sees your PowerPoint slides and hears your voice.
- Are easy to do well at because (since no one can see you) you can have your notes in front of you the whole time with no one knowing. It is also less intimidating to speak in front of an audience you cannot see.
- Often have international audiences, which means you can select from a range of time slots (such as after work) and widen your net of influence.
- Typically have a moderator present who can help you with any technology questions and field questions the audience submits.
- Give you a speaking credit to list on your CV without the expense of travel.
- Are often recorded, which means you'll have a link to the recording you can submit if other conference organizers require video evidence of your prior speaking (as TED Talk submissions usually require).

Once you have some online conferences under your belt, you will find it much easier to present the same material before a live audience.

> ### SCRAPPY TIP
>
> Find the CVs of professionals you admire (on their websites or www.LinkedIn.com) and see which conferences they have spoken at, which awards they have won, and where they have published. Then apply to the opportunities that match your own expertise.

POSTER PRESENTATIONS

If you've just completed your dissertation or study, a common way to share your findings is through a poster. These are typically presented in a large room displaying many people's posters over the course of a conference. There is often a designated time when presenters must be present for interaction with visitors.

Poster's Nature

A good research poster grabs viewers from 10 feet away and draws them in to learn more about your study. The sections are similar to that of a dissertation: your information (title, name, email address, and affiliation), abstract, introduction, purpose and hypotheses, methods, results with visualized data, conclusion, and references. However, rather than dense write-ups, these sections should use succinct summaries viewers can scan and digest quickly.

Use bullets, callout boxes, images... whatever it takes to make key points stand out, because most viewers won't read your whole poster to find those points. Include plenty of empty space to cushion text and sections; this will help content appear digestible and inviting. Use a pleasing color scheme (Google "modern color schemes") rather than dull or chaotic coloring. Pick a layout that best suits the communication of your particular ideas (even if it deviates from the sections and order I provided in the previous paragraph). For example, if your study is best shared with a photo of a brain in the middle and seven text boxes shooting out from that image in a circular array, then go for it. Unique posters can still communicate all of the standard poster components, and chances are they'll be more appealing and memorable.

Most research posters land somewhere between 36" (91 cm) to 48" (122 cm) on their shorter sides, and 72" (183 cm) to 96" (244 cm) on their longer sides. Headings should be around 40–100 point font size (with headings larger than subheadings, but both within this range), and body text should never be smaller than 18 point font. Use fonts like Arial or Helvetica that are more streamlined than Times New Roman.

Google "poster presentation" to reveal many free templates and examples after which you can model your poster. Some of these make all text look the same (which renders the words forgettable for many viewers), but you can enhance these posters with design tricks (mentioned earlier) that make key points stand out.

Poster's Display

Some venues provide tacks and bulletin boards to hang posters, but others offer easels to prop stiff posters. I opted for a poster I could roll up and then post, but inside the tube I carry it in I kept four thin slats of wood and large bull clips so I could fashion a hard frame in cases where it had to be propped. This allowed a single poster to function in either display environment. Check with conference organizers ahead of time so you'll know what will be provided but note you might show your poster at other venues in the future that will have different setups.

Tack your business card next to your poster (this also saves your cards, as people can simply take a photo of your information) and have the actual dissertation on hand, as well as other literature viewers might ask about. You might even match your attire to your poster's color scheme, which Keegan and Bannister (2003) found made more visitors approach a poster.

CONFERENCE KEYNOTES

Use this book's "List of Conferences" eResource to find conferences for which you could give an appropriate keynote. Whenever you believe the conference organizers will begin planning for the next conference (perhaps three months after an annual conference's last conference, and often before a call for regular session presenters is announced), email the conference organizers and officials. You can often find their email addresses on the conference organization's webpage or on emails relating to the previous year's conference.

SCRAPPY TIP

Search social media sites (Twitter especially) and the internet for calls for keynote speakers. I search phrases like "call for keynote" and "suggest keynote speaker". I often add "-if -my -me" to these Twitter searches to exclude tweets in which people are proposing themselves as speakers (there are many, and they typically include those words). Be sure you are on pertinent conferences' emailing lists to be made aware if they put out a call for keynotes.

Don't turn up your nose at giving your first keynote presentation at a venue that won't reach many in your target audience(s). Once you are able to say (and add to your CV) that you're a keynote speaker, this opens the door to countless future keynote speaking opportunities where you can reach tens of thousands of appropriate listeners, through whom your words can touch the lives of kids. If you have valuable knowledge to share, any keynote speaking venue that launches this journey will be worth it.

Even if you suspect the keynote has already been selected, it doesn't hurt to approach conference organizers. Once I was told the keynote had already been booked, but I was offered $3,000 (plus paid travel and hotel) to be one of the conference's "Featured Speakers". While this didn't give me the whole conference's audience, it still gave me hundreds of listeners with which to share my work (and funds for future travel to reach more audiences). Even small audiences add up to a bigger influence on students than you will have if you never reach out to conference teams.

Another response I received, from another conference's organizer, essentially read, "Thank you for reaching out about being a keynote presenter. We already have a tentative keynote speaker lined up. However, if that should change, I will enlist your help." This can position you to step in at the last minute, or to be considered as keynote for the organizers' future events.

See the "Sample Email" text box (note the underlined words are hyperlinks, which the reader can click for more information online). Compose a similar email in which you suggest yourself as an event's next keynote speaker. Some key points to make include:

- ❏ Your experience with the keynote topic.
- ❏ Your experience speaking and (if applicable) giving keynotes.
- ❏ Why your topic is of importance to the conference audience (timely, impactful, etc.).
- ❏ How your topic works well with the conference theme (if there is one; otherwise, relate your topic to the hosting organization's mission and values).

SAMPLE EMAIL I SENT A CONFERENCE PRESIDENT TO BOOK A KEYNOTE

Dear Dr. [Name]:

I hope your week is off to a great start. I have been presenting at [Conference] every year since [year] and love the conference. I teach the Masterclass at University of Cambridge each year as a visiting lecturer, but I spend most of the year writing books for educators. I am a former teacher (honored by the White House for my dedication to students), assistant principal, school district administrator, and chief education and research officer. Anyway...

187

I humbly propose that I deliver a keynote at [Conference] 2017 titled *Leveraging Partnerships to Beat **Teacher Burnout*** for these reasons:

- I cover this topic in my latest book, *First Aid for Teacher Burnout*, for which I just returned from receiving the Outstanding Book Award Honorable Mention from the Society of Professors of Education at the American Educational Research Association (AERA) annual meeting.
- I am a skilled public speaker who has given a TED Talk at TEDxTUM, speaks extensively and regularly, and just returned from teaching the AERA PD course "Strategies for Sharing Your Research" in which I taught other academics how to best give a killer keynote. In fact, my next book covers how educators can rock public speaking.
- I have given very successful, engaging (e.g., with audience participation) keynotes on teacher burnout to a wide range of educators. For example, last month I gave a keynote on teacher burnout in the African DR Congo, and this week I'll give a keynote on teacher burnout to 1,200 educators at the Association for the Education of Young Children (AEYC) annual conference in Ohio.
- Teacher burnout is a timely topic of pandemic proportions (yet too rarely talked about in research circles). A pair of articles I wrote for *Psychology Today* provides a sampling of statistics.
- The emphasis on the power of partnerships to help beat burnout is a clear complement to the 2017 conference theme of "[conference theme]".

I hope you find this proposal intriguing and appropriate for a [Conference] 2017 keynote. My CV (with bio) is available at www.JennyRankin.com/bio. Thank you very much for your consideration.

Sincerely,

Dr. Jenny Grant Rankin

Sometimes conference organizers put out an open call for keynote speakers, and you'll want to heed those calls. For example, in the past ASCD posted a "Suggest a Keynote for an ASCD Conference" form on its website. I only found the link after it had expired, and I regretted not having checked the site monthly (ASCD conferences are huge and well respected).

SCRAPPY TIP

Sometimes event organizers come under fire for the absence of diversity in their keynote lineup. For example, CES is the largest technology convention in the world (and one many involved in educational technology attend). In 2017, CES was called out by Gender Avenger (www.genderavenger.com) for featuring zero women in its extensive keynote lineups for both 2017 and (as announced for) 2018 (Captain, 2017). Within a month of that criticism, CES added five women to its nineteen keynote speaker lineup for 2018.

If an event only has one keynote speaker and that speaker is a White man, no one should criticize the choice. However, if the event has six keynote speakers who are all White, or if the event has hosted only male keynotes since its first annual conference twenty years ago, this raises diversity red flags (and the same goes if the keynotes were always women or always from another single racial or ethnic group).

When event organizers are called out, you can help. Email organizers immediately to suggest yourself or a respected colleague (if either would break the homogeneity) as keynote speaker. Even if organizers deem it too late to change the upcoming lineup, they can save your information to offer a more inclusive keynote offering the subsequent year. Once in that position, use your voice. Let your unique wisdom shine and share your unique perspective.

Targeting smaller conferences first will increase your odds of acceptance. Consider events hosted by academy trusts, local educational authorities, or school districts, which love to open with a respected keynote. Once you have done a keynote at a smaller venue, your odds of being accepted at a larger event increase.

Tell professional acquaintances of your desire to book keynotes. My first keynote (which opened the door to more keynotes) happened because the scheduled keynote speaker got sick. Because he knew I would be interested and qualified, he asked me if I could take his place. I agreed and quickly sent him my short bio, CV, and sample slides from a previous presentation to ensure he could easily convince event organizers to give me a chance. He was then able to arrange for me to take his place at the last minute.

As soon as you have given one keynote presentation, add "keynote speaker" to your description on social media sites, your business card, and anywhere else that feels appropriate. If your keynote was filmed, try to obtain a link to the recording, which you can place on your website and provide when seeking other opportunities.

SCRAPPY TIP

Lori (2017) suggested that upon finishing a presentation you ask your audience about other venues at which you should speak and ask that audience members tell those venues about you, too. You can ask attendees who approach you after your talk rather than ask the whole audience from the podium.

BOOKING AGENCIES

If you want to wholeheartedly jump on the speaking circuit, you might want to join a list of keynote speakers, which some organizations maintain to facilitate booking. When folks such as conference organizers, event planners, large corporations, or government branches want to book a keynote speaker or hire a consultant, they often turn to these one-stop-shops for likely candidates.

Such list maintainers come in many forms. See Table 8.1 for some examples.

SCRAPPY TIP

If there is a particular event at which you aspire to give the keynote, linger after a current keynote presentation and politely ask the presenter (privately) how she landed the job. Then pursue the same path.

Education experts who dislike searching and applying for individual speaking opportunities find this avenue favorable (they don't have to go to the prospects; the prospects come to them). Meanwhile, if there are key events where it would be beneficial to share your work, you can continue to apply to individual conferences while also sitting on one of these booking lists.

If you pursue a booking agency, you'll apply through the entity's submission process. If accepted, you will typically get to choose which speaking gigs you undertake and can turn down any that don't fit your goals. This way you can ensure your time is spent speaking to applicable audiences where your words can ultimately benefit the most learners.

Table 8.1 Types of Speaker Booking Agencies

Type	Example
Company	Coleman (https://experts.colemanrg.com) and Geniecast (https://geniecast.com)
Organization	National Association for Gifted Children (NAGC) Expert Speakers Program (ESP) (www.nagc.org/professional-learning/expert-speakers-program)
Publisher	ASCD Resource Speakers (www.ascd.org/about-ascd/Affiliates/Affiliate-Community/Resources-$-Forms/Resource-Speakers.aspx)

IF YOU PREFER TO START SLOW

As covered earlier, I highly recommend online conferences as a great place to begin presenting. However, if you don't feel ready to apply or present in front of a large audience of education stakeholders, consider some of these less intimidating options for your early foray into speaking:

❑ Talk to your principal, dean, or others about presenting your work to colleagues. You could present during staff development time or during an optionally-attended session.

❑ Local service organizations and clubs (such as Lions Club, Chamber of Commerce, and Rotary clubs) need content for their meetings, and it would help them if you offered to speak there; www.meetup.com and www.eventbrite.com also list meetings by area (Lori, 2017), and these are sometimes related to education. Keep in mind that many adults are parents, and you can gear your topic to ways parents can help their kids thrive.

❑ Events that are not education-specific can still pertain to your specialty. For example, a session on what is happening in our brains when we learn would interest business professionals who train staff, and a presentation on giftedness would interest an IQ-based society like Mensa.

Reach out to these venues and ask if they would like you to speak at any meetings or events. Even when these engagements lack prestige within our field, this approach will let you practice your content before live audiences before you present at a within-field event.

❑ Community centers have a huge impact on students. Denzel Washington is one of thousands who credits the Boys & Girls Club as being a prime reason he stayed on a positive trajectory while his friends did not (Boys & Girls

Clubs of America, 2018). You can offer to speak (at no cost) to a community center's staff on strategies that will help them help children.

❏ Reach out to non-traditional schools like charters and non-public schools. An investigation by the U.S. Department of Education (2018) concluded that early-career teachers in charter schools reported having less access to beginning teacher seminars and classes than early-career teachers in traditional schools reported. Yet non-traditional schools often have fewer formalities to jump through to get a seminar to happen. You could present your wisdom to these schools' teachers in order to help their students.

PLAN A CONFERENCE

Care to go big? If an important facet of the field would benefit from an event yet none is already offered, consider planning a conference of your own. When I used to plan the Illuminate Education User Conferences, I found it was a lot of work but well worth the effort.

If you can get a school or university to host outside of class hours, the expense can easily be covered by registration fees. Also consider an online venue (Google "Steve Hargadon" to explore his successful education conferences, which are offered online and included in this book's "List of Conferences" eResource). Speak with organizations who might want to get involved (they can also promote the event to members) and other like-minded folks to form a conference committee.

YOUR TURN

"Chapter 6. Speaking Anywhere" and "Chapter 7. Preparing Slides for Anywhere" provided guidance to present well. This chapter provided added tips, as well as multiple opportunities to share your expertise at conferences and other events. Select an event (use the "List of Conferences" eResource for suggestions) to which you will apply to present. Then complete Exercise 8.1 to plan your submission and presentation. Reference sections in this chapter and the previous two chapters as you complete the exercise.

EXERCISE 8.1: EVENT SPEAKING PLAN

1. What type of presentation will you be presenting?
   ❏ In-Person Conference Session
   ❏ Online Conference Session
   ❏ Poster Presentation
   ❏ Conference Keynote
   ❏ TED Talk (covered in the next chapter)
   ❏ Other:

2. At which event will you apply to speak?

3. Read the event's submission guidelines. What is on the rubric that reviewers use to determine acceptance, required description word count, etc.?

4. Note any details that will influence what you present.
   - ❏ Event theme:
   - ❏ Presentation strand:
   - ❏ Presentation type:

5. Who is your audience made up of? This can be one main audience or a few key groups.

6. What does your audience need from you?

7. What are your key purposes in delivering this presentation?

8. With what new understanding will your audience leave your presentation?

9. What will your audience be able to do after your presentation?

10. Describe what your style will be (humorous, casual, formal, etc.).

11. What will your presentation's title be?

12. What is your session's description? Multiple descriptions might be required (such as a short description for the conference app, list of objectives, and abstract for the program).

13. What magic will you use to make concepts resonate? Remember Table 6.1.

14. Create a PowerPoint template and use it to outline your presentation (or outline separately from the template). Then add and improve slides, gradually turning your template into a set of polished slides.

15. Practice your presentation, and proof and revise your slides and content as necessary. Ensure your speech matches what you promised in your submission, as well as criteria described in this chapter and the previous two chapters (actively engages the audience, communicates your core message, doesn't overload your reader, etc.).

REFERENCES

Boys & Girls Clubs of America (2018) *Alumni Hall of Fame*. Retrieved from www.bgca. org/about-us/alumni-hall-of-fame/denzel-washington

Captain, S. (2017, December 4). CES slammed for not including any female keynote speakers this year. *Fast Company*. Retrieved from www.fastcompany.com/40503227/ces-slammed-for-not-including-any-female-keynote-speakers-this-year

Keegan, D. A., & Bannister, S. L. (2003). Effect of color coordination of attire with poster presentation on poster popularity. *Canadian Medical Association Journal*, *169*(12), 1291–1292.

Learning Forward. (2017). *Justify your attendance kit for Learning Forward's conference.* Retrieved from http://lf.informz.net/z/cjUucD9taT03MDI0MTYwJnA9M-SZ1PTEwOTg0MDQzOTTkmbGk9NDg0MzY4NDc/index.html

Lori, L. (2017). 17 ways to find speaking opportunities. *Famous in Your Field*. Retrieved from http://famousinyourfield.com/17-ways-to-find-speaking-opportunities

U.S. Department of Education. (2018). *Preparation and support for teachers in public schools: Reflections on the first year of teaching*. Retrieved from https://nces.ed.gov/pub-search/pubsinfo.asp?pubid=2018143

Chapter 9

Speaking on Air
and Recordings

Few topics get more technical than particle physics. Steven Goldfarb is part of a team of scientists that works on the particle collider at the European Organization for Nuclear Research [translated from French] (CERN) and discovered the Higgs boson. Upon naming the Higgs boson Particle of the Year, *TIME Magazine* declared, "Forget Person of the Year – the discovery this summer by the Large Hadron Collider of the Higgs Boson particle was one of science's greatest achievements" (TIME staff, 2012, p. 1).

Wow! So, Goldfarb could consider the news of his discovery shared and stick to discussing particle physics with his colleagues at CERN and through scientific journals. Surely many a researcher of education, physics, or any other topic would have no qualms about sticking to familiar circles after such recognition for a discovery. But Goldfarb is an exception from which we all can learn.

Goldfarb and I became friends in 2015 when we gave TED Talks at TEDxTUM in Munich. "That's so cool," I thought then, "to see a physicist of such acclaim doing something to share his ideas and findings with the general public." I didn't know at the time what an understatement that was.

When I returned home to California, I turned on *60 Minutes* (one of my favorite television shows) and *wow!* There was Goldfarb, up on the screen, talking to Leslie Stahl about the Higgs discovery ...again, taking the time to share his findings with a new and varied audience. Throughout that week I noticed Goldfarb's ample use of social media to share more. The following week I was perusing TED-Ed lessons (where often-complicated concepts are explained to students in engaging ways) and stumbled across one featuring Goldfarb: he and another member of his team at CERN provided voices for an animated short in which they explained the Higgs boson to kids.

...and I'm not even done yet. Last year Goldfarb enthusiastically co-taught the Post Doc Masterclass at University of Cambridge with me. I spent the first half of class teaching Life Science doctoral students how to best share their research findings with the world, and then Goldfarb joined us from Geneva via video conferencing software, took us on a virtual tour of CERN, and answered questions about particle physics and his team's findings.

It should come as no surprise that Goldfarb chairs the International Particle Physics Outreach Group and is a fellow of the American Physical Society Forum for Outreach and Engaging the Public. What might surprise you, though, is how impactful his sharing of very technical findings is on mainstream audiences where folks come from a wide range of backgrounds.

We education experts have a well-known tendency to communicate in silos. Primary and secondary school educators talk about things like *differentiation* with folks who know exactly what terms like that mean. Education professors and researchers talk about things like *confirmatory analyses* with folks who know what terms like that mean. When we step outside these silos, like broadcasting can help us do, we can reach countless people both within and outside of our silos. The impact of this act can be huge.

Consider that episode of *60 Minutes* I mentioned, where correspondent Leslie Stahl and Goldfarb discussed an online webcast that announced and described the Higgs discovery. Stahl (2015) said, "Goldfarb told us that he was amazed at how many people went online to watch the meeting at which the discovery was announced." Then Goldfarb said, "You know, one billion people by the end of that week had seen video from that webcast. So, a significant portion of our planet was interested enough to watch something which was a very technical seminar."

One *billion* people in one week. If we educators dismiss the idea that people outside our field can understand and find value in the very specialized information we have to share, we have to remember our knowledge is surely no more complicated than particle physics. Plus, many TED Talks, video blogs, news media, radio shows, podcasts, webcasts, television shows, and videos also reach those working within our field (and many of these target education experts, in particular).

Speak on air and in recordings to reach all types of audiences. Believe in people's potential to do good things with your wisdom and findings. You never know how people's connection to your ideas is going to spark an idea that can change the world. Step onto the live or recorded stage to share your ideas and see what happens.

HOW THIS CHAPTER WORKS

(You Need Chapter 6)

"Chapter 6. Speaking Anywhere" provided you with the fundamental guidelines that apply to all speaking opportunities described in this book. The speaking guidelines provided in this chapter are supplemental and are meant to be considered *with* the guidelines in "Chapter 6. Speaking Anywhere".

SCRAPPY FAST TRACK

If you want to skyrocket to appearances on huge-audience media (for example, you have never been interviewed but are anxious to be heard on NPR), I recommend you use the information in this chapter (including its eResource to find opportunities) to take this route:

Step 1. Apply to broadcasts devoted entirely to the education field, such as BAM! Radio, Education Talk Radio, and Educators Lead (see the "List of Broadcasting Opportunities" eResource for details on these programs and others). As this chapter explains, field-specific broadcasts offer better acceptance odds and reach the best audience for your work. The facilitator or interviewer is likely to be another education expert, which usually means insightful questions and dialogue. This experience can also help you land and perform well for larger audiences.

Step 2. Perfect your speaking skills (covered in "Chapter 6. Speaking Anywhere") and pursue the wide range of opportunities covered in this book. For example, awards, books, and fellowships don't relate to radio but will enhance your CV and make you more guest-worthy to those deciding whether or not to feature you in a broadcast. Also work on your branding (covered in "Chapter 2. Image") so the specific expertise you offer is clear, and maintain a press page (covered in "Chapter 13: Multiply Your Impact").

Step 3. Apply to appear on NPR and other big producers covered in the "Other Radio and Podcasts" section. If you are familiar with NPR and the other organizations' huge audiences, you might be taken aback by the notion you should apply before you are an icon in our industry. In this book I encourage you to be scrappy and aim high. Being featured on NPR – something that carries much clout – will likely open countless doors for you. Those opened doors mean more chances to help kids. So why not go for it? See the "National Public Radio (NPR)" section of this chapter to see how many ways such a privilege can be made possible.

Step 4. Make your NPR (or similar) experience obvious to anyone visiting your social media sites, reading your email signature, visiting your website, or reading your CV. This will lead to even more opportunities to share your message on behalf of improving education for students.

LIST OF BROADCASTING OPPORTUNITIES (PODCASTS, RADIO, TELEVISION, VIDEOS, AND WEBCASTS)

LIST OF BROADCASTING OPPORTUNITIES

This book lists 109 broadcasting opportunities (such as podcasts, radio, television, videos, and webcasts) for you in an electronic file that makes it easy to find and pursue opportunities. You can sort the file by broadcast type and visit each website with a simple click. The list contains details like submission link, type, and manipulation-friendly fields you can use to track your submissions. Note TED Talks are included on the "List of Conferences" eResource, covered in the previous chapter, since Talks are organized like conference keynotes (and submission processes are like that of conferences). See the "eResources" section near the start of this book for details on accessing and using this "List of Broadcasting Opportunities".

TED TALKS

If you are not familiar with TED Talks, you'll want to visit www.ted.com right now and watch a few. Bill Gates, Stephen Hawking, Serena Williams, Sheryl Sandberg, Bill Clinton, Herbie Hancock, Carol Dweck, Pope Francis, and more have all done TED Talks. These are live presentations of 18 minutes or less that usually center on a unique, world-changing idea. The speeches are recorded and distributed widely for avid TED fans (typically a worldwide intellectual audience that spans ages, backgrounds, and fields).

Doing a TED Talk (which is considered highly prestigious) will open count-less doors for you. I believe I never would have been selected as lecturer of the Post Doc Masterclass at University of Cambridge if I had not done my Talk at TEDxTUM. Also, TED will expose a large audience to your work. My Talk reached over 500 viewers when I delivered it on stage, then thousands of viewers within its first month online on TED's TEDx site, and then thousands more over time. Just one of Sir Ken Robinson's TED Talks on education has passed the 50 million viewer mark.

Educators change lives every day, are able to see firsthand (and thus vividly describe) the impact of new approaches they employ, and are experienced orators. Educator researchers contribute to life-changing innovations, merge inspiration from varied fields, and can have large-scale impact. If you are either, it's likely you can share something unique and highly valuable with a larger community. TED is looking for speakers who will inspire viewers with original, powerful ideas.

You can see some TED opportunities listed in this book's "List of Conferences" eResource (described earlier). Sort the file alphabetically by "Conference" to find TED speaking prospects. You can be selected to give a Talk in any of the follow-ing ways:

- ❏ Get invited (usually if you're already famous).
- ❏ Apply (or have someone nominate you) to speak at TED or TEDGlobal (https://speaker-nominations.ted.com) or a less regular TED event like TEDFest (www.ted.com/about/conferences).
- ❏ Apply (or have someone nominate you) to speak at a TEDx event (www. ted.com/tedx/events). If a TEDx listing you pick has an event website, you can often find a submission form there (timelines vary, but organ-izers tend to select speakers 3–10 months before the event). Note that TEDxYouth events are only for kids, universities sometimes limit speakers to their faculty and students, and city-specific talks often limit speakers to residents.
- ❏ Apply to bring TED Institute (www.ted.com/about/programs-initia-tives/ted-institute) to your company, foundation, or organization. This will involve working with TED to identify internal idea-makers, polish ideas, and prepare TED Talks.
- ❏ Apply (or have someone nominate you) for the TED Prize (www.ted. com/participate/ted-prize/nominate) to execute your world-changing idea. The deadline is usually in March.
- ❏ Apply to become a TED Fellow (www.ted.com/participate/ted-fellows-program), which puts you in the pipeline to give a TED Talk. The deadline is usually in September.

❏ If you can live in Soho for four months, consider TED Residency (www.ted.com/about/programs-initiatives/ted-residency), which also puts you in the TED Talk pipeline.

❏ Apply (or have someone nominate you) to develop an animated TED-Ed lesson (http://ed.ted.com/nominate_an_educator).

Acceptance

These qualities will help you pass the competitive screening process to give a TED Talk:

❏ Have an idea "worth spreading" (unique, interesting, inspiring, and impactful).

❏ Pick a TEDx event with a location, focus, and theme that match your message and circumstances. For example, my Talk took place at the Technical University of Munich ("the MIT of Europe"), which matched my topics of design, data, and technology, not to mention my focus on education and students. The event's theme was Facets, and my research involved a facet of data use that is too often overlooked. Conversely, I was also selected to give a Talk at a local university's TEDx event but was dropped after higher-ups ruled speakers could only be from their own university.

❏ If picked to audition, be as prepared and passionate as if you were giving an actual, polished Talk.

❏ Keep your slides highly visual and as word-free as possible. If you ultimately give a Talk, many of your slides will get cut in the editing stage when a camera angle focuses on your face rather than what's projected, so your words should be able to stand on their own.

❏ Make your concept clear enough to summarize in one sentence (your pitch).

❏ Watch a lot of TED Talks and consider what has already been done.

Other ways to get involved with TED include:

❏ Organize a TEDx event (www.ted.com/participate/organize-a-local-tedx-event). You can informally plan a simple "viewing party" where you and colleagues view a lineup of Talks you select for attendees. Alternatively, you can apply to host a full-fledged TEDx event for which you are trained to select, coach, and host speakers whose talks could end up on the TED website.

❏ Create your own TED-Ed lesson (http://ed.ted.com/videos) that integrates an existing Talk. For example, my Talk became a data visualization lesson for students.

❏ Facilitate a TEDxYouth event (www.ted.com/participate/organize-a-local-tedx-event/before-you-start/event-types/youth-event) for students.
❏ Apply to offer TED-Ed Clubs (http://ed.ted.com/clubs) at your school.

NEWS MEDIA AND TELEVISION

Education news coverage influences how policymakers and the public think about educational issues and helps to frame which of these issues are deemed important (Coe & Kuttner, 2018). Other coverage on air and film is meant specifically for stakeholders in the education field. Establishing a presence through these media can help you inform professional and public dialogue to ultimately improve education for kids.

When Media Matters analyzed education coverage on cable news programs (CNN, Fox News, and MSNBC) during a 10-month timespan, only 9% (16) of the 185 guests discussing education policy were actual educators or had advanced degrees in education (Tone, Power, & Torres, 2014). Voices from experts such as you are missing from discussions that shape the public's view of our field and influence policies that affect students.

Timing

Inserting yourself into education news coverage involves widening your networks and establishing yourself as a credible expert (such as through publications) so you are ready when chances to share that expertise open. In *The Public Professor: How to Use Your Research to Change the World*, Badgett (2016) describes how Stephanie Coontz's work on American families was relegated to academic audiences until Coontz published a book in 1992 to counteract the public's misconceptions. That same year, Vice President Dan Quayle happened to criticize the fictional TV character Murphy Brown for being a single mother. This alignment of current events with Coontz's sharing of research catapulted Coontz into the media as the topic's go-to expert.

Consider how your message might squeeze into current media coverage of education topics. See Table 9.1 for ideas. Your wisdom could shed light on a highly publicized topic or fill an information void.

Pitch

News shows, where stories revolve around current events and issues, are always looking for important topics to cover. Education is rife with such fodder, but coverage will better serve students if expert perspectives such as yours are included in the dialogue. Getting included usually involves a pitch. This is similar to the pitch discussed in "Chapter 1: Introduction" (you'll want to whittle your

Table 9.1 Finding Entry Points for Your Message in Media

Current Media Coverage	Motivation to Contribute
In an analysis of 25 years' worth of news coverage, involving more than 5,000 sources, Campanella (2015) found most education coverage concerns sports (the clear winner with 14% of all coverage), followed by school events and funding (allotted 5% each).	Is your topic outside the scope of sports, school events, and funding? If so, it is missing from current media dialogue. You can work to change that.
Eng (2016) found that when covering education, media tend to focus on problems more than successes.	Though uncovering problems is a crucial component to our push for equitable education, *solutions* are especially valuable in treating injustices and other problems. Do you have answers the public can benefit from hearing? You can share them to help students while also shifting public conversation.
Hanford (2018), senior correspondent for American Public Media (APM), shared that more news coverage is needed on the following topics: how people learn and how those findings can be applied in schools, the gap between research and practice, the best ways schools can teach children to read, how financial interests (private donors, political donors, publishers, etc.) shape the country's conversation about education, and how education can best promote social and economic mobility.	Is there a way in which your practice or your research relates to the topics Hanford listed? What about topics other reporters express wanting to know more about? If you read interviews with journalists and attend panels on which they speak, you can find topics on which your knowledge is needed.
Local, regional, and state media outlets devote 7% of their coverage to education, whereas national media outlets devote only 2% (and this percent drops at election time), and 80% of news consumers get the majority of their news from local television, which they trust more than national sources (Campanella, 2015).	Outlets like BBC, CNN, *60 Minutes,* and NPR are fantastic platforms; definitely shoot for national and international media stages. However, don't neglect local media outlets in the process. The fact that education news consumers value local sources most can enhance your impact through these channels. You can also pursue local media in multiple geographic areas.

(Continued)

Table 9.1 Continued

Current Media Coverage	Motivation to Contribute
Eng (2016) found that when media do cover solutions they perpetuate "silver bullet" answers that emphasize individual groups or acts (ignoring systemic dynamics), such as characterizing Michelle Rhee as reforming Washington, DC schools by taking on the teachers' union.	Simple, single-stroke endeavors are rarely the answer for schools, which are complex ecosystems involving many moving parts and people. While sharing your message, you can emphasize (in an easy-to-digest way) the group effort involved in implementing solutions, and the roles multiple factors play.

idea down to a compelling core) but is different in that it's not just about getting a message across; it's also about convincing someone to broadcast that message.

You can send producers your pitch, couching your expertise within a story you can imagine will interest viewers or relate to current hot topics. Aim to offer something new, such as new information or a new perspective on an existing topic.

Most of a television show's viewers will not be teachers, and (even if they were) there wouldn't be enough time in a typical segment to cover all you know about a topic (such as to teach all key teaching strategies). Thus, when you pitch a story for a television show, find an angle with mass appeal and communicate clearly (without jargon).

See the text box for an example of how a successful education story pitch:

- ❏ couches the topic in an intriguing way in the subject line.
- ❏ shares a timely problem immediately (for example, teacher burnout just reached an all-time high), as neither a news story nor its pitch should bury the lead under a load of text.
- ❏ is angled to be public-centered (for example, ways the public can help with teacher burnout).
- ❏ is actionable and arms readers to combat the problem shared.
- ❏ includes a link to a key term (for example, teacher burnout) so more information can be accessed if needed without cluttering the pitch.

SAMPLE PITCH TO PRODUCERS THAT LED TO AIRTIME

Subject: Teacher Burnout is a Pandemic

Dear [Contact's Name],

I would love to see you produce a segment on teacher burnout, which just reached an all-time high. Teachers experience burnout more than any other profession. 15% of teachers leave the profession every year (20%

in low-income neighborhoods, meaning historically underserved students are hurt most). Nearly half of teachers leave the profession within five years of starting, and teacher attrition is rising. Teacher turnover costs the U.S. $2.2 million every year. There are two pages of cited stats like these in my recent, award-winning book *First Aid for Teacher Burnout.*

Teaching is a society-changing profession in need of the public's help. There is much that parents and community members can do to better support their neighborhood school teachers. I can provide the names and contact information of people in the U.S., U.K., and Africa (as this is an international problem) who are taking steps to protect their teachers' wellbeing so teachers can find success and sustainability in their jobs. Please let me know if you'd like a free copy of my book for support in your investigation, and if there is anything else I can do to support a story. My cell is __, and my email is __. Thank you.

Picking a show you respect and watch will help you understand what its producers' want. Many networks are driven by ratings and air stories that tap into fear, shock, or another sensation, but this isn't always the case. Even if you do supply the statistics and case studies to catch an audience's attention through worry, I encourage you to also provide details (including contacts reporters can use) on current efforts to solve the problem, and where hope can be found. If a story rattles an audience but doesn't point anyone in the right direction, then it doesn't align with your purpose of helping students.

Some networks stand out in their prioritization of a story's merit over ratings. For example, *60 Minutes* does not select its segments based on ratings, public demand, or whether most viewers will side with them; rather, the show relies on good stories that give the audience something interesting and important (Dommerholt, 2012). The approach appears to be working. *60 Minutes* regularly ranks the #5 show or better on Nielsen's weekly Top 10 List and averages 12.4 million viewers (CBS Interactive Inc., 2018).

Likewise, Public Broadcasting Service (PBS) is prone to broadcasting shows that celebrate teachers and explore our field, with series like *Only a Teacher* and specials like *Ted Talks Education.* The public isn't necessarily asking for such education coverage, but PBS presents these stories in a way that's engaging for anyone.

Networks differ in how stories should be pitched to them, so search show and network webpages for details. For example, CBS' *60 Minutes* receives concise story suggestions via email (60m@cbsnews.com) or mail (Story Editor, 60 Minutes, CBS News, 524 West 57th Street, New York, NY 10019), and the correspondents and producers find stories rather than someone dictating journalistic direction from above them. NBC's *TODAY* show and CNN's programming, however, have forms (www.today.com/news/send-us-your-uplifting-inspiring-story-our-everyone-has-story-t39496) through which viewers suggest features they'd like the show to cover.

Use this book's "List of Broadcasting Opportunities" eResource to find television venues to which you can pitch your expertise in contributing to a segment. Searching network and programming websites and social media can render additional opportunities, which you can save to the "List of Broadcasting Opportunities" file once you've saved it to your own computer.

For example, an "Advanced Search" on Twitter allowed me to specify tweets only made by @PBS that featured the phrase "looking for". This immediately rendered a tweet by PBS (2012) reading, "PBS is looking for people to feature in on-air spots..." A web search revealed a PBS LearningMedia (2017) post announcing, "We're looking for educators who love what they do, and who have found creative and thoughtful ways to integrate technology and digital media" (p. 1), with details to become a PBS Digital Innovator and share one's ideas in national settings. Though they ended up not needing me, I was on standby for a PBS documentary all because of Twitter.

If you're passionate about being featured on a particular network or show but aren't getting a response from its staff, get scrappy to pitch your idea through additional avenues. For example, consider CNN. There is a form for you to submit ideas, but CNN reporters can also be reached via Facebook (like Anderson Cooper at www.facebook.com/AC360 and John King at www.facebook.com/JohnKingCNN) or Twitter (like Nancy Grace at @NancyGrace and Don Lemon at @DonLemon). Pitching to a specific individual can often render you more consideration and success than pitching to a social media account devoted to an entire station. You can also use CNN's feedback form (www.cnn.com/feedback), an individual CNN show's feedback form, a general CNN email address (cnn.feedback@cnn.com or community@cnn.com), or the email signup form in case pitching opportunities are shared there (www.cnn.com/login.html).

You should never harass a station or person by pursuing contact avenues repeatedly, but you can contact a venue in new ways over time in case it might interest a new recipient when it failed to strike a chord with the last. Though I've never tried this approach with CNN, it worked for me with NPR.

SCRAPPY TIP

Regularly interacting with your favorite reporters within social media, a strategy pushed elsewhere in this book, can also prompt reporters to reach out to you. For example, reporter Michael Koenigs (2013) tweeted to a single Twitter user: "we're looking for an expert for

> an upcoming segment for ABC News. Please reach me at ... " (p. 1).
>
> Reporters such as Koenigs often invite people to send them news stories via Twitter. Put "send me news stories" in Twitter's search field, then select the "People" option to filter results by people using those words in their profile, and you'll see plenty of reporters (from BBC News, in particular) asking you to pitch them stories. Changing your search to "send news stories", "looking for news stories", and other variations will render additional reporters.

Local networks, news shows, and talk shows are worth contacting whenever their nature suits your message and can help bring about positive change for students. Their proximity makes it easier for them to film you in your classroom, school, or lab, and your work in their viewers' neighborhood makes you more relevant to their audience. Local stations allow you to target your area's residents, such as prompting parents to sign up for your opportunity on their children's campus or encouraging community members to volunteer for your student-helping program.

Since "scrappy me" likes to aim high, I suggest submitting your suggestion to local stations *and* larger networks wherever your story fits. The same message can be written once and then tweaked in small ways to suit each network. Thus, after you've written the message once for one venue, it costs you negligible work to also reach out to others. Visit "Chapter 13. Multiply Your Impact" for tips that can prompt news stations to come to you for your opinion and sound bites.

The next few sections in this chapter cover some broadcasting venues that cover education news and more.

NATIONAL PUBLIC RADIO (NPR)

NPR is a non-profit syndicator of programs to individual public radio stations around the U.S. Public radio stations can apply to become members of NPR, but not every show you listen to on such a station is produced by NPR. Educators (and others) view NPR as prestigious, and being heard on NPR can open many doors for you.

My journey to get on NPR was a scrappy one.

Academics don't end up on NPR or the *PBS NewsHour*, at the White House, or in front of lawmakers by accident or blind luck. Making a difference by engaging in the public conversation or debate about the issues that your work addresses ... [is] a matter of being effective and strategic.

(Badgett, 2016, p. 8)

I tried all of the strategies below, and finally two approaches landed me on NPR.

Buckle up, because the list below conveys a highly scrappy ride. I happen to be very techy and fast (or a hyperactive nerd, depending on how you view it). I keep my pitches on my smart phone, so if I check Twitter while in line at the grocery store and spot a reporter to contact, I'll have emailed her easily before I ever reach the cashier. Thus, the efforts below did not infringe on my time as one might expect. If a journey this scrappy doesn't fit you or your time, that's no problem. This book offers plenty of other, more direct routes to airtime for you to pursue. At the very least, let this account reiterate there are many failures and almost-worked-but-didn'ts on the road to reaching big audiences with your expertise:

- ❏ I visited www.npr.org/sections/author-interviews and noted which NPR staff and shows included author interviews. I then contacted these staff and shows with the suggestion they cover my latest book.
- ❏ I visited www.npr.org and clicked "Contact". This took me to a page where I could contact NPR shows, blogs, and departments, as well as opt to pitch a story. I used every avenue that seemed a good match for the expertise I wanted to share.
- ❏ I found NPR broadcasts at www.npr.org categorized as "Education" and reached out to reporters and hosts who seemed a good match for content I wanted to share.
- ❏ I found the NPR webpages of shows that could appropriately cover my topic (such as www.npr.org/programs/all-things-considered) and looked at the "Meet the Hosts" section of each. I then clicked on each person's profile to see if their background fit my topic and if they broadcasted near me. I then reached out to some hosts.
- ❏ I attended an AERA session where an NPR education reporter spoke on the panel. Afterwards, I tracked down his email address and reached out to him.
- ❏ I tweeted messages to @NPR, @NPR_ed, and @youthradio (NPR programming) on Twitter, mentioning one of my books and proposing a related story.

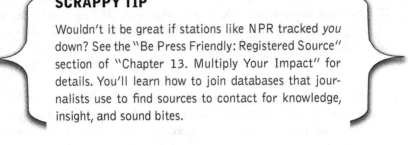

SCRAPPY TIP

Wouldn't it be great if stations like NPR tracked *you* down? See the "Be Press Friendly: Registered Source" section of "Chapter 13. Multiply Your Impact" for details. You'll learn how to join databases that journalists use to find sources to contact for knowledge, insight, and sound bites.

❑ I joined the NPR Listens community (nprlistens@npr.org), which sometimes surveys members for programming suggestions.

❑ Since NPR welcomes book submissions and provides on-air reviews, I submitted one of my books (the one with the most mainstream appeal) for consideration by addressing it to an appropriate program and mailing it to [Name of Appropriate Program], NPR, 1111 North Capitol Street NE, Washington, DC 20002.

❑ I used NPR's station finder search tool at www.npr.org/stations, found my nearest NPR broadcasting station, and reached out to it about interviewing me on its related, NPR-affiliated shows.

❑ I visited Youth Radio's Contact page at https://youthradio.org/contact and shared my pitch in case any of their reporters wanted to cover my work.

❑ I signed up for the Youth Radio Newsletter (related to NPR programming) at https://youthradio.org/newsletter to watch out for opportunities to contribute.

❑ I kept an eye out for prospects through organizations that partner with NPR. For example, the Muslim American Leadership Alliance (MALA) (2017) issued a call for Muslim heritage stories, some of which are produced in partnership with NPR's StoryCorps podcast. Though I didn't qualify for the opportunity, I shared it with my Muslim friends who did.

❑ I follow @NPR, @NPR_ed, and @youthradio on Twitter. When these accounts posted opportunities, I pursued them.

• Example of opportunity NPR's Education Team (2017) posted on Twitter:

Do you have a voucher success or horror story? We want to hear from you. Tweet or message us @npr_ed (p. 1)

❑ I follow NPR on Facebook (www.facebook.com/NPR). When this account posted prospects, I pursued them.

• Example of opportunity NPR (2018) posted on Facebook:

Are you a teacher whose TEACH grant was converted into a loan? If so, we want to hear your story. Email us at npred@npr.org, and we might contact you for a story (p. 1)

Posted opportunities are time-sensitive, so watch social media regularly to find invitations in time to pursue them.

❏ I signed up for NPR Ed's weekly e-newsletter at www.npr.org/sections/ed and watched for chances to contribute.

- Example of opportunity NPR Ed (2017) emailed me:

  NPR Ed is launching a new longform project, aimed at everyone who has a young person in their lives. And we need your help. Has there been a time when you, as a parent, educator or caregiver, wished that a fairy godmother could give you some magic words to answer a young person's question? ... How did you explain something complex or hard or funny? Reply to this email or send to npred@npr.org and please include your contact information so we can get back to you.

TECH TIP

Richard Reddick (2016), an education professor who has appeared on NPR and the Associated Press, suggests asking for a digital copy of interviews and other audiovisual media opportunities, since "many news organizations keep these media for a short time only on their sites. With archival media sites like YouTube and SoundCloud, these appearances can be kept and referenced to well after the original airdate" (p. 62).

NPR also produces written (off-radio) work. The remaining bullets in this section relate to those:

❏ A professional acquaintance of mine was interviewed on an NPR blog called *MindShift*. I congratulated her, and she offered to introduce me to the NPR reporter. After our email introduction, the staffer invited me to pitch some ideas to her.

❏ I Googled things like *NPR.org submit deadline* and found obscure NPR programs where stories and other contributions could be submitted.

❏ I emailed the host of NPR's TED Radio Hour and proposed my Talk from TEDxTUM be included on the show.

❏ I emailed nprEd (npred@npr.org) with a story idea related to my work.

❏ I visited nprEd at www.npr.org/sections/ed, clicked "Connect with Us" at the bottom of the page, and noted each reporter's Twitter account where an email address was often displayed. I then contacted each reporter via Twitter and email, pitching my research topic as a story for nprEd.

Notice I didn't stop at the first bulleted approach. Some approaches *almost* paid off (an NPR staffer and I would email for a bit or talk on the phone, but a production never came to fruition), but it took me many creative tries to finally get featured on NPR. Note even when I wasn't ultimately heard on a show, I still had the benefit of sharing my perspective with reporters, which might have shaped their coverage.

Note how none of the above approaches was pushy. For example, I did not harass any NPR reporter with repeated requests, as that would be inappropriate. Rather, I thought outside of the box, searched for new ways in, and tried one approach after another over time. If you want something to happen, you shouldn't just wait for the opportunity to land in your lap.

This book's "List of Broadcasting Opportunities" eResource has a single row devoted to NPR. As I tried each of the approaches described above, I created a new row to track that specific approach. You can use the spreadsheet in whatever way works best for you.

BRITISH BROADCASTING CORPORATION (BBC)

BBC dominates broadcasting in the U.K., with a strong presence on TV, radio, and other formats. For example, BBC Radio (just one of BBC's arms) reaches 34.85 million listeners per week (BBC, 2018).

BBC is like NPR in that there are multiple ways to request an appearance. Visit www.bbc.com as a starting point to visit show sites, use contact options, find reporters, and more (in the scrappy way described in the previous section). Also, BBC reporters make extensive use of social media, and many BBC reporters put "send me news stories" in their Twitter profiles; pursue these invitations with your pitch if BBC is a good fit for your message.

OTHER RADIO AND PODCASTS

Other broadcasts are also worth pursuing. Open this book's "List of Broadcasting Opportunities" eResource (described earlier) and note the assortment of broadcast types, as characterized in the "Category" column. Those categorized as "Radio" can be heard live (as they occur) on the air, whereas shows categorized as "Podcast" are recorded so listeners can download and listen to them anytime, though it's common for a show to function in both formats these days. Many of these stations are devoted entirely to the education field. Approaching education-specific broadcasts first can offer better odds of acceptance and allow your work to reach the most appropriate audience.

Note opportunities that are labeled as "Radio Org" in the "Category" column. These producers of broadcasted content reach massive audiences. For example, American Public Media reaches 20 million listeners per week (American Public

Media, 2018), and Radiotopia (just one Public Radio Exchange podcast collection) garners more than 17 million downloads per month (PRX, 2017). Getting featured on one of these organizations' shows can bless you and your work with great exposure, particularly if your research holds mainstream relevance (for example, how much "screen time" our brains can productively handle). Like webinars and online conferences (covered in the previous chapter), radio interviews can often be held from your own home, where you "phone in" to participate with an interviewer who is physically elsewhere.

While some opportunities offer clear "Contact" or "Pitch Page" links (like https://airmedia.org/resources/the-pitch-page) on their websites, not every station offers an obvious path to being featured. You might thus need to get scrappy in your approach. Sometimes this means finding the host or the producer of an airing and Googling the person to find his contact information. When you reach out, provide your succinct pitch, related literature (such as a study you just published), and a link to your press page (covered in the last chapter) so what you offer listeners is clear.

Of course, you can also create your own podcast. An estimated 112 million people have listened to podcasts, 24% have listened to a podcast in the last month, and 86% of listeners finish most or all of the podcasts they hear (Edison Research, 2017). Google *create your own podcast* and you'll find lots of information on how this can be achieved. NPR recently released a call for new podcasts and anyone could submit their podcast for consideration to join NPR's lineup.

SCRAPPY TIP

Look for radio show or station booths at conferences you attend. Many shows pre-record a series of shows (or broadcast directly from) events, as there they can easily interview one expert after another. They are often on the lookout for people to interview or have gaps in their schedule where they could easily accommodate another expert.

Don't be shy: Politely inquire as to whether the program would like to interview you. Be ready with your quick pitch and an accomplishment or two ("I devised a way for dyslexics to easily read, and Forbes Magazine named me Education Researcher of the Year"). Even if there is no time at the event, your interview could be scheduled for another date.

Preparation

Because the audience can't see you when you're on radio, you can have notes in front of you. Having your message, pitch, and talking points from "Chapter 1. Introduction" can help you stay on topic and prevent you from overlooking key points (you can check off talking points as you share them). I find it most helpful to keep statistics and names I plan to cite nearby. If there's anything you want to share but might not be able to remember accurately or entirely, have those details in front of you.

Well before an interview, I always ask if I can have a copy of the questions I'll be asked. These are usually provided (sometimes the host even asks me to write possible questions). I draft answers ahead of time (in abbreviated, bullet form) to be sure I don't miss anything on the air. If callers will be asking questions, I consider what those questions might be (especially questions skeptics might ask) and plan answers to those, as well. I've usually written such answers in some article or correspondence before, so assembling answers is easy. Just be sure you speak naturally and in the moment, covering the answers' key points but not reading them.

WEBCASTS AND OTHER WEBINARS

Webcasts such as webinars run more like online conference presentations than they do like this chapter's other broadcasts. For example, you might upload PowerPoint slides and use your computer's or phone's audio and mic to narrate progression through your slides with or without the audience seeing your face. Companies and organizations in the field of education often run webinars as one form of ongoing professional development for their followers.

EdTechTalk: Collaborative Open Webcasting Community (http://edtechtalk.com/ttt) is listed as one webcast venue you might approach to offer to appear in a webcast. So many of the organizations on the next chapter's "List of Organizations" eResource also offer webinars that it's worth approaching the groups you're familiar with first.

When you learn of a webinar being offered through a group that suits your expertise area, ask its announcer how you can get involved in the future. Those who offer webinars are eager for expert content and you can expect the reception to be warm. In fact, as scrappy as I am, I've never contacted anyone about giving a webinar because they've always reached out to me, first. Surely a webinar provider won't be able to resist your pitch, talking points, and willingness to give your time so its followers can benefit.

DOCUMENTARY

Filmed documentaries, aired in theaters and on television, have the power to shift a nation. For example, the documentary *Waiting for "Superman"* caused a surge of charter school support and teachers union opposition in the U.S. when it was released in 2010. You can agree to be featured in someone else's documentary, or (if you have the time, resources, and skills) film your own (see www.desktop-documentaries.com for guidance).

VIDEO BLOGGING

Blog posts don't always have to be written. You can set up a free video channel on YouTube (www.youtube.com) or Vimeo (https://vimeo.com) to post videos you create. This is especially appealing to those who hate to write, or who find it faster to just say what they're thinking.

While YouTube gets more traffic, Vimeo contains no adult content and is thus more education-friendly (and less likely to be blocked by schools' or universities' internet firewalls). Create a channel on both platforms and post your videos to each.

These videos need not be lengthy or polished to be effective. In a study involving 110 undergraduate student participants and the review of 270 peer-reviewed articles, Carmichael, Reid, and Karpicke (2018) found shorter videos increased engagement (with 6 minutes per video or segment established as the optimum time period), and a conversational style was found to be more beneficial than a more formal speaking approach. And Berger (2013) found "most [videos] that go viral are blurred and out of focus, shot by an amateur on an inexpensive camera or cell phone" (p. 6).

If you'd like to produce something more elaborate, you might find help with filming, lighting, audio, or editing from:

- Production class students or teachers if you're based at a school.
- Technology Department team if you're based at a local educational authority or school district.
- Campus audio/visual labs or Communications Department if you're based at a university.

VIDEO LIBRARIES

Video allows you to show and demonstrate skills in a way written formats can't capture. Carmichael et al. (2018) found video to be superior to written materials when it came to visually demonstrating "how-to" processes and helping the audience to develop practical skills.

When I filmed my first 15-minute video for the SAGE Video Collection, I was hooked. This library of videos, which features academics speaking about specific research topics, reaches an international audience of university educators, researchers, and students. I was paid for my time, I got to plug my related books, and the filming took place in conjunction with a conference I was attending, so I incurred no travel costs. I kept in contact with organizers and quickly signed up to film more.

Open this book's "List of Broadcasting Opportunities" eResource (described earlier). Sort the file by "Category" and find opportunities listed as "Video". Reach out to those collections that seem a good fit for your areas of expertise.

YOUR TURN

"Chapter 1. Introduction" and "Chapter 6. Speaking Anywhere" provided guidance to speak well about your area of expertise. This chapter provided added tips, as well as multiple chances to share your expertise on the air or in recordings. Select a broadcast (use the "List of Broadcasting Opportunities" eResource for suggestions) you will approach with the desire to present. Once accepted, complete Exercise 9.1 to plan for your talking points. Reference sections in this chapter, "Chapter 1", "Chapter 6", and "Chapter 7" as you complete the exercise.

EXERCISE 9.1: BROADCASTING SPEAKING PLAN

1. **On what type of broadcast will you be speaking?** Use Exercise 8.1, instead, for a TED Talk.
   - ❏ Podcast
   - ❏ Radio Show
   - ❏ Television Show
   - ❏ Video
   - ❏ Webcast
   - ❏ Other:

2. **For which broadcast will you speak?**

3. **What are the broadcast parameters?** video conferencing site to log in ahead of time, host name, show length, etc.

4. **Who is your audience made up of?** This can be one main audience or a few key groups.

5. **What does your audience need from you?**

6. **What are your key purposes in joining this broadcast?**

7. **What primary message will you communicate in this broadcast?**

8. **What will your talking points be?** List these by importance. Alternatively, if you were provided with interview questions ahead of time, write the questions with your answers below.
   1.
   2.
   3.
   4.
   5.
   6.

---

9. **What magic will you use to make concepts resonate?** Remember Table 6.1.

10. **Plan any supplementary materials as required** (slides, list of online resources, images for pre-broadcast advertising, etc.).

REFERENCES

American Public Media. (2018). We're everywhere you listen. *American Public Media*. Retrieved from www.americanpublicmedia.org.

Badgett, M. V. L. (2016). *The public professor: How to use your research to change the world.* New York, NY: NYU Press.

BBC. (2018). *Record BBC Radio 6 music listeners and increased BBC digital radio audiences.* Retrieved from www.bbc.co.uk/mediacentre/latestnews/2017/rajar-q3

Berger, J. (2013). *Contagious: Why things catch on.* New York, NY: Simon & Schuster.

Campanella, A. (2015). *Leading the news: 25 years of education coverage: How local, regional and state news sources cover education and schools.* Campanella Media and Public Affairs, Inc. Retrieved from www.scribd.com/document/268980834/Leading-the-News-25-Years-of-Education-Coverage

Carmichael, M., Reid, A., & Karpicke, J. (2018, February). *Assessing the impact of educational video on student engagement, critical thinking, and learning: The current state of play.* SAGE Publishing. Retrieved from https://us.sagepub.com/sites/default/files/hevideolearning.pdf

CBS Interactive Inc. (2018). *About us: 60 Minutes airs Sundays at 7 p.m. ET/PT.* Retrieved from www.cbsnews.com/60-minutes/about-us

Coe, K., & Kuttner, P. J. (2018, January 11). Education coverage in television news: A typology and analysis of 35 years of topics. *AERA Open, 4*(1). Retrieved from https://doi.org/10.1177/2332858417751694

Dommerholt, T. (2012, January 17). *60 Minutes: An inside look with producer Shari Finkelstein.* Retrieved from www.wjpitch.com/print/2012/01/17/60-minutes-an-inside-look-with-producer-shari-finkelstein

Edison Research. (2017). *The podcast consumer 2017 report.* Retrieved from www.edison-research.com/the-podcast-consumer-2017

Eng, N. (2016). Education inequality: Broadening public attitudes through framing. *CUNY Academic Works.* Retrieved from http://academicworks.cuny.edu/cc_pubs/346

Hanford, E. (2018, March). APM Reports' Emily Hanford discusses what she looks for when covering education research. *AERA Highlights.* Retrieved from www.aera.net/Newsroom/AERA-Highlights-E-newsletter/-em-AERA-Highlights-em-March-2018

Koenigs M,. [@mcckoenigs]. (2013, July 9). *@MoneyConfidante we're looking for an expert for an upcoming segment for ABC News. Please reach me at* [omitted]. *thanks!* [Twitter moment]. Retrieved from https://twitter.com/mcckoenigs

Muslim American Leadership Alliance. (2017). *Submit your story.* Retrieved from www. malanational.org/submit-your-story

National Public Radio. [NPR]. (2018, March 30). *NPR* [Facebook status update]. Retrieved from www.facebook.com/NPR/photos/a.315515951755.185285.10 643211755/10156779793306756/?type=3&theater

NPR Ed. [email@et.npr.org]. (2017, June 11). *NPR Ed is launching a new project -- and we need your help!* [email].

NPR's Education Team. [@npr_ed]. (2017, May 28). *Do you have a voucher success or horror story?* [Twitter moment]. Retrieved from https://twitter.com/npr_ed

PBS. [@pbs]. (2012, October 31). PBS is looking for people to feature in on-air spots. Has PBS helped you explore new ideas or worlds? Visit www.pbs.org [Twitter moment]. Retrieved from https://twitter.com/pbs

PBS LearningMedia. (2017, January 12). Networking - Kentucky Educational Television. *PBS LearningMedia.* Retrieved from blogs.ket.org/networking/?tag=pbs-learning media

PRX. (2017). About PRX. *PRX.* Retrieved from www.prx.org/about-us/what-is-prx

Reddick, R. J. (2016). Using social media to promote scholarship. In M. Gasman (Ed.), *Academics going public: How to write and speak beyond academe,* (pp. 55–70). New York, NY: Routledge, Taylor & Francis.

Stahl, L. (Writer). (2015, November 8). *The collider* [Television series episode]. In A. Court, K. Sharman, & S. Fitzpatrick (Producers), *60 Minutes.* Meyrin, Canton of Geneva, Switzerland: CBS News.

TIME Staff. (2012, December 19). The Higgs boson: Particle of the year. *TIME Magazine.* Retrieved from http://poy.time.com/2012/12/19/the-higgs-boson-particle-of-the-year

Tone, H., Power, L., & Torres, L. (2014, November 20). Report: Only 9 percent of guests discussing education on evening cable news were educators. *Media Matters.* Retrieved from www.mediamatters.org/research/2014/11/20/report-only-9-percent-of-guests-discussing-educ/201659

Part IV

Participating

Chapter 10

Connecting

I got to volunteer in the Democratic Republic of the Congo (DRC) at a school called Africa New Day [translated from French] (UJN). The DRC is the rape capital of the world (Wilén & Ingelaere, 2017), and violence and crime are commonplace, so you can imagine it's difficult to run a school for impoverished kids who walk miles for an education. UJN could keep their eyes solely on teaching, but how could their students learn on long-empty stomachs? when they have been traumatized? when they worry for their moms and siblings who have been violated? when they have no clothes or shoes to wear to class?

A child's education is influenced by so many variables that we can't help kids if we view our work through tunnel vision. The UJN change-makers recognize this, so they further their goals by connecting with others. They collaborate with business leaders, the community, soldiers, peacekeepers, outsiders, and more to provide what is needed for the whole child: food, safety, shelter, counseling, a job for Mama, career training for an older sibling, self-defense lessons, side businesses and donations that make outreach programs sustainable, and a steady stream of volunteers to work with teachers and students. This approach pays off: I saw children beaming and thriving despite personal stories that would bring you to your knees.

Like UJN, your mission is helping students. Like UJN, your contributions will expand and multiply when you connect with others. Tunnel vision – just looking forward and not interacting with those around you on your journey – will shortchange you and the students you hope to help. You're able to contribute more to your field when you share and learn from a wider network of professionals. Connecting with new people exposes you to ideas and resources you wouldn't otherwise find and gives you more avenues to spread your own contributions. Many connections lead to friendships in which you regularly lead one another to new information-distribution opportunities.

Yet when I hear the term *network*, my natural response is to cringe. And I'm not even an introvert. This is because my initial understanding of networking was that it meant having awkward, forced conversations with strangers in which everyone is only trying to get something from one another.

It wasn't until I actually engaged with strangers within my field that I found relationships taking form without ever trying to do the dreaded act of "networking." I wasn't "after" anything – I was just swamping ideas with the goal of helping students. I learned what effective networking really is: it is about connecting with others over shared passion.

I favor Brené Brown's definition of connection (see text box). If you approach others in our professional arena with a synergistic spirit in mind, your connections will be more authentic, more enjoyable, and more likely to benefit the field.

DEFINITION OF NETWORKING

Merriam-Webster (2017, p. 1) defines *networking* as:

"the exchange of information or services among individuals, groups, or institutions; specifically: the cultivation of productive relationships for employment or business"

DEFINITION OF CONNECTION

Brené Brown (2010, p. 19) defines *connection* as:

"the energy that exists between people when they feel seen, heard, and valued; when they can give and receive without judgment; and when they derive sustenance and strength from the relationship"

TO MAKE CONNECTING EASIER (EVEN IF YOU HATE IT)

This section's strategies encourage connections without a "forced" feeling.

Connecting at Events

❏ **Visit discussion tables** or other arrangements made at some conferences to facilitate interaction. You can always sit quietly and listen, so the risk for a shy person need not be high. Though once you have gotten comfortable, your interest in the issue being discussed could prompt you to participate.

❏ **Set goals low enough to reach.** Curtin (2016) suggests aiming to make just one new connection at an event, as this takes the pressure off, provides a clear metric, and makes later follow up with contacts more manageable.

❏ **Get someone you know to attend with you.** A friendly security blanket can put you at ease, and a more-assertive friend can initiate conversations of which you can then be part even if you are shy.

❏ **Volunteer for a conference you're attending**, such as working the information booth or chairing a panel. This positions you for engagement with participants and presenters, even if you wouldn't normally initiate conversation on your own.

Connecting Anywhere (Online, by Phone, at Events, Etc.)

❏ **Give something.** Ask for someone's email address to send her a resource related to a shared area of interest. This could lead to further dialogue. My motivation when I give and help is simply that I like to give and help (for those who've read Malcolm Gladwell's *The Tipping Point*: I'm one of those eager Mavens), but those who don't naturally volunteer resources to others can be convinced by research to do so. According to the *norm of reciprocity* founded on the research of Kunz and Woolcott (1976), people are motivated to do things for you when you do things for them (Smith, 2017; Tannenbaum, 2015).

❏ **Put out a call for participation or invite feedback.** This is how I met Margie Johnson, who has become a dear friend and remains one of my most frequent collaborators. She lives in Tennessee and I live in California. We met nonetheless (first over the phone) when I was conducting a study and asked EdSurge to post a call for participation in their e-newsletter. Margie called me because the study related to work she was doing. We connected well over the phone and were soon presenting together at conferences. Margie connected me with state-level educators who then applied my research, adding to my credibility (for those who've read Gladwell's *The Tipping Point*: Margie is a Connector). When I landed the chance to lecture at University of Cambridge, I arranged for Margie to co-teach the first class with me. When you find someone whose ideas and character you respect, it is natural to want to help her succeed. It does not feel forced and it is not insincere; it is simply enjoying a friend who shares your passion and enjoying the chance to help good ideas spread.

SCRAPPY TIP

Don't have the money or time to attend a particular conference? You can still take part in its twitter conversations. Search Twitter for the conference's designated hashtag (this is often the organization abbreviation and conference year, like "#ISTE2018") and follow along. You might find opportunities to contribute your own thoughts, too.

❏ **Join social media dialogue during events.** This is a great way to connect at the conference and also afterwards (through new social media followers and followed). Education conferences often announce a designated hashtag (such as "#NSPRA2018") for the event, otherwise you can search likely hashtags and find the one most people are using. Add this hashtag to any tweets and other social media messages you post in relation to what you are learning or doing at the conference.

In a study on educators' Twitter use, Alderton, Brunsell, and Bariexca (2011) found that educators' use of Twitter for backchannel conversations during conferences supported networking; for example, one participant stated that while using Twitter at "professional conferences like ASCD and NCTE, I have met and collaborated with other educators from around the country to share ideas and best practices. These kinds of exchanges strengthened my experiences... socially and professionally" (p. 7).

TWITTER CHAT DEFINITION

A *Twitter chat* is a conversation between users of the social media tool Twitter, who are brought together by the use of a unique hashtag. These users include the same hashtag (example: #edchat) in their tweets and follow the stream of texts using this hashtag in order to view and participate in a single discussion. These discussions are often formally organized and recurring, such as at the same time and on the same day of every week.

❏ **Join social media dialogue anytime.** Posting comments and work that interests you, and reading the same from others, lets you connect with people across geographic boundaries. Chances are it won't feel like networking; it'll just feel like enjoying a shared passion with others, which is what this chapter is all about.

You can also participate through planned social media discussions. Every week there are hundreds of scheduled chats on Twitter related to education. If you visit https://sites.google.com/site/twittereducation-chats/education-chat-calendar or Google *education twitter chats* you will find plenty to choose from. This allows you to converse from the comfort of your own home with people who share your field interests.

GOOD CONNECTING HABITS

The previous section gave you low-risk ways to put yourself out there, even if you hate networking. But once you are *in* the throes of connecting, there are some additional guidelines to encourage success:

❏ **Carry business cards with you.** If your employer does not provide them, order or make your own. If you're handy with your computer's printer, you can use perforated business card paper (available at office supply stores) to print your own.

> **MONEY-SAVING TIP**
>
> Sites like www.VistaPrint.com often run promotions where you can order professional-looking business cards for free.

If you hear a presenter or conference attendee mention something that correlates with your work, you can approach her afterwards, state what you appreciated hearing, and hand her your business card while adding you would love to talk more. Writing a note on the back of the card can help this person remember what you said.

If she gives you a business card, as well, note on the back of it what sparked the connection. Then send this person an email or call within the week initiating a conversation. If you give this person something, such as a link to a related article, this can help you feel less awkward about reaching out.

❏ **Write notes on the backs of business cards you receive.** Even if you think, "I'll never forget this person!" when she hands you a business card, figuring out later who's who in a stack of collected cards can be daunting.

Whenever I get a business card from someone, I write a note on the back related to our connection. For example, "working on a book like my fourth" or "has brother at BBC Radio who might want to interview me". These notes are a huge help when I follow up with people later.

❏ **Determine if an expert you admire will be making an appearance you can attend.** Just as I recommend you list your upcoming presentations and media appearances on your website, you'll find that other education experts often do the same. If you admire someone's work, look for her upcoming engagements. If you can attend one of these, reach out to the expert in the way described below.

❏ **Reach out to speakers prior to events.** When a conference's program is released in advance, you will likely spot session topics and speakers devoted to your area of expertise. These can be great folks with whom to connect, but speakers could be drowning in a crowd of other interested attendees if you wait to approach them at the conclusion of their talks.

Send a speaker a message by email or through social media well before an event if you want to connect there. Succinctly explain how your ideas might correlate and politely ask if the speaker would have some time for you over the course of the conference (for example, to grab a cup of coffee or sit at the same table during the conference lunch buffet). Posting some positive social media messages (such as tagging the speaker while expressing excitement about her last book or upcoming keynote) around the same time can help your invitation stand out.

I receive emails like this regularly (one just popped up in my inbox as I wrote the previous paragraph), and I have yet to turn anyone down. Like you, most speakers are seeking to have a positive impact on the world. Swapping ideas with other education experts is yet another way to do this.

SCRAPPY TIP

The first time I taught a course on this book's topic at the AERA Annual Meeting, I mentioned I was working on this book. After class, Norman Eng (2017) handed me a free copy of his book, *Teaching College: The Ultimate Guide to Lecturing, Presenting, and Engaging Students*, which relates to presenting one's education expertise. I read the book on the plane and promptly gave it a 5-star review on Amazon, recommended it to colleagues, and cited it several times in this book.

Handing a speaker a paper, article, or other resource you wrote (paired with a mention of why you believe she would find the work helpful) can increase the odds that she will read it, benefit from it, and share it with others.

> If this speaker's words carry impact in the field, informing her with your work will benefit students impacted by those the speaker teaches.

❏ **Follow up.** Sheryl Sandberg (2013) of Facebook, Google, and *Lean In* fame tells of meeting a social media expert at a conference who shared impressive ideas and over time would reach out to Sandberg with some interesting information, but never asked to get together or infringe on Sandberg's time. When Sandberg later left the Starbucks board of directors, Sandberg suggested this woman as a replacement. This conference contact was then invited to join the Starbucks board of directors at only 29 years of age.

New you follow up with those you meet in helpful (not overbearing) ways, this can lead to collaboration in ways that benefit students. It can also open you up to new opportunities to share your expertise.

❏ **Facilitate sharing.** If your sharing potential outgrows the way you and contacts correspond (such as emailing back and forth), graduate to another mode for sharing, such as using a free Gmail account to use Google Docs (www.google.com/docs), where multiple people can collaborate on the same items. Steve Waters of the Teach Well Alliance created a collaboration site on Basecamp (www.basecamp.com) for people to discuss and share resources on teacher wellness. Every day that site propels international efforts to support teachers.

GOOD CONNECTING MINDSET

Approach connection-making with the right state of mind. For example:

❏ **Be in it for students.** One of the reasons people cringe at the thought of networking is that we've seen so many superficial, what-can-you-do-for-me networkers. Ugh. I definitely don't want you to be that, and I don't think there's any benefit — to you or students — to being primarily focused on your own advancement.

When your core motivation is helping children, and you're making connections in order to help more children, this intention shines through. In these cases, you are connecting with others over ideas and altruistic plans. You are just as excited to offer a way to help someone else share an idea that can help kids (you say things like, "Let me introduce you to a blogger I know who writes about that same topic!") as you are to advance your own ideas. Some people are still suspicious of the well-intentioned, but most people will recognize your goodwill as they get to know you.

❏ **Conscientiously strive for diversity.** Steve Jobs once said, "If you're gonna make connections which are innovative ... you have to not have the same bag of experiences as everyone else does" (Baer, 2015). Being around people who are different from us provokes thought, makes us more industrious, exposes us to added information and perspectives, and even makes us more creative (Phillips, 2014). Even if your intention when connecting with others is to share rather than to receive, you and your work will benefit substantially if you open yourself to learning from a wide range of fellow experts.

Don't miss that I wrote *if you open yourself to learning from*. It's key that no member of a group is added as a mere token. Rather, every member will have a unique viewpoint and knowledgebase from which you can and should learn. As Leslie Odom, Jr. (2018) wrote, "If you have a person from an underrepresented group on your team and you aren't tapping them for their unique and varied perspectives and contributions, it may be tokenism. And if it's tokenism, it's always a missed opportunity" (p. 93).

When I attended an education authors' cocktail reception, I noticed all the Black authors in the room were sitting at the same table. So, I (a blonde White lady ... OK, fine: *artificially* blonde) joined them. One woman there told me how her early experiences – different from mine and from everyone's at the table – shaped her current work in both urban and rural schools. Her journey was a formidable one, and hearing it gave me insight into why she applied particular strategies for optimum success with students. I walked away with a deeper understanding of our shared field of work than I would have if I had only conversed with someone with a similar life story to mine. In another conversation, one of the table's gentlemen happened to share insights about raising a daughter of another race. We compared and contrasted this with my White mother's experiences being raised by a Black woman in the American South back in the 1940s and 50s. You can't gain a lifetime of understanding from what you hear secondhand (let alone during the span of a dinner conversation), but each person's experience is only their own anyway; the goal is to learn from as many different people as we can to get as mindful as we can about the wide array of circumstances in our world.

Yet as much as we talk about diversity in this field, we are still subconsciously drawn to people who look just like us: the hip youngsters in the room gather at one table, the alternatively-dressed folks are at another, etc. This tendency limits us and requires conscious effort to avoid.

If you're not a member of the Association of Latino Administrators and Superintendents (ALAS), you could still benefit from hearing about their latest endeavors, and you'll most likely hear about these by sitting next to a Latinx educator. Aiming for interaction with people of all backgrounds, races, ethnicities, genders, creeds, ages, and sexual orientations exposes us to a wider range of perspectives and — with that — ideas and opportunities that can help us better serve our field.

❑ **Be approachable.** If someone initiates discussion with you online, do you give a curt answer? As you await the start of a conference session or enjoy the lunchtime buffet, are you hunched over your cellphone or salad? I hope not.

Whether you interact with someone in person or not, give thoughtful responses and ask questions that invite discussion. When you attend events, sit up, display open body language, and smile to people who pass by or join you. These habits communicate you're open to talking, which is required if you're going to swap ideas that can better kids' lives.

❑ **Be positive.** In our field, people connect in hopes of finding, sharing, and expanding upon solutions. If you're discussing a topic like school lunches and all you do is rant about the meals' shortcomings, you aren't offering anything to your discussion partner.

As a vegan who is bewildered by the junk food on my daughter's school lunch menu, I can accept that many school lunches have shortcomings. I also know, however, there are many people trying to make improvements. Even if I don't have a solution to improving school lunches when I discuss this topic, I can propose possible ideas and questions worth investigating, or I can name other people concerned with the topic and suggest we get together to brainstorm solutions. I can be focused on solutions.

The same goes for other educators connecting over other topics. Discussing problems and frustrations is important, but pair these discussions with words that move dialogue forward toward improvements.

A DIFFERENT KIND OF MENTOR

This section is not about the mentor who helps you get better at your job, like a teacher who helps you perfect your teaching, or a researcher who helps you perfect your research. Rather, this section is about the mentor who helps you share your expertise with the world, such as through helping you land opportunities to reach a wider audience. Having the latter type of mentor is a huge asset for an education expert seeking to share knowledge.

You don't have to have a single mentor in this endeavor. Maybe there is someone who can help you navigate the book publishing world, someone who will teach you to use technology and social media, and someone who will help you book speaking gigs. All these areas, and more, are part of maximizing your work's reach, but you might not meet a single person with vast expertise in all these areas. There could be numerous people who, together, provide you with comprehensive support in sharing your education expertise.

Finding a Mentor

Don't ask a stranger to be your mentor (Sandberg, 2013). Rather, let mentorship begin organically (someone starts helping you in small ways, and the relationship develops), though it is fine to label the relationship eventually if you'd like. Sometimes this prompts the mentor to provide you with increased assistance.

To identify your mentor(s), consider:

- Who has the career, influence, or visibility you desire?
- Who might not be ahead of you, but is scrappily finding and landing great opportunities for herself?
- Who seems genuinely interested in your success?
- Who seems willing to help you?
- Are you looking at all of your options?

People are often drawn to those who remind them of themselves, but that tendency leads to limitations (covered in the previous section). I'm a White woman, whereas my current mentor is Black. My mentees are all either Asian, Black, Hispanic, gay, male, or half my age, and would never consider me their twin in appearance or life experience. We would all miss out on the value of mentorship if we only forged connections with those who look or live like us.

LOOK BENEATH THE SURFACE

You don't have to have mentors who look like you. Had I been waiting for a black, female Soviet specialist mentor, I would still be waiting. — Condoleezza Rice, first Black female Secretary of State (Jackson & League, 2015, p. 4).

Keeping a Mentor

Being a desirable mentee will help you:

- Acquire a mentor.
- Keep a mentor.
- Inspire your mentor to help you as much as she is able.

I have a fabulous mentee named Colette Boston. If I offer to bring a printout of something to our meeting, she offers to bring it, instead. If I suggest something online, she says she'll find it on her own. When she asked me to be her mentor, she wrote, "I am very low-key (don't need a lot of attention)." I could not refuse someone who appreciates my time and clearly has the self-sufficient, go-getter qualities that tell me this woman will go far (as she quickly has), and thus any time spent helping her would mean a great contribution to the education field.

Be like Colette Boston. Mentors are typically busy people who don't have time for excessive hand-holding (Sandberg, 2013). If someone is generous enough to step up to mentor you (which can be as casual as sending opportunities your way), show appreciation and respect this person's time. This means:

❑ When getting to know the mentor, share your pitch (covered earlier) on your expertise and a sentence that captures your background. Do not share a rambling account of all your life experiences.

❑ Be flexible. If your mentor wants to talk in 10-minute blocks when she drives to work, don't insist on long dinner meetings.

❑ Be as self-sufficient as possible. For example, if your mentor suggests you should attend a certain conference, don't expect the mentor to email you the website link, submission details, etc. Instead, find the details online yourself.

❑ Do not lean on your mentor for emotional support, such as asking to meet for pep talks. You can speak with friends or a counselor for that.

❑ Do not ask your mentor to introduce someone you know to someone the mentor knows (for example, an editor). Making a professional introduction is often perceived as an endorsement of that person, which is hard to do for someone your mentor doesn't know. If the introduction results in conflict (for example, your friend fails to meet the editor's deadlines), it could reflect badly on your mentor.

You might have a mentor friend who is fine if you violate the above guidelines, but at least consider the possibility that she is not. Otherwise, your mentor could view you as unappreciative, too time-intensive, or as someone who lacks the motivation to make the most of mentorship. Your mentor could be less likely to offer you guidance in the future, because such interaction would mean a strain on the mentor's time.

Mentorship Ideas

Consider the following activities with your mentor:

❑ Go through your mentor's CV together and ask her to highlight any opportunities you should also pursue (for example, a publication for which you should also submit your work) and identify any introductions your mentor might make (such as to a broadcast journalist who might want to also interview you).

❏ Meet up with your mentor at conferences and attend sessions together. This will make it easier for your mentor to introduce you to people she knows.

❏ Ask your mentor to forward prospects to you. Express special interests (for example, you've done plenty of writing but are looking for more speaking engagements).

❏ If your research areas match, your mentor might be able to bring you in as a co-presenter or co-writer for an opportunity she lands.

Finally, pay the help back when you can. I have had mentors throughout my life, and I found the most exciting stage of mentorship to be when I, as the mentee, came into a position to help my mentors. It can be easy to miss these opportunities, as we are used to seeing ourselves as the less-expert half of the partnership, so look carefully. Is there an opportunity you learned about that your mentor would also like to pursue? Is there a new journal paper on your mentor's research topic? Have you met someone who can help your mentor if introduced? There is a wonderful feeling of having met a milestone when you pay some help back to your mentor.

CLOSE TO HOME (UNIONS, SPECIAL INTEREST GROUPS, AND MORE)

This book covers some far-reaching types of opportunities, both geographically and in terms of wow factor. However, it is also worth considering what you can do *within* your workplace and circles to share your expertise. While such possibilities are endless, a few include:

❏ Step up for a leadership role (department chair, committee head, union representative, professional association leader, etc.).

❏ Form or join a special interest group (SIG) (for example, a Lean In circle, http://leanincircles.org).

❏ Collaborate with coworkers on a new study.

❏ Arrange to conduct training sessions for your colleagues.

Brainstorm on what other options are possible within your specific organization and pursue those that interest you. If such opportunities are difficult to secure (such as if you are new to the field and are being overlooked due to lacking experience), you can improve your professional image and thus your chances of being taken seriously by pursuing prospects elsewhere in this book. Many of those opportunities (writing, speaking, and more) take place online, making them "close to home" as well.

It's common to aim for roles within groups that currently reflect your same ideology. However, you can also select groups you wish were on a different trajectory. For example, "unions ... need to evolve with the times. There are incredible, solution-oriented state and local union leaders leading the way on this ... and there are others who are struggling to move into the twenty-first century" (Coggins, 2017, pp 31–32). If your union leaders fit the latter description, you have the potential to get involved in the union to spearhead efforts to protect good teachers while simultaneously doing what's best for kids and what's realistic in light of budget constraints and other realities. Maybe there's a group within your university, lab, neighborhood, office, or school that could similarly host you as a source of positive change.

LIST OF ORGANIZATIONS (JOINING AND SUBSCRIBING OPPORTUNITIES)

LIST OF ORGANIZATIONS

This book lists 220 organizations for you in an electronic file that makes it easy to find and pursue organizations to join or to subscribe to its publications. You can sort the file by type or visit each website with a simple click. The list contains details and manipulation-friendly fields you can use to track your subscriptions and memberships. See the "eResources" section near the start of this book for details on accessing and using this "List of Organizations".

ORGANIZATIONS

Organizations offer pathways to meet and interact with professionals who share your specific interests. View this book's "List of Organizations" eResources (described above) for a list of organizations within the education field, as well as their websites, to consider joining and setting up a member profile page. A "Guide to Hunting and Harvesting" eResource (introduced in this book's last chapter) covers many benefits you can get from organizations.

Blaze Your Own Trail

If you find a necessary organization to be nonexistent, consider founding it yourself. When Chris Moggia was a school district administrator, he noticed how increasingly complex data analysis and state reporting was becoming in California, whereas staff who work extensively with student data did not have adequate support in this endeavor. Chris thus founded the nonprofit California Association of School Data, Assessment, and Accountability Professionals (CASDAAP) to support district data staff. Projections based on similar projects suggest CASDAAP will have 330 members within its first year. Chris left his district position and now runs CASDAAP fulltime, making a difference for students statewide.

Another option is to start a new Special Interest Group (SIG) within an organization that offers them if you find your specific passion isn't addressed by an existing SIG. Starting a new SIG is typically a petition process in which you must establish that 75-or-so current members of the organization want the SIG to exist. Search the organization's website or speak with its representatives for application specifics.

CALLS FOR INPUT

Government bodies, companies, research institutions, organizations, and more put out a "call for input" when they want experts or other stakeholders to contribute feedback. This often relates to a problem they seek to solve or an endeavor they seek to implement.

Calls for input are chances for you to contribute to decisions and affect policies in quick, convenient ways. Some calls allow you to include your contact information and can lead to more extensive, follow-up involvement in an endeavor.

Keep an eye out for calls for input from your professional affiliations. Various factions of the U.S. White House, U.K. Parliament, U.S. Department of Education, and U.K. Department for Education often announce calls for input, as do educational research organizations like the American Educational Research Association (AERA) and British Educational Research Association (BERA). On such entities' websites, search for "call for input" (using the search field and placing the phrase in quotes) to produce a list of upcoming calls. Searching "call for knowledge" and "call for findings" is also worthwhile.

The "List of Serving Opportunities" eResource, covered in the next chapter, contains specific calls for input with the details needed to pursue them. Some calls are one-time occurrences, but those issuing the calls often issue different calls in the future. Note some government administrations issue requests for feedback more frequently than others, so if you don't see many calls during one leader's term, it's worth checking again after the torch has been passed.

News publications also issue calls for input to collect quotes and leads for stories. You can search your favorite news sites for terms like "to Hear from You" (usually preceded by "We'd like", "We want", "[this publication] would like" etc. For example, *The New York Times* (2017) issued this call with a short form for educators to complete: "If you are an educator who works with undocumented students, we'd like to hear from you. We may follow up with you to hear more about your story. Your name and comments might be published" (p. 1). Also keep an eye on a publication's social media, where such invitations are commonly released.

POLICYMAKING

If you are intimidated by the prospect of addressing politicians and other poli-cymakers, note that Elmo (a Muppet from Sesame Street) testified before U.S. Congress on behalf of education, resulting in $225,000 in federal funding allotted to research on music and the brain (Ward & Suk, 2018). All education field roles (meaning you) offer a unique perspective to inform decisions that impact kids and those who serve them.

Teacher voice, in particular, is underrepresented in – yet of critical impor-tance to – policy decisions (Gozali, Claassen Thrush, Soto-Peña, Whang, & Luschei, 2017). As Teach Plus founder and Entrepreneur in Residence at Harvard University Celine Coggins notes, "When education decisions are made without teachers at the table, students suffer the consequences" (Coggins, 2017, p. 6). Whatever your role, I encourage you to consider how you might lend your voice to policymaking.

Where Decisions Are Made

In most countries, regional government entities make at least some education policy decisions (and national decisions affect different regions within the coun-try differently); in countries with federal education systems, regional authorities are the primary decision-makers and managers of education programs (OECD, 2014, p. 34). For example, only 6% of U.S. federal spending (as opposed to 49% of state spending) goes to education, and "very little decision making happens in Washington DC ... most of the power to set direction in education resides at the state and local levels" (Coggins, 2017, p. xvi).

Getting face time with politicians is easier than many people guess. Just pick-ing up the phone can land you an appointment with a state assemblyperson in the U.S. (it did for me here in California), member of the Lords in the U.K., etc. I found it very easy to have one-on-one conversations with state assemblypersons, state and federal departments of education representatives, city councilpersons, school board members, ambassadors, and other people in government positions. Likewise, getting discussion time with members of organizations devoted to my areas of expertise (even founders and CEOs) was remarkably simple. These peo-ple generally want to know new findings related to their missions, so remember you have something to offer them.

Also, consider more than just your own country. For example, if your exper-tise on the "school choice" debate matured too late to inform Britain's 1988 Education Reform Act, timing could have still placed you at the forefront of the U.S.'s No Child Left Behind (NCLB) Act of 2001 (or in the voucher drama U.S. Secretary of Education Betsy DeVos has stirred). Those acts bore similar implica-tions for poor performing schools (such as losing students to higher performing

233

schools), even though they were enacted in different countries. Students in other parts of the world are just as worthy of your voice, and the internet makes it easy to stay abreast of education developments all over the planet.

Opportunities to Impact Policy

There are many ways to impact policy. First, consider current public dialogue and debate on your area of expertise and determine where you fit in and what you have to offer. If such public discourse is missing entirely, consider what aspects of your topic are most important to bring to policymakers' and the general public's attention first.

Next, consider the following approaches to inform those whose votes or decisions shape educational reform:

- ❏ The previous "Calls for Input" section covers one way political bodies collect feedback to inform policy.
- ❏ Reach U.S. Congress members through www.house.gov/representatives/find or www.govtrack.us. Reach U.K. Members of Parliament, Lords, and officers at www.parliament.uk/mps-lords-and-offices. Reach members of U.K. Parliament's Education Committee at www.parliament.uk/business/committees/committees-a-z/commons-select/education-committee/membership. Call offices and make appointments to meet about specific issues and current policies.

  Congressional staff (mainly in the majority party's interests) determines who gives in-person testimonies before U.S. Congress by speaking with insider networks, advocacy organizations, and other experts for names of likely witnesses (Badgett, 2016). By that point, members generally have their minds made up on an issue and simply seek to prove their points. Thus, there is much value in speaking with politicians early and informally to influence their stances before legislation is being enacted.
- ❏ Unlike congressional hearings, state and city level hearings are often open to the public. Call ahead of time to determine what the signup process is, then show up and share your professional opinion on a related topic.
- ❏ The "Internships" section of the next chapter covers another way in which you can work closely with policymakers (such as at The White House or House of Commons).
- ❏ Email Britain's Secretary of State for the Department for Education (DfE) at ministers@education.gov.uk and the U.S. Secretary of Education at press@ed.gov.

RESOURCE TIP

For Primary and Secondary School Educators:

- *How to Be Heard: 10 Lessons Teachers Need to Advocate for Their Students and Profession* by Celine Coggins (2017)
- Teach Plus (www.teachplus.org), Teach to Lead (www.teachtolead.org), and ASCD Educator Advocates program (www.ascd.org/educatoradvocates) empower school teachers to be more involved in policy.

For Professors and Researchers:

- *The Public Professor: How to Use Your Research to Change the World* by M. V. Lee Badgett (2016)
- The American Educational Research Association (AERA) offers webinars on how to effectively communicate education research to congressional district offices. Search AERA's Virtual Research Learning Center (https://eo3.commpartners.com/users/aera) for titles like "Speaking Up for Education Research" and "Insights on Sharing Education Research with Capitol Hill", and watch AERA newsletters for announcements of upcoming webinars.

For All Education Experts:

- *Policy Making in Britain* by Peter Dorey (2014)
- ASCD offers *Policy Priorities* (www.ascd.org/publications/newsletters/policy-priorities/archived-issues.aspx). The quarterly publication provides insight into current education policy topics, and its "Dig Deeper" links lead to additional resources to supplement your research on each topic.

❏ Watch state or regional entities' websites (like www.doe.k12.de.us) for invitations to provide feedback on new initiatives. For example, in 2016 when all U.S. states were charged with forming their own implementation plans to reflect the Every Student Succeeds Act (ESSA), state Departments of Education collected community input before drafting their plans. It can also help to determine who is on state or regional advisory teams, then reach out to members to offer your expertise. Also build relationships with regional and state department of education officials within a division that matches your area of expertise (student data, gifted education, etc.).

❏ Think tanks, federal research programs, and other players in the research arena are go-to sources of input for government policymakers. *The Guardian* maintains a list of U.K. think tanks at www.theguardian.com/politics/2013/sep/30/list-thinktanks-uk. For the U.S., Comprehensive Centers are listed at www2.ed.gov/about/contacts/gen/othersites/compcenters.html (this list can change, particularly after a 5-year period), and Regional Educational Laboratories are listed at https://ies.ed.gov/ncee/edlabs. Google searches and use of this book's "List of Organizations" eResources will direct you to more.

You can email a program in your area to learn how you might get involved (organizations are regularly looking to forge partnerships) or look for calls for participation in their publications and at national conferences. For example, a research group will sometimes offer a session at the National Center for Education Statistics (NCES) STATS-DC Data Conference focused on how education experts can get involved in writing standards, collecting educator input, etc.

❏ Some events are devoted entirely to education policymaking and advocacy. For example, ASCD hosts an annual conference called the Leadership Institute for Legislative Advocacy (LILA) (details are listed in this book's "List of Conferences" eResource).

❏ Join an organization that helps mobilize, empower, and position education experts to influence education reform in positive ways. Bad Ass Teacher (www.badassteacher.org) and the Network for Public Education (www.networkforpubliceducation.org) are examples. See the text box for more.

❏ Some programs are devoted (partly or entirely) to enhancing education experts' influence on policy. Some can be found listed as "Fellowships/Programs" in this book's "List of Serving Opportunities" eResource (introduced in the next chapter). For example, the ASCD Educator Advocates program (www.ascd.org/educatoradvocates) will put you in touch with what is happening in Congress, state boards of education, and more. ASCD

"Educator advocates have access to invitation-only briefings and Q&A sessions with policy experts[,] ... webinars with ASCD's Government Relations team[,] and customizable policy and advocacy resources" (ASCD, 2017, p. 7). See the text box for more.

❑ When you are aware of a new policy in the works or a policy revision, write an op-ed with research-backed and expert-voiced suggestions. "Chapter 4. Writing Short-Form" contained a "Newspaper" section and introduced this book's "List of Writing Opportunities" eResource, containing a wealth of places to submit commentaries.

❑ Visit education governing bodies' regional websites for opportunities to contribute. For example, the Alaska Department of Education & Early Development (2017) posted, "We are looking for educators ... who demonstrate outstanding instructional and leadership abilities ... These distinguished educators are considered for special recognition programs. Additionally, these educators are considered for statewide and national advisory boards and task forces" (p. 2). This led to a Talent Pool Recommendation Form which educators could submit to join this pool for opportunities.

❑ University news and public relations offices often maintain a list of faculty experts to share with media and policymakers. If you work at a university, get on such a list.

❑ Write a letter to top officials. When President Bill Clinton won his presidential election, Teresa Ghilarducci wrote him a congratulatory note that offered her help and some ideas on reform; the letter was passed around among Clinton's insiders and led to Ghilarducci's invitation to be on important boards (Badgett, 2016). You can use the same verbiage in letters you send elsewhere, so it costs you negligible added time to reach high with your correspondence. Go for it!

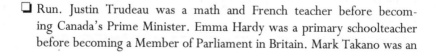

SCRAPPY TIP

Twitter is the social media platform favored by policymakers (Badgett, 2016). Join dialogue with influencers there.

❑ Run. Justin Trudeau was a math and French teacher before becoming Canada's Prime Minister. Emma Hardy was a primary schoolteacher before becoming a Member of Parliament in Britain. Mark Takano was an

English teacher before becoming a U.S. Congressman. If you believe you can help more kids through a political appointment, consider stepping into the arena. Resources like Run for Office in the U.S. (www.runforoffice.org) and The Electoral Commission in the U.K. (www.electoralcommission.org.uk) offer support.

Approach

When speaking with policymakers, avoid long-winded or negative rants. Policymakers are busy people looking for solutions. Your ideas should be presented and backed up succinctly, just as you learned to do with your pitch and talking points in "Chapter 1. Introduction".

Be open to listening and to entertaining compromises, as policymakers face constraints that determine what can and cannot be done. When speaking with legislators, educators should plan to help them balance budgets, spend tax dollars in a way voters would find wise, identify prospective funds (such as grants), and ensure an equitable distribution of resources across the system; consider that 49% of U.S. state budget dollars are already spent on education (health care gets 25%, public safety gets 11%, and 15% goes to other causes) (Coggins, 2017). Decision-makers won't listen to you because they want to help you; rather, they will listen to you because they want *you* to help *them*, and they'll continue to listen if you provide that help in a timely, accommodating way.

BRIEFING PAPERS AND EXECUTIVE SUMMARIES

A briefing paper (for which you write a brief summary, outline facts, and suggest action) can help whomever you speak with to understand your points and respond as you recommend.

If you provide policymakers with a research report, some might request an executive summary. An executive summary states the problem the report addresses, your purpose in writing the report, and your findings, conclusions, and recommendations. It is like a report abstract (covered in "Chapter 7. Writing Short-Form") except it is meant for non-academic audiences. Also, unlike an abstract, an executive summary is typically a full page and sometimes spans up to ten pages if the report it summarizes is long.

Timing

Policymaking experts suggest waiting for a "policy window" to open, which means a time when your area of expertise becomes a hot topic in the media. "As the window opens, new ideas and voices will find it easier to get into the mix" (Badgett, 2016, p. 41). This is great advice and worth following; this is often how someone goes from quietly working at her school to suddenly testifying before congress and being quoted in major papers as the "go to" expert.

However, don't sit back and *only* wait for a policy window. By the time politicians are debating a topic for the cameras, they have typically already consulted experts and have already made up their minds on an issue (and politicians get raked over the coals for changing their minds, so by then they are reticent to change their public stances). While you're on the lookout for a window to open, speak with policymakers, establish yourself as an expert, widen your network of folks who know you know your topic. That way you can make some progress while you await the opening of a policy window, and you'll be ready to stick your head through that window when it opens.

FINAL THOUGHTS

Part of using your connecting powers for good is championing others who have important insight to share in the field. As you connect with others, find ways to introduce colleagues to like minds, point colleagues in the direction of new opportunities, and share tips and venues you've found to be effective in spreading your own work. These endeavors will allow you to bring even more benefit to students.

REFERENCES

Alaska Department of Education & Early Development. (2017, May 5). *Information Exchange: Vol. 45 No. 18 - 5/5/17*. Retrieved from https://education.alaska.gov/news/infoexch/ix170505

Alderton, E., Brunsell, E., & Bariexca, D. (2011, September). The end of isolation. *Journal of Online Learning and Teaching, 7*(3), 1–14.

ASCD. (2017, June). Participate: Do you have what it takes to advocate? *Education Update, 59*(6), 7. Alexandria, VA: ASCD.

Badgett, M. V. L. (2016). *The public professor: How to use your research to change the world.* New York, NY: NYU Press.

Baer, D. (2015, February 20). In 1982, Steve Jobs presented an amazingly accurate theory about where creativity comes from. *Business Insider*. Retrieved from www.businessinsider.com/steve-jobs-theory-of-creativity-2015-2

Brown, B. (2010). *The gifts of imperfection*. Center City, MN: Hazelden Publishing.

Coggins, C. (2017). *How to be heard: 10 lessons teachers need to advocate for their students and profession*. San Francisco, CA: Jossey-Bass.

Curtin, M. (2016, May 23). A networking trick you'll like even if you hate networking. *Inc.* Retrieved from www.inc.com/melanie-curtin/a-surprisingly-effective-networking-trick-for-introverts.html

Gozali, C., Claassen Thrush, E., Soto-Peña, M., Whang, C., & Luschei, T. F. (2017). Teacher voice in global conversations around education access, equity, and quality. *FIRE: Forum for International Research in Education, 4*(1), 32–51.

Jackson, A. E., & League, L. (2015). 8 successful people share how not to find a mentor. *Fast Company.* Retrieved from www.fastcompany.com/3052068/8-successful-people-share-how-not-to-find-a-mentor

Kunz, P.R., & Woolcott, M. (1976). Season's greetings: From my status to yours. *Social Science Research, 5,* 269–278.

Merriam-Webster (2017). *Dictionary: Network.* Retrieved from www.merriam-5. Ships

The New York Times (2017, September 7). Do you have DACA students? We'd like to hear from you. *The New York Times.* Retrieved from www.nytimes.com/interactive/2017/09/07/multimedia/formacist-opinion-daca.html?smid=tw-nyt opinion&smtyp=cur

Odom, L. (2018). *Failing up: How to take risks, aim higher, and never stop learning.* New York, NY: Feiwel and Friends.

OECD. (2014). *Education at a glance 2014: OECD indicators.* OECD Publishing. Retrieved from http://dx.doi.org/10.1787/eag-2014-en

Phillips, K. W. (2014, October). How diversity makes us smarter. *Scientific American.* Retrieved from www.scientificamerican.com/article/how-diversity-makes-us-smarter

Sandberg, S. (2013). *Lean in: Women, work, and the will to lead.* New York, NY: Alfred A. Knopf.

Smith, R. (2017, February 25). Exploiting the norm of reciprocity on Bourbon Street. *Psychology Today.* Retrieved from www.psychologytoday.com/blog/joy-and-pain/201702/exploiting-the-norm-reciprocity-bourbon-street

Tannenbaum, M. (2015, January 2). PsySociety: I'll show you my holiday card if you show me yours. *Scientific American.* Retrieved from https://blogs.scientificamerican.com/psysociety/i-8217-ll-show-you-my-holiday-card-if-you-show-me-yours

Ward, A., & Suk, A. (2018, February 28). The surprising stories of Sesame Street. *Scatterbrained @ Mental Floss.* Podcast retrieved from http://mentalfloss.com/article/533609/surprising-stories-sesame-street

Wilén, N., & Ingelaere, B. (2017, August 31). War-torn Congo has been called the "rape capital of the world." *The Washington Post.* Retrieved from www.washingtonpost.com/news/monkey-cage/wp/2017/08/28/what-do-rebels-think-about-sexual-violence-in-congo-we-asked-them/?utm_term=.5e93d0c0c701

Chapter 11

Serving

Which of the following answers reflects a myth? Internships, fellowships, and similar programs:

A. are only for novices in our field.
B. don't carry any prestige.
C. make amateur additions to a resume or CV.
D. All of the above.

The answer is D. All of the above assumptions about internships, fellowships, and similar programs are common yet misguided.

An internship at the White House is something to crow about. Becoming National Board certified can mean an automatic salary increase and give you added clout in any U.S. state. The Albert Einstein Distinguished Educator Fellowship (AEF) Program sends primary and secondary school educators to work in U.S. Congressional offices – hardly a trifling feat. Other countries offer equally impressive programs. This chapter will share such ways to learn while also serving the field in compelling ways.

This chapter covers other chances to serve the field, as well. You can mentor, share lessons (an opportunity for teachers), become an edupreneur, teach at the university level, join a board or panel, or judge a competition in the field. These offer ways to share your expertise but can also open new networking channels and lead to additional opportunities to contribute. No matter which of this chapter's prospects you pursue, one could become or lead to your proudest achievement.

LIST OF SERVING OPPORTUNITIES (CALLS FOR INPUT, CALLS FOR PARTICIPATION, FELLOWSHIPS, PROGRAMS, INTERNSHIPS, PANELS, BOARDS, AND OPPORTUNITIES TO BE A JUDGE OR REVIEWER)

LIST OF SERVING OPPORTUNITIES

This book lists 107 serving opportunities (such as calls for input, calls for participation, fellowships, programs, internships, panels, boards, and opportunities to be a judge or reviewer) for you in an electronic file that makes it easy to find and pursue opportunities to serve the field. You can sort the file by category or deadline, and you can visit each website with a simple click. The list contains details like publication type and manipulation-friendly fields you can use to track your submissions. See the "eResources" section near the start of this book for details on accessing and using this "List of Serving Opportunities".

FELLOWSHIPS AND PROGRAMS

Fellowships and similar programs are great ways to learn. They often also mean connections with people who can help your ideas spread, advanced certification, funnels into new opportunities, and chances for you to contribute to the field in new ways (such as through influencing education policy). Even if a program doesn't meet where you live, some offer virtual or flexible options to accommodate your ties to a home base.

RESOURCE TIP

Cornell University Graduate School offers a robust fellowship database at https://gradschool.cornell.edu/fellowships

Open this book's "List of Serving Opportunities" eResource (described earlier). Sort the file by "Category" and find items categorized as "Fellowships/Programs". Some examples include:

- American Educational Research Association (AERA) Congressional Fellowship

- Harvard University Center for Education Policy Research (CEPR) Strategic Data Project (SDP) Fellowship Program
- TED Fellowship
- U.K. Department for Education (DfE) Policy Fellowship
- U.S. Department of Education School Ambassador Fellowship
- White House Fellowship

Many more are listed on the eResource. Apply for programs that suit your interests and goals.

INTERNSHIPS

Want to work at the White House or somewhere else exciting? Government bodies and initiatives (such as the White House Initiative on Asian Americans and Pacific Islanders), companies, research institutions, and organizations seek interns of all ages. Government bodies in particular often stress the desire to groom people who are undergoing a career transition rather than requiring interns to be a particular age.

Internships are chances to contribute and grow in a new area (for example, education policy). Some internships come with a high level of prestige. Visit www.ed.gov and search "internship" within the search field to find numerous U.S. Department of Education internships. Visit www.whitehouse.gov/participate/internships for White House internships, though note some administrations offer internships more than others. You might also check this book's "List of Organizations" eResource (introduced in the previous chapter) and approach groups for which you're interested in interning.

MENTORSHIP

The previous chapter covered how you might benefit from a mentor who helps you land new opportunities to share your expertise with the world. However, you can also mentor a mentee at your work or in your field. Benefits to serving as a mentor include better job performance, recognition, and a rewarding experience (Eby, Durleya, Evansa, & Ragins, 2006).

Consider which colleagues already come to you for guidance and make a conscious effort to share more of your wisdom with them. You can also pursue formal mentorship opportunities, for example, through Beginning Teacher Support and Assessment (BTSA) Induction programs or a professor/student pairing.

LESSON SHARING AND SELLING

Teachers can expand their impact by sharing lessons with other teachers. This is common for school teachers but also occurs at the higher education level. You can offer your lessons for free or to earn money; either approach is worthwhile.

Refining your lesson explanations prior to sharing (include standards addressed, pre-lesson preparation, examples to model on board, etc.) also helps you reflect on your own instruction to improve your next delivery of each unit. Consider these ways to share your lesson plans:

❏ Many school districts and academy trusts utilize Curriculum Management Systems (CMSs), Learning Management Systems (LMSs), or other edtech with lesson housing features. Check with your leadership team member who oversees technology to see what is available or use EdSurge's Product Index (www.edsurge.com/product-reviews) if advocating for multi-school adoption of a system to house lessons.

❏ Whether your workplace adopts a CMS/LMS or not, there are open educational resources (OERs) online to which you can upload lessons for educators everywhere to benefit from. Examples are categorized as "Share Teacher Lessons" on the "List of Serving Opportunities" eResource (described earlier).

❏ You can also share directly with colleagues at your school. When I was a teacher I organized all my lessons and their components by standard-specific binders in the staff lounge. Though some view hard copy systems as archaic, the style of my lessons (game-based, with lots of pieces like cards and game boards) fit the need for teachers to use the copy machine to build their own game pieces for these interactive lessons. I invited colleagues to add their own lessons to these binders based on which ones they found (by observation, student feedback, and performance data) to be successful. Some teachers relied solely on these best-from-everyone binders to determine how they would teach each unit.

❏ You can sell your lesson plans. Teachers Pay Teachers (where teachers from the preschool through college levels sell their materials) wouldn't release exact amounts, but sources like Korbey (2016) reported that by 2015 Teachers Pay Teachers had already earned 14 teachers more than $1 million each and 300 teachers more than $100,000 each. Money like that could always be used for conference travel and other efforts to improve the field. Places teachers can sell their lessons are categorized as "Sell Teacher Lessons" on the "List of Serving Opportunities" eResource (described earlier).

❏ Create your own TED-Ed lesson that integrates an existing TED Talk. If you give a TED or TEDx Talk (covered in "Chapter 9. Speaking on Air and Recordings"), you can even build upon your own Talk. I found this to be a great way to make my Talk accessible to a young audience. Visit http://ed.ted.com for details.

Before selling lessons you created while employed as a teacher, determine whether your job contract specifically assigns copyright ownership of such materials to the teacher. If not, investigate what you are permitted to sell without violating copyright laws (see sites such as www.copyright.gov or www.gov.uk/copyright for more information).

EDUPRENEURSHIP

While the term "edupreneur" is used in a number of ways, here I mean it in the sense of someone who starts a business in the education realm. Examples include creating and offering educational technology products, professional development for educators, or new student curricula. Edupreneurship allows you to lend your expertise to the field in the form of needed products or other resources. Some edupreneurs do this while maintaining their "day jobs" at the same time. Others (like my husband, Lane Rankin) jump from the education field into full-time pursuit of expanding their impact through edupreneurship.

If you're interested in edupreneurship, I recommend exploring (and subscribing to news from) EDUKWEST (www.edukwest.com) and EdSurge (www.edsurge.com). Resources such as these can keep you abreast of industry news and opportunities (including funding). The next Chapter's "List of Honors" eResource also shares some edupreneurial funding and support sources (such as the Milken-Penn Graduate School of Education Business Plan Competition, known for its prestige and prize pool, and the Camelback Fellowship, which specifically backs ventures led by people of color and women). Browse the "Fellowship/Program" category on the "List of Serving Opportunities" and the "Contest/Competition" category on the "List of Honors" eResource for similar endeavors.

UNIVERSITY TEACHING

Teaching a class of your peers allows you to impact students on a broader scale. Whether you want to transition into full-time faculty or teach part-time as adjunct while maintaining a school job, there are a variety of ways to get involved:

- ❑ Search your local university's website (look for "job" or "career" links) to apply for a job within its School of Education or separate teaching program. Most tenured professorships require a PhD or an EdD, but there are lecturer positions or other support roles that don't always require a doctorate.
- ❑ Search your local university's "extension" or "continuing education" webpage. These often offer classes for teachers but often don't list their job openings within the university's regular website.

245

❏ When you strike a rapport with university faculty (for example, while at a conference) or are connected by a mutual acquaintance, inquire about teaching opportunities.

❏ Search the Higher Education Recruitment Consortium (HERC) website (www.hercjobs.org) for U.S. positions and www.jobs.ac.uk for positions in the U.K. and abroad. You can filter jobs by location and keywords (for example, if you only want to teach online).

❏ Search the American Educational Research Association's (AERA's) career page (http://careers.aera.net). You can also find non-teaching (such as research) positions in the field this way.

❏ Join the email list of your regional educational research associations. These often announce higher education employment opportunities.

❏ Consider teaching for a massive open online course (MOOC) or other platform that allows teachers to earn money teaching classes of their own design. The top 10 teachers at Udemy (www.udemy.com) earned an average of $500,000 each, meaning some earned even more (O'Dell, 2013). Within five years, teacher Scott Allen earned over $1,800,000 selling classes on Pluralsight (www.pluralsight.com), where teachers' average royalty is $40,000, the top 10 teachers' average is $250,000, and the top five teachers' average is $400,000 (Lacy, 2013). Skillshare (http://blog. skillshare.com) is another popular venue used to teach peers online. The added income could fund travel to share your knowledge internationally or in other cost-intensive venues.

ADVISORY BOARDS

Companies (such as edtech vendors) and educational organizations (such as non-profits) often have advisory boards through which they garner experts' feedback at regular intervals. Education consultants are often called to assemble advisory boards and could be looking for someone like you.

Board members get to help shape an organization's direction and collaborate with other thinkers. Commitment time varies, as does compensation.

If this role appeals to you, consider where your expertise could help. Are you an edtech tool's "power user"? Did you conduct a study on the specific population a nonprofit is targeting?

Leverage any contacts you have at your chosen organization to find out if they have a board and would consider adding you. If you don't know anyone involved, visit the organization's website for contact information. Some organizations post invitations to participate. For example, Public Broadcasting Service (PBS) (2018) posted this invitation for the NOVA Education Advisory Board: "The NOVA Education team is always looking for educators who would like to test our resources and provide us with feedback. If you would like to join the NOVA

Education Advisory Board, please email NOVAeducation@wgbh.org for more information" (p. 1).

Share your willingness and qualifications, whether a board is already in existence or not (you never know what plans are in the works). Also, your other activities (speaking at conferences, writing, etc.) will improve your chances of being approached with a request to join a board.

SCRAPPY TIP

I recently met with a colleague who wants to get on some boards. I showed her an article (see Johnson, 2017) on the top educational technology boards that are completely devoid of women. My colleague happens to be female. I suggested she contact the companies with all-male boards and offer her considerable expertise with the chance to add diversity to their boards. My colleague is also Black, another demographic that is underrepresented on most educational boards and deserves a larger presence. Once aboard, she will share her unique wisdom and perspective and will continue to push for a more heterogeneous and inclusive board.

SCHOOL BOARDS

Professionals within the education field tend to make superb school board members. Primary and secondary school educators, researchers, professors, and other education experts all have specializations to enhance a board in their area. Each U.S. state sets its own procedures for running for local school boards, so contact your state's school boards association if you are interested in this form of service. U.K. local education authority (LEA) councils, which replaced school boards in 1902, offer similar opportunities.

Visit Run for Office (www.runforoffice.org). There you'll find the nonprofit's free database of more than 80,000 school board positions across all 50 states, which you can search to find when nearby school board seats are up for election, whether you are eligible to run, and how to launch your campaign (Fay, 2017).

ELECTED POSITIONS AND GOVERNING BOARDS

Education organizations often have annually elected positions such as president and treasurer. Examples of such organizations include American Educational

Research Association (AERA) and Computer Using Educators (CUE), but there are many more. Divisions and Special Interest Groups (SIGs) within such orgs often have elected positions, as well.

Some organizations have governing boards. For example, the ASCD Board of Directors (www.ascd.org/about-ascd/Governance/ASCD-Governance.aspx) governs ASCD. Some boards are charged with special tasks, such as the National Assessment Governing Board, which Congress created to oversee the National Assessment of Educational Progress (NAEP).

Consider running for a position to lead or govern organizations in which you are involved. Search the organization's website, subscribe to its newsletters and announcement lists, and attend its events to learn of possible openings. A contact is usually provided when openings are announced, and you can ask this person about prerequisites, the election process, and the work such a position would demand of you. If the organization (such as a union) is located in your area, meet with representatives to learn more about involvement and express your interest.

SCRAPPY TIP

When an organization's members vote on leadership roles, they are usually given a bio or statement for each candidate. Being a highly active participant in the organization (volunteering on its committees, moderating its conference sessions, working its booth at events, etc.) will make you a more electable candidate.

JUDGE

Nonprofit and institutional efforts in the education space allow students, educators, or edupreneurs to compete for accolades, mentorship, or funds. These often rely on judges with field expertise. Consider applying to serve on one of these judging panels.

Find opportunities categorized as "Judge" in this book's "List of Serving Opportunities" eResource (described earlier) by sorting the file by its "Category" column. You will see several examples listed but note there are even more chances to judge the work of your peers. For example, the awards and competitions listed on the "List of Honors" eResource (described in the next chapter) typically rely on judges with backgrounds like yours.

Consider approaching the organizers of any honors for which you are interested in judging. Often the award's website will have an application form or directions specific to potential judges. If you find none, you can likely locate a contact page or email address to send an inquiry with a very concise account of your qualifications.

REVIEW PANELS

Reviewers are regularly needed to evaluate submissions for journals, books, conferences, and more. Reviewers influence which contributions are selected, and their feedback helps to shape published work. As a reviewer, your expertise could improve the way important concepts are communicated and could prompt others to address topic aspects they might otherwise overlook. For those new to academia, seeing one's name published in a respected journal as one of an issue's reviewers can boost your confidence and desire to submit your own papers in the future.

SCRAPPY TIP

If the "Awards and Honors" portion of your CV is sparse, serving as a judge, reviewer, or any other role covered in this chapter can be listed as an "honor" on your CV. Don't mistake listing achievements as a self-serving act. Rather, strengthening how you appear on your CV can help you secure opportunities to share your expertise in ways that can ultimately benefit kids.

Open this book's "List of Serving Opportunities" eResource (described earlier) and find prospects listed as "Reviewer" in the "Category" column. You will see several examples, but there are even more chances to review the work of your peers.

Additional ways to find reviewer prospects include:

❑ Join an organization that hosts education conferences. Watch its website and emails for invitations to review presentation submissions and contact conference organizers to volunteer your services as a reviewer. Even if entries aren't being reviewed during the time of year you reach organizers, you can ask to be included when potential reviewers are contacted later in the year.
❑ Visit the website of a journal relevant to your expertise (the "List of Writing Opportunities" eResource described earlier can help you find one). Look for

links like "Become a Reviewer". If there are none, follow a link to the editorial board members' contact information. Use this to email editors and propose yourself as a reviewer.

❏ Join an organization that publishes education journals. Examples include AERA (such as *American Educational Research Journal*) and National Association of School Psychologists (such as *School Psychology Review*). Journals' publishing organizations often reach out to members when they're in need of reviewers, or they include invitations to review in their communications to members.

❏ If your mentor has served as a reviewer, published in journals, or presented at peer-reviewed conferences, ask if he would be willing to recommend you to that venue's editor or event organizer.

In any of these cases, be ready to provide your CV, short bio, and an explanation of how you are qualified to review the venue's submissions.

If you are female, I encourage you to give reviewing added consideration. Women are recommended for peer review panels for scholarly journals less than men and far below the gender ratio of published female authors, regardless of age category (this

> **Peer review** is a process in which a group of experts evaluate a work's (for example, a journal paper's or book chapter's) merit, such as to determine its publication, inclusion in a collection, or qualification to be presented by its author at a conference. Reviewers commonly submit recommended revisions for the author to consider.

is true among both editors' and authors' recommendations), but women more frequently decline these invitations when they are extended (Lerback & Hanson, 2017). As a result, women are greatly underrepresented in the scholarly review process, yet field literature and conference offerings benefit when varied perspectives are involved.

STUDY PANELS

Readers with research backgrounds (such as Ph.D.s) have conducted studies and are likely familiar with how to conduct or participate in more. Readers without research backgrounds, however, also have chances to get involved and expand the research section of their CVs. There are many calls for participation that educators can answer. Organizations, universities, and individuals announce the need for study participants meeting particular criteria.

Even as a participant, studies can lend you credibility. For example, when the Common Core State Standards (CCSS) and Smarter Balanced Assessment Consortium (SBAC) were new and U.S. school districts were scrambling for CCSS and SBAC experts, my involvement as one of the educators who reviewed SBAC CCSS assessment questions and recommended achievement level scores for the actual tests opened doors for me. This participation resulted from my answering a call on the SBAC website to serve in its alignment study. I checked the website regularly for such an opportunity to arise.

Studies are timely opportunities with end dates. You thus won't see them listed on one of this book's opportunity eResources. Joining emailing lists for field news (see the "List of Organizations" section in "Chapter 10. Connecting") can help you hear of new studies. For example, e-newsletters from EdSurge, Edutopia, and ERIC have all included details for study participation in the past.

If you Google or run a twitter search for *study "call for participation"* (put the last three words in quotes) you can find opportunities. Add a word like *teacher* to your search to cater your search to your role or research area. If you know a group is going to roll out new standards or some other field-rocking endeavor, watch its website regularly for any committees or studies that form.

RESOURCE TIP

If you want to conduct your own study but don't know where to start, read *Doing Your Research Project: A Guide for First-Time Researchers* by Bell and Waters (2018) for support.

REFERENCES

Bell, J., & Waters, S. (2018). *Doing your research project: A guide for first-time researchers.* Maidenhead, United Kingdom: Open University Press/McGraw-Hill.

Eby, L. T., Durleya, J. R., Evansa, S. C., & Ragins, B. R. (2006, January). The relationship between short-term mentoring benefits and long-term mentor outcomes. *Journal of Vocational Behavior, 69*(3), 424–444. Amsterdam, Netherlands: Elsevier.

Fay, L. (2017, October 23). Want to Run for Your Local School Board? New Database Makes It Easy. *The 74.* Retrieved via www.the74million.org/want-to-run-for-your-local-school-board-new-database-makes-it-easy

Johnson, S. (2017, July 26). Edtech's hidden shortage: Women directors. *EdSurge.* Retrieved from www.edsurge.com/news/2017-07-26-edtech-s-hidden-shortage-women-directors

Korbey, H. (2016, January). Millions of teachers minting millionaire teachers. *Spectrum Equity*. Retrieved from www.spectrumequity.com/news/millions-of-teachers-minting-millionaire-teachers

Lacy, S. (2013, July 8). Lessons from the first millionaire online teacher. *PandoDaily*. Retrieved from http://pando.com/2013/07/08/lessons-from-the-first-millionaire-online-teacher

Lerback, J., & Hanson, B. (2017, January). Journals invite too few women to referee. *Nature: International Weekly Journal of Science*. Retrieved from www.nature.com/news/journals-invite-too-few-women-to-referee-1.21337

PBS. (2018). *About NOVA Education*. Retrieved from www.pbs.org/wgbh/nova/education/about.html

Chapter 12

Awards

Awards can open new world-helping opportunities you never anticipated. Consider when Nikos Giannopoulos won Rhode Island's Teacher of the Year in 2017. President Trump had just taken office and his administration had already revoked protections for transgender students and removed the LGBT+ rights webpage from the White House's website. Giannopoulos, who is gay and has gay and transgender students, made a deliberate choice to not tone down his style for his photo op with President Trump and the First Lady. Giannopoulos wore a rainbow lapel pin, nose ring, and gold anchor necklace, cocked his head and hips to one side, and (despite a White House aide's objections) splayed his partner's black lace fan in one hand for the camera. The photo was an internet sensation and, more importantly, sent a strong message that LGBT+ educators and advocates would not shrink back when faced with the new administration.

When you win awards, what you do with the resultant platforms is up to you. People will be watching and listening, and you can seize the moment to have a positive impact in yet more ways.

Some professionals in the education field have mixed feelings about applying for awards. They worry it means they are conceited, or they feel guilty devoting time to the endeavor. However, since awards can make a CV more impressive, and since a more impressive CV can open doors for you and allow you to share your knowledge on a larger scale, earning accolades can help you to ultimately help more students. Often awards are tied to specific works (such as a paper you wrote or a program you developed) and increase the work's credibility and circulation, and thus its impact.

This chapter will help you in in your award-related endeavors. Traditional awards, badges, book awards, contests, competitions, dissertation awards, grants, and other honors are all waiting for you to apply. Don't keep them waiting!

SCRAPPY FAST TRACK

I was honored by the U.S. White House before I ever earned another CV-worthy award. This is because the path to big honors is different than paths to other accomplishments. To land a book deal, you commonly need to have published smaller works first. To land a major speaking gig, you need to have first performed at smaller speaking venues. But when it comes to major awards, the judges and reviewers typically don't care whether or not you collected other awards along your way to them.

Thus, this scrappy fast track is different from others. What will matter most is the quality of your contribution(s) to the field. If you want to skyrocket to snagging a major award (such as the MacArthur Genius Grant or the Varkey Foundation's Global Teacher Prize), I recommend you use the information in this book to take this route:

Step 1. Be devoted to students. The "Good Connecting Mindset: Be in it for students" section of "Chapter 10. Connecting" can help.

Step 2. Have a clear brand. In order to award you, judges need to understand what you're all about. "Chapter 2. Image" can help.

Step 3. Craft a submission that makes your contribution clear. This is less about cramming as many assets as you can into the allowed word count than it is about telling a story that intrigues the reader, gets to the core of your message and merit, and moves and persuades the judges. To hone these skills, see the parts of

Chapter 1. Introduction" concerning message, pitch, talking points, and packaging, and see all of "Chapter 3. Writing Anything".

Step 4. Follow this chapter's guidance in award acceptance and proofread critically before hitting a "submit" button.

Step 5. Apply for many awards; this statistically increases your odds of winning. If you electronically save all of your submission answers and explanations, you'll have a pool from which to simply copy and paste information for reuse (revising as necessary), making future award submissions easier and faster. Sort the "List of Honors" eResource by its "Month to Apply" column to pick new prospects every month.

Step 6. As you await verdicts, busily pursue the other opportunities in this book to expand your impact. Speak at conferences, write op-eds for newspapers, serve on panels, and so on. Many of the highest honors (Nobel Peace Prize, MacArthur Genius Grant, etc.) have a closed nomination process, and this book's opportunities to share your work loudly and widely will increase nominators' chances of knowing about the important work you're doing. For example, though far from a Nobel, my highest honors (winning Teacher of the Year and having the U.S. flag flown over the White House in my honor) were arranged by others to my surprise. I still encourage applying for awards on your own, but if you don't win those you try for you can know that good work is often recognized eventually, one way or another.

LIST OF HONORS (AWARDS, BADGES, BOOK AWARDS, CONTESTS, COMPETITIONS, DISSERTATION AWARDS, GRANTS, AND OTHER HONORS)

LIST OF HONORS

This book lists 383+ honors (such as awards, badges, book awards, contests, competitions, dissertation awards, and grants, as well as award lists containing additional awards) for you in an electronic file that makes it easy to find and pursue honors. You can sort the file by submission deadline and visit each website with a simple click. The list contains details like deadline to apply, submission link, award type, and manipulation-friendly fields you can use to track your submissions. See the "eResources" section near the start of this book for details on accessing and using this "List of Honors".

AWARDS

Remember that by promoting yourself and your work, you are promoting knowledge that can help kids. If you believe in your research or your professional expertise, and you believe it can help the education field, then get out there and rack up some honors.

There are all kinds of awards waiting for you: traditional awards, book awards, dissertation awards (applicable if you recently completed your PhD), and a wide variety of purposes and focus areas within each of these categories. For example, school teachers might shoot for the Varkey Foundation's Global Teacher Prize (known as the "Nobel Prize in Teaching" and meaning $1,000,000 in prize money that could fund student-helping endeavors), whereas education professors and researchers might shoot for the Scottish Educational Research Association (SERA) Estelle Brisard Memorial Prize. Many more options abound.

SCRAPPY TIP

Sometimes nominations are not collected for awards, and it is up to a committee or judging panel to select work to review. Judge identities are sometimes secret, but when they're known you can put your work on a judge's radar without being pushy. For example, knowing an economy reporter was judging for an award relevant to my book, I sent her a single tweet that read:

@[*judge's Twitter handle*] 15% of teachers quit each year, costing U.S. $2.2mil per yr; teacher burnout issue might interest you: www.[*link to my book on teacher burnout*]

Open this book's "List of Honors" eResource (described earlier). Sort the file by "Category" by clicking the arrow atop that fourth column and sorting in ascending order. Find the opportunities that are listed as "Award", "Book Award", or "Dissertation Award" in this column to note all the options available.

I also recommend sorting the file by "Month to Apply" to determine what you can apply for at any given time. Check this list monthly to apply for all prospects that fit your situation. Since award winning is a very subjective game, applying for many awards increases your odds of winning them.

TIME-SAVING TIP

Award applications often ask for the same types of information (what inspires you, what has your impact been, why is your book's topic timely, etc.). When you enter to win an award (typing your bio and other information on an online form), always save the information you enter on a Word document on your computer, as well. I have a single "Awards" folder on my computer that contains a separate folder (within it) for each honor for which I apply (such as "SPE2017BookAward"). This way I can quickly find and then electronically copy and paste my entry information (from different places as needed) to reuse it in the future. Also, since composition takes time, an online form can "time out" during the entry process (losing your information) if you take too long to submit.

Acceptance

This section will help you win awards but can also be applied to the other opportunities featured in this chapter. For most awards, competitions, or other honors, you will submit an entry or someone else will submit a nomination on your behalf. Submission requirements vary, even when the type of award is the same. You might have to submit a simple bio, write a complete paper, or complete rounds of interviews.

MONEY-SAVING TIP

Beware of scams. If an award requires an entry fee over $25, investigate whether the award is truly prestigious and worth pursuing.

Other experts will review your submission to determine if you win an award, how you place, etc. Guidelines to increase your odds of acceptance vary by award type, so apply those that suit whatever you are shooting for (such as a dissertation award vs. an outstanding educator award):

❑ Determine what the award acceptance criteria is and be sure you meet eligibility requirements. Sometimes the rubric judges will use to score entries is shared with applicants. Before, during, and after you prepare your application, consider how your entry will meet all criteria.

❑ Determine the award's purpose (this often involves its history). For example, the National Council on Measurement in Education's (NCME's) Alicia Cascallar Award honors Cascallar's history of encouraging new academics in the area of educational measurement. If paper entries are not written by early career scholars or do not relate to educational measurement, they will not win this award. Be sure you, your work, and your entry match the award's purpose.

❑ Tailor your answers to the questions asked. When we paste answers we've provided for other award entries in the past, it's easy to miss this step. Check your answers and tweak them as necessary to be sure they directly address what the awards committee wants to know.

❑ Avoid dry descriptions of your work. Judges want to get excited about the people or projects they select to win. Your passion should come across in a way that is contagious.

Write to intrigue your entry's reader, capture the core of your merit and message, and move the judges to win them over. For help, see the parts of "Chapter 1. Introduction" concerning message, pitch, talking points, and packaging, and see all of "Chapter 3. Writing Anything". For example, anecdotal stories and other magic from Table 3.2 make the power of your work come alive.

❏ Favor phrases like "The program I led" over phrases like "My program". You'll want to acknowledge group contributions and indicate the collaboration that is crucial to effective implementations and school culture.

❏ Use statistics to communicate impact. Consider how weak this statement is: "Our school's Sober Is Cool initiative helped prevent student intoxication." Consider how much stronger this is: "By the end of the first year our school implemented the Sober Is Cool initiative, instances of on-campus student intoxication dropped from nine per month to two for the entire school year." The same goes for communicating a problem your work addresses.

❏ Look at previous years' winners (read winning papers and note topics covered, learn about the educators who won, familiarize yourself with the education companies that earned funding, etc.). Consider ways you can make your message and merit stand out like they did.

❏ If you know a colleague is submitting a nomination on your behalf, provide her with sample answers to all nomination form sections. Your colleague can then tailor responses to fit what she wants to say. If someone is kind enough to nominate you, this person should not have to search for your credentials, scramble to find your phone number, etc.

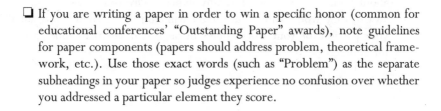

SCRAPPY TIP

If you see "deadline extended" for an award, consider applying! This often means not many people applied, or not enough of those who did apply were deemed appropriate winners. In such cases, it's likely there will be reduced competition if you apply, which increases your odds of winning.

❏ If you are writing a paper in order to win a specific honor (common for educational conferences' "Outstanding Paper" awards), note guidelines for paper components (papers should address problem, theoretical framework, etc.). Use those exact words (such as "Problem") as the separate subheadings in your paper so judges experience no confusion over whether you addressed a particular element they score.

❏ Write with enough clarity that even people unfamiliar with your efforts or the problem you seek to solve (as judges might be) can easily understand your contributions and their importance.

❏ When you paste your entry information into an online form after first composing and saving the information on your computer (as previously recommended), check to be sure all text pastes correctly. Sometimes special characters (even basic ones, like apostrophes) are automatically replaced with peculiar characters, and sometimes words with special formatting (such as bold) are omitted entirely. These problems are rare, but you will want to check for them.

SCRAPPY TIP

Many awards or contests use volunteers to judge the winner. Around the time the entry window is announced, the award committee's website or emails may call for people to apply to volunteer as judges. Serving as a judge will give you an inside peek into the judging process. This inside scoop can help you prepare an entry that is selected for this award in the future, but also for other honors. Plus, you can include your service as a judge as an honor in the "Awards and Honors" section of your CV if that section is sparse.

❏ Address every aspect of every question (after you answer the question, reread the question and your answer to ensure this). Applicants fail to do this surprisingly often, and this oversight is especially damaging if judges use a rubric to judge submissions.

❏ This is not the time for modesty. The judges likely don't know anything about you, so if you don't vividly explain why you're worthy of the award, they won't know you should win. You won't sound arrogant if your passion for your work comes through stronger than your passion for yourself.

If you don't win an award, don't lose heart. Sometimes that year's judges don't connect with your work like next year's judges will, or sometimes your work isn't as developed as it will be the following year. Lengthy lists of awards on others' CVs can intimidate us, but if these CVs also listed awards that were lost, the lists of failures would be longer. Keep trying.

KEEP TRYING

I've missed more than 9,000 shots in my career. I've lost almost 300 games... I've failed over and over and over again in my life. And that is why I succeed.

– Michael Jordan (Goldman & Papson, 1998, p. 49), considered by many to be the greatest basketball player of all time

CONTESTS AND COMPETITIONS

A 1976 Special Olympics moment was commemorated as a poignant commercial. During a track race one athlete took a hard fall. Rather than capitalizing on the moment, two of the competitors stopped, turned around, helped the boy up, and then ran together to cross the finish line as one. Many mistake the scene as evidence the mentally challenged are all blessed with an angelic nature, which is a myth (news flash: people with cognitive challenges are just as varied in nature as the rest of the population). Rather, this scene captures the beautiful side of *competition*, in which we all have the opportunity to bring out our best selves, encourage those around us to succeed, and celebrate a love for whatever it is we're doing.

Open this book's "List of Honors" eResource (described after this chapter's introduction) and find opportunities categorized as "Contest/Competition" to note available options. Sort the file by "Month to Apply" to determine what you can apply for at any given time, and apply to the contests and competitions that match your situation.

HONORS

You'll notice some opportunities are listed as "Honors" in the "List of Honors" eResource (described earlier). These aren't exactly awards yet are nonetheless prestigious achievements to mention in the "Awards and Honors" section of your CV and can open many doors for you. Examples include being inducted into the National Teachers Hall of Fame, being knighted by the British government, being named on the Forbes 30 Under 30 List, being invited to attend the Teacher Appreciation White House Social, and being named one of the CNN Heroes. Education experts have achieved each of the listed honors. Maybe you could join their ranks.

SCRAPPY TIP

Do you have an organization, online community, or other group you'd like more people to know about? Create an annual collection of awards. You need not award money; education professionals will apply and nominate others just for the honor of winning.

Awards allow you to celebrate good practice in the field while simultaneously spreading the word about your group or resource. Winners and runners-up put the awards on their CVs and websites, post about them in social media, mention them to others, and more ... which spreads the word to others in the field who might want to be involved in your project.

Also consider determining the winner by popular vote (for example, teachers each submit a specific type of lesson to your site, and anyone visiting the site can view all the lessons and vote on the best one based on criteria you post). Since people will want to win, they will tell others to visit your website and vote for them. This exposes more people (many of whom are likely in the field) to your website and thus your message. If the judging rubric you post is tied to best practices you want to spread, those who use it will learn the practices as they vote.

SERVING AND PANELS

"Chapter 11. Serving" covered many opportunities that can also be considered honors. For example, serving as a judge, on a panel or board, in a fellowship or other program, in an internship (for example, at the U.K. Parliament House of Commons), as a reviewer, informing policy, or as an elected official are sometimes mentioned in the "Awards and Honors" section of one's CV. This practice can help if you feel a lack of awards is holding you back from landing other prospects to share your work.

BADGES

Badges are digital proof an organization gives you as you accomplish specific tasks. For example, Academic Experts might give you its Published Badge for contributing a specific resource or Connected Educator Month (CEM) might give you its CEM Socialize Badge for completing a specific series of education social networking tasks. Universities and programs sometimes offer badges to students to represent micro-credentials or certifications, or they offer instructors badges for specific training or contributions to a department.

Some badges are directly tied to opportunities. For example, at the California Association of School Data, Assessment, and Accountability Professionals (CASDAAP), the badges members earn for non-monetary contributions to the organization are used to determine who is eligible to serve on the organization's board.

Not everyone in the education field is familiar with badges, but these accomplishments can still be listed on your CV as evidence of new skills and achievements. Badges can also give a welcome boost to a new CV, when the "Awards and Honors" section is likely to be sparse.

Open this book's "List of Honors" eResource (described earlier) and find opportunities listed as "Badge" in the "Category" column. Your university and professional organizations might also offer badges you can earn. The Badge Alliance (www.badgealliance.org) has working groups you can join to stay up to date with the topic of badges in the education field.

GRANTS

A variety of grants are available to help kids. The U.S. Department of Education (2018) offers three types of grants: student loans or grants that assist students with college costs, formula grants awarded based on formulas set by Congress (rather than an application process), and discretionary grants awarded through a competitive process. States also offer grants, many of which are competitive (such as the federal discretionary grants), meaning you can apply to win them. The "List of Honors" eResource, covered earlier in this chapter, contains details for applying for the discretionary grants and state grants.

Many grants are available for U.K. schools, as well. Visit the "List of Honors" eResource to find these, as well as grants from nonprofits, companies, and private parties that will fund schools in the U.S., U.K., and other countries. Philanthropically funded education grants, offered by groups like the Bill and Melinda Gates Foundation (with its $45 billion endowment), exceed $1 billion annually (Coggins, 2017).

The Bill and Melinda Gates Foundation (2018) does not award grants to individuals who apply (rather, it awards funds to organizations identified by the foundation's staff). However, many grant awards are based on applications an education expert like you can submit (for example, on behalf of a program or study you are running). Some of these grants are listed in this book's "List of Honors" eResource. Others can be found on sites like GrantsAlert (www.grantsalert.com/grants) and The Grantsmanship Center (www.tgci.com/funding-sources).

Grants also enhance your CV and credibility, thus leading to more opportunities to share your expertise. "Getting a grant from an influential foundation like Ford, Rockefeller, or Gates also legitimizes the work that's funded, and it enhances the status of grantees" (Badgett, 2016, p. 58).

YOUR TURN

Select an award or other honor (use the "List of Honors" eResource for suggestions) for which you plan to apply before an upcoming deadline. Then complete Exercise 12.1 to plan your submission, referencing this chapter's previous sections as necessary. If the application involves writing a paper, use "Chapter 4. Writing Short-Form" for added support.

EXERCISE 12.1: AWARD PLAN

1. **Pick an award or honor (with an upcoming entry deadline) for which you will apply** (use the "List of Honors" eResource for suggestions). What is the honor?

2. **Visit the honor's website (e.g., as provided on the "List of Honors" eResource) and locate all of the following that exist** (not all honors have all of these):
   ❏ Application form or description of information you must submit
   ❏ Rubric that reviewers will use to judge submissions and determine winners
   ❏ Information on previous winners
   Use the above items to help you with the rest of this exercise.

3. **Describe the award's purpose.** This often involves the award's history. Keep this purpose in mind when crafting your entry.

4. **Write a response for one of the main descriptor components of your entry.** The application might specify a maximum word count for responses. Make sure your passion is clear and contagious. There should be a connection to the award's purpose. Insert statistics (related to the impact or the problem being solved) as appropriate. Include anecdotal stories or other magic from Table 3.2 as appropriate.

5. **Before submitting your entry, check to be sure it meets all submission requirements.** I print the rubric and submission instructions, place a checkbox next to every requirement, and then read my entry (checking off boxes as I go) to ensure my entry conforms to all requirements.

REFERENCES

Badgett, M. V. L. (2016). *The public professor: How to use your research to change the world.* New York, NY: NYU Press.

Bill and Melinda Gates Foundation. (2018). *How we work: Grant opportunities.* Retrieved from www.gatesfoundation.org/How-We-Work/General-Information/Grant-Opportunities

Coggins, C. (2017). *How to be heard: 10 lessons teachers need to advocate for their students and profession.* San Francisco, CA: Jossey-Bass. Goldman, R., & Papson, S. (1998). *Nike culture: The sign of the swoosh.* London, United Kingdom: SAGE Publications.

U.S. Department of Education. (2018). Funding: Grants: Overview. Retrieved from www2.ed.gov/fund/grants-apply.html

Part V

Extra Credit

Chapter 13

Multiply Your Impact

If you have gone to the trouble of writing a piece, delivering a speech, getting interviewed by the media, or sharing your expertise in some other way, you can make this effort far more impactful by increasing the audience that consumes it. This chapter will help you maximize each of your endeavors by promoting and spreading it further. This isn't about self-promotion or hubris; this is about ensuring your wisdom reaches as many people — and thus helps as many students — as possible.

Of course, if you're not careful, your efforts to *spread* your ideas and research could cut into your time spent furthering your work. As you follow this chapter's strategies, remain conscientious about striking a healthy balance between your work in the field and sharing that work with others. You don't have to do everything in this chapter; just do what you can accomplish without sacrificing your professional practice.

SCRAPPY FAST TRACK

If you want to catapult the reach of your ideas (for example, if you have done limited branding and have limited social media presence but want much exposure for your work), I recommend you use the information in this chapter and "Chapter 2. Image" to take this route:

Step 1. At very least, establish your pitch and a professional website (even if it's just your workplace profile page) where journalists can find your bio and press information (including contact information). The book's first two chapters will help you with this.

Step 2. If you have published a book or work at a university, your publisher or university likely has a PR Department. Engage with its team members to plan efforts to promote your work. Try to get a list of journalists they feel will be most interested in your work and approach them about interviewing you, doing a feature on your findings, or quoting you. If a journalist in the public eye shares your work, it will instantly reach far more people than you are likely to reach on your own.

Step 3. From the comfort of your home or office, use this chapter's strategies to engage with targeted journalists regularly (but not overbearingly). Share your work with them as you produce articles and other outreach pieces recommended in this book.

Step 4. Regularly be on the lookout for reporters to interact with them in person. Kat Stein (2016), Executive Director of Communications at University of Pennsylvania's Graduate School of Education, suggested looking in the working pressroom of a major academic conference for journalists who are there looking for news.

Ask them about what they are finding interesting about the conference and establish a relationship. If a reporter calls you at any point, keep their contact information! ... This is perhaps one of the most useful and rarely used communication strategies.(p. 108).

At a casual AERA "Speaker's Corner" session with journalists, *Education Week* editor Debra Viadero told me her story interests include social-emotional learning, pathways to STEM, and group-learning strategies for digital classrooms. Information like this can highlight ways your expertise intersects with journalists' needs.

Step 5. Don't stop aiming for other "vast reach" opportunities covered in this book, like doing a TED Talk or getting interviewed on *PBS NewsHour*. Opportunities like those will gain your work much exposure.

BE PRESS-FRIENDLY

Since publications have slashed staffing in order to survive, journalists are more under pressure than ever and thus have less time than ever (Stein, 2016). If you don't make things easy on the press, journalists are likely to pass you over to cover news elsewhere. Being press-friendly will help you get your ideas out into the world where they can help more students.

Press/Media Page

Publicist Devin Boyle taught me to add an obvious link to the top of my website that leads to a Press/Media webpage (I'll use the terms "press" and "media" interchangeably here, though some prefer to distinguish between them). Boyle explained that journalists and reporters who visit the site will want a clear indication that I'm quote-worthy and am used to working with the media. Seeing a list of previous press experience on a devoted webpage will help assure them of this. This page should also make it easy for reporters to contact me.

Your press/media webpage can contain:

- Your easy-to-spot email address and/or phone number.
- Short list of topics you specialize in.
- Brief bio summarizing your most impressive and relevant qualifications.
- Links to your full bio and CV, appearances, and publications.
- List of your media interviews, expert quotes, etc.
- "Media Assets" (photos of you the press can download and use).

For an example, check out my press page at www.jennyrankin.com/press.

Twitter

"The number one reason to be on Twitter? That's where the journalists are – all day, every day – talking to each other" (Badgett, 2016, p. 148). A *PBS NewsHour* education editor took interest in my stance on President Trump's proposal to arm teachers with guns only because I private messaged her about it on Twitter.

If you want your voice shared through news media, it behooves you to join journalists in their Twitter dialogue. Interaction can involve liking and retweeting reporters' posts you admire, replying to their posts with an insight or resource (promoting others you admire as much as your own work), and occasionally private messaging them with a pitch or news tip.

SCRAPPY TIP

On Twitter, search #journorequest and #journorequests to view tweets that use either hashtag (sort by "Latest" to see recent tweets first). Journalists (mainly in the U.K.) use these to tag requests for people to be part of their stories. You can add terms like "education" and could find a request related to your topic!

Registered Source

Register with Education Writers Association's (EWA's) SourceSearch (www. ewa.org/sourcesearch) as a journalist's source for knowledge and insight. More than 3,000 reporters are EWA members, and they search this directory to find experts like you for input.

Also register with Public Insight Network (PIN) (www.publicinsightnetwork. org) as a journalist's source. PIN is used extensively by TV stations and networks (like PBS), public radio stations (including NPR), commercial news organizations (like *The Washington Post*), and universities (Briggs, 2016).

Conduct

When interacting with press, be:

❑ **Timely.** Return a call or email immediately. Even if you don't have time to talk that day, note you are available to talk that night (or at other suggested times) so you can be counted on as a contributor. Scott Jaschik (2016), editor and co-founder of *Inside Higher Ed*, wrote, "Reporters remember who called back promptly – and few things are more likely to make you a regular than responsiveness. You can win a Nobel Prize and, if you don't call back, you won't get the calls" (p. 14) from press again.

❑ **Helpful.** Even if you are not qualified to address what a journalist is looking for, e-introduce her to someone you know who is. This is a great way to ensure quality information is shared by the press while simultaneously helping others in the field. Boyle noted this approach also encourages reporters to see you as their "go to" person.

❏ **Precise and understandable.** Being misquoted by journalists is a problem spanning centuries. Even Abraham Lincoln, in the wake of his 1858 "House Divided" speech, visited the newspaper office to personally check the galley proofs because he worried the newspaper would inaccurately print the copy he gave reporters.

The press will typically not share your level of expertise in relation to your topic. Reporters will try to condense and summarize anything elaborate you say, so be very succinct and very clear (avoid jargon like the plague). Unlike President Lincoln's, "your words" will typically be published without your having a chance to approve a journalist's version of them, so you want to make sure the press thoroughly understands what you say or write.

Following pitch guidelines will help you achieve coherence when reporters accept pitches. See the "News Media and Television" section of "Chapter 9. Speaking on Air and Recordings" for details.

❏ **Commit to a stance on issues.** A major reason an expert never makes it onto NPR or other media outlets is that the media want either of the following combinations of guests: one opposed to the discussed issue and one in favor, or one conservative and one liberal (Etzioni, 2010). If you waver back and forth between two opposite stances, you are often deemed a less-desirable guest.

❏ **Listen carefully to what your journalist's story will focus on** so you can offer a response that will fit well within the piece (or speak up if the angle is misinformed). For example, most news publications focus on a consumer perspective, so journalists are more likely to ask an education expert about something like whether parents can expect their kids to get into top colleges than something like whether the state university system is equitable (Jaschik, 2016). In those cases, if you consider ways your topic relates to the general public, you can find access points to share with the press.

❏ **Amiable.** Thank the reporter for the opportunity to share, don't be condescending, etc.

BE PROMOTION-FRIENDLY

Promote Others

When I first attended AERA with Gail Thompson, we constantly ran into people who knew her (she is very accomplished and prolific). Dr. Thompson would excitedly introduce me like this, "You have to meet Dr. Jenny Rankin, who teaches a class at Cambridge. Do you know *five* of her books were published just this year? You might have seen her TED Talk." Each person exchanged business cards with me and was surely more interested in what I said than if Thompson had not given me such a generous endorsement. Thompson's example inspired me to pump up the passion with which I introduce people I respect.

If you are female, people of any gender are likely to be overly critical of your promotion efforts. Women often avoid touting their accomplishments due to society's discouragement of this trait in women; for example, a woman can lower her chances of getting hired if she explains her qualifications or accomplishments in a job interview (Sandberg, 2013). But Sandberg described how a group of women at Merrill Lynch circumvented this stigma and rose to the executive level by bragging about *one another's* accomplishments at meetings. Now that they're leaders in their institution, they are in stronger position to make it a place where women can speak about their own successes without repercussions. Promoting colleagues' efforts can be equally powerful in the education field. We can find many ways to support one another when we look for the chances.

I have met the opposite of Dr. Thompson: people who fear praising others will somehow hurt their own chances to shine. Examples include speaking in a presentation as if a group study were that person's sole project; giving weak excuses to not mention some people's sessions in an SIG email meant to detail all member presentations at an upcoming conference; publicly posting, "How did *you* get that?" when a colleague posts an accomplishment on social media. The worst offender I've personally encountered in our field (having done all of the above slights and more) is a woman, so groups commonly facing bias can also be the ones guilty of slamming doors on others.

Let's all try to compensate for these disparagers by lifting up one another. As you promote your work, liberally promote others' quality work, too. Since our greatest goal is helping students, championing any information that can help kids is worthwhile.

Promote Your Work

Make it easy for people to promote you. For example, anytime you are giving a keynote and will be introduced or have written an article for which a publication will include a byline, provide the bio and byline to your contact person even if you are not asked for it. Otherwise that person might find information on you online from an outdated site or might write one that does not mention the achievements you most like to promote. This is not about arrogance; rather, the better you look, the more likely people are to listen to and learn from you, increasing your benefit to children.

Throughout your promotion efforts, avoid these pitfalls:

❏ Being excessively humble (if you are a woman who struggles with this, read *Lean In* by Sheryl Sandberg for inspiration).

❑ Only being interested in promotion (not in meeting people, discussing or learning about your topic, etc.).

❑ Being pushy or disregarding others' needs (this includes not catering your presentations to your audience).

❑ Taking sole or misleadingly large credit for a group effort (remember the "Honesty and Integrity" section guidelines in "Chapter 1. Introduction").

❑ Appearing arrogant or promoting yourself rather than your work.

Though this book recommends confidence, you don't want to be pushy. When we sense people are trying to persuade us, such as influencing us through unbridled confidence, we raise our mental shields against them (Grant, 2016). Let your confidence stem from knowing you have something valuable to share and that you've crafted a compelling way to present it. That kind of preparation and sureness will prevent an overly aggressive delivery.

Grant (2016) found you can even point out problems with your idea that you're still trying to solve; this establishes you as trustworthy and also shifts the audience away from self-defense and into problem-solving mode. Suddenly your idea becomes their idea, too, which is what you want.

EXPOSURE FOR YOUR ANYTHING

When you have an upcoming speaking engagement, your program will be highlighted on the news, or you published another article or paper, your knowledge-sharing will ultimately help more students if more stakeholders know about it. Do each of the following, depending on your resources:

Social Media

Announce your new endeavor on each of your social media accounts (see the "Social Media and Presence" section of "Chapter 2. Image" for help). This shares the work with your networks and also creates more backlinks (to raise the work's search engine ranking).

For some accounts, like Facebook and LinkedIn, there are also groups and pages where you can announce your work. For example, when I publish something new related to giftedness, I commonly share it on Mensa's private "Exceptionally & Profoundly Gifted SIG" Facebook group page (which has 170 members) and I visit the Mensa group page on LinkedIn that I follow and post it as a new conversation on that page (which has 25,000 followers).

In Twitter, "pin" your tweet so it remains at the top of your profile. For example, I will pin a tweet of my latest book to the top of my Twitter profile for about a month so that my additional tweets and retweets don't push the book tweet down during that time.

Note the area of your Twitter screen where trending topics (in the form of #hashtags) are shown. If your work relates to one of these, use it in your tweets. This will dramatically increase the number of users who see your post.

If an organization facilitated your endeavor (the magazine your article is in, the publisher of your book, the association hosting the conference you'll be speaking at, etc.), check if that organization has a social media account. Include a tag or reference to that account (such as a Twitter handle) in your post so they can see your marketing efforts, "like" the posts, and repost or retweet them with their expansive networks. Knowing you're actively hustling on behalf of your work can also keep you in promoters' minds when new opportunities arise. For example, a radio station asks your publisher for an expert to interview, and your publisher's staff thinks of you for the task, knowing you'll likely accept.

Twitter Chat

Offer to moderate (or get interviewed during) an education-related Twitter chat (see "Chapter 10. Connecting" if you're unfamiliar with Twitter chats). Being the moderator is like being the invited guest on a radio show; your involvement will be promoted, and visitors will be eager to interact with you. When I moderated an Edutopia (@Edutopia) Twitter chat on teacher burnout, over 4,600 different people participated in the 1-hour chat. That meant thousands of people I could interact with and impact with my ideas

Some chats even ask for moderator suggestions. For example, a tweet from NBC Learn (@nbclearn) once read, "If you or another educator want to be involved in our next #NBCLearnChat, let us know!" (NBC Learn, 2015). You can volunteer by tweeting your willingness with the chat hashtag (for example, #NBCLearnChat) or by reaching out to whoever is listed as managing the chat (private message him on Twitter or track down his email address).

Author Pages

Update your author pages (covered in the next "Exposure for Your Books" section) with the new item if you do not already have a link there to direct people to where new presentations, publications, etc. are listed on your webpage. I try to include a link whenever possible so that I only have to keep one location (my website) up-to-date.

Marketing and PR Teams

If you have written a book, your publishing house likely has a marketing team or public relations (PR) contact you are invited to consult. Find out who these people are and introduce yourself. Ask if you can have a phone conversation to talk about ways you can best promote your work (not just your book, but your other endeavors, too). I have learned a wealth of strategies this way and have also landed additional opportunities (for example, my PR contact delivering my article straight to her magazine editor contact, resulting in a speedy publication).

Regularly notify your editor and publisher's marketing team of anything newsworthy you are doing (such as a symposium where you'll be speaking, or a new paper you wrote). They will typically use their newsletters, social media, correspondence with reporters and other authors, and other outlets to help you spread the word. For example, this book's publisher operates over 60 different social media accounts devoted to different subjects and audiences (Routledge, Taylor & Francis Group, 2017), so when I notify Routledge of something I'm doing they tweet and post to the audiences that might be interested.

If you work at a university, you might also have access to a marketing team or a PR contact there. Meet with this person for valuable promotion tips and prospects. Also utilize your university's interdisciplinary center and resource information managers (RIMs) to share your work across disciplines.

You can share this book with your marketing and PR contacts. Teaming up can help you tackle the book's recommendations in an efficient way and avoid unnecessarily duplicating efforts.

Press Release

Issue a press release. If you work at a university, it likely has a Press Office, PR staff, or a communications team that will write and issue press releases for you, yet you'll still need to provide information to the writers and will want to proof the piece before release.

DEFINITION OF PRESS RELEASE

A **press release** – also called a media release, news release, or press statement – is a document sent directly to journalists and news editors of all media (magazines, newspapers, radio, television, etc.) to announce something newsworthy. Press releases are commonly issued for completed research studies and planned events, but other occasions qualify if they would be of high interest to those reading and visiting news outlets.

A press release is unbiased, whereas a pitch (covered in earlier chapters) tries to persuade a reporter to run with a particular idea for a story. A press release and pitch may be sent together or alone, depending on what you deem most appropriate for your ideas and which each journalist prefers.

Just like other modes of writing, in a press release you'll want to hook the reader and use a tantalizing headline (such as, "98% of Students Try Harder When Teachers Love Them"). Your first sentence (and typically your title) should convey whatever is most newsworthy about your announcement (such as a study's key findings). From there, briefly introduce key information (who, what, why, where, when), add details and findings, offer a couple of quotes from experts involved in the project, and conclude with a short summary.

Present the event or findings in a jargon-free way that's of public interest. In fact, aim for a press release that could be printed by a newspaper without any major changes. Be super concise: you're trying to grab journalists' interest, and they can always ask you to elaborate when they contact you.

Include a brief bio of each expert involved, as well as contact information journalists can use for more information and quotes. Reporters also like receiving a low-resolution headshot, an infographic or other public-friendly image, or a link to a video or other item the reporter can opt to embed in the story (Stein, 2016).

Email your press release to journalists. Don't miss the Associated Press (AP), which has journalists devoted to all levels of education. Many news outlets get their news from AP; in fact, more than 50% of the world's population sees AP's content every day (Associated Press, 2018). There is a "submit press release" option on the contact form at www.ap.org/contact-us.

See the "Newspaper: Pitch" section of "Chapter 4. Writing Short-Form" for help including a pitch in the body of your email. Also share your press release through social media and place it in research repositories, covered later in the "Exposure for Your Other Writing" section.

Virtual Signatures

Adjust your virtual signatures (automatic email signature, online forum signatures, etc.) to feature a link you are particularly passionate about sharing (for example, to your TED Talk) below your name. You can also add these links to your bios (appearing at the end of your articles, in your social media profile, etc.).

Resume and CV

Immediately update your resume (including online resumes, such as at https://chroniclevitae.com), CV, and website with the new publication, event, or honor. I do this immediately upon acceptance so that I am never behind or overwhelmed by a growing mountain of additions. The only exceptions are my resumes in job hunt repositories, which (in the interest of saving time) I will only update when I hunt for a new job.

Discussions of Your Work

Visit the comments section, which often appears under an article or appearance you post online, and converse cordially with those who comment there. This is a great chance to share free online resources to help readers implement your ideas.

Academia.edu has a "reason for downloading" message center you can treat in the same way. This, many blog software tools, and other writing venues will automatically notify you when someone posts a response to your work.

"At times, other experts and commenters of note (public figures, other academics) will join the discussion – providing another opportunity to link to their thoughts (and even connect to them via social media networks such as Facebook, LinkedIn, and Twitter)" (Reddick, 2016, p. 62). You can use the comments section to further inform and engage readers in ways that can help them implement your recommendations to help students.

Some websites track who is interested in your work. Elsevier's Mendeley Stats displays who cited each journal article, who tweeted it, and more. Elsevier publisher Jennifer Franklin told me authors can use this information to make connections with their readers.

Discussions of Others' Work

You likely read a lot of online content about your topic. There is often an option at the bottom of the webpage to comment on online articles. Use those fields to share your thoughts on the topic. Sometimes mentioning one of your articles or resources here is appropriate. Just be sure the work you mention is highly relevant, and that your post adds to the discussion rather than sidetracks the author's message. Posting a link to content on your website can also boost your site's search engine ranking through establishing what's known as backlinks from related sites.

On the same note, when you engage in Twitter chats, forum conversations, or other online discussions, mention one of your resources when it will help readers (for example, "For a reference sheet on Dabrowsky's overexcitabilities, visit www...."). Since much online content is "forever up," it's fun to see how comments you made years ago still bring new people to your website and resources you offer the field (if your website's analytics tool reveals how people were brought to your site).

Reference Sites

Recall the "Short Answer and Reference Sites" section of "Chapter 4. Writing Short-Form" and consider whether your piece should be referenced on articles within Wikipedia, answers within Quora, or other reference sites. As long as your references conform to site policies (such as furthering conversations versus furthering self-interests), you can introduce visitors to your work so it can affect more lives.

Alerts

Set up Google Alerts (www.google.com/alerts) and Talkwalker Alerts (www.talkwalker.com/alerts) to send you an email anytime your name, book title, or specialized research concept is mentioned on the internet. Another approach to the above is to Google your name or work every now and then. Either approach will connect you with other people and organizations who are following your work, doing similar work, etc.

Also search for your name and any recent endeavor (such as a reading program you launched, a keynote you've been scheduled to give, etc.) on social media platforms. Interact with those who are posting about it.

Content Curration

You can spread your (and others') online content with tools like Digg (http://digg.com), Newsvine (www.newsvine.com), Reddit (www.reddit.com), Scoop.it! (www.scoop.it), and StumbleUpon (www.stumbleupon.com).

Handouts

At presentations, add web addresses to key resources (such as your book, a resource you made, etc.) to your presentation handout and mention these during your presentation. I always give my audience online access to the session handout (I house the PDF beside where I mention the presentation on my website) and I upload the handout to my session details on the event app (when this function is available).

If you are scheduled to present in a "roundtable" format where slides are not used, handouts become especially crucial. Apply the same design savvy to your handouts that you learned in this book concerning image, branding, and slides.

Newsletters

Any time you can get mention of a publication or an appearance into a newsletter or e-newsletter, you expose a whole new list of subscribers to your work. Consider every organization of which you're a member, every publishing house for which you're an author, and every institution for which you work. Many of these have newsletters or e-newsletters in which industry news is shared.

Reach out to the organization or its news editor to request that your latest publication or appearance be added. Reach out to them as soon as the terms of the accomplishment are solidified so they have time to place the listing in their newsletters.

Member Updates

Note which organizations you've joined communicate news specifically about members. For example, the National Communication Association (NCA) publication *NCA Insight & Out* has a recurring "Member News" segment. Divisions and SIGs within larger organizations often mention members' new work (in emails or newsletters, like *AERA Division H News & Announcements*).

These groups will often display directions for submitting your own updates to be shared with all members. Notify the appropriate people in these groups whenever you have a new endeavor from which they could benefit. Provide a title, one-sentence synopsis of the work, and a link to where the piece (or at least more information on it) can be found online. Your wording should match the way such announcements are sent to members so it can simply be pasted into an email or newsletter without being reworked.

SCRAPPY TIP

Reaching out to journalists (such as with a press release) before 10:00 AM will allow you to catch them before they begin writing their stories for the day (Stein, 2016).

Spokesperson

Empower others to carry your message for you. People will resist your message when it doesn't align with their current beliefs, such as:

- parents hearing that spanking kids is ineffective, whereas these parents were raised being spanked "and turned out just fine, thank you!";
- students hearing they should tell an adult if they are bullied, when they see bullying worsen after parents or principals get involved.

You can bypass disbelief if listeners receive your message from someone they view as sharing their belief systems. For example, anti-littering ads in which

Native Americans and wildlife decry environmental damage don't put any dent in rates of littering, because folks who throw trash clearly don't care about the environment or those they hurt within it. Conversely, Texas solved its massive littering problem only after airing ads in which Dallas Cowboys athletes, whom the typical litterer admired, pick up and crush a littered can and say, "Don't mess with Texas" (Heath & Heath, 2008). Littering in Texas finally plummeted, and that 1980s ad campaign was so successful that its catchphrase is well known even today.

The spokesperson strategy is particularly powerful when reaching students, as long as the right message is communicated. Berger (2013) wrote of a "Just Say No" anti-drug commercial that showed a teenager going about her day and being offered different drugs by different people, which she declined, yet the ads *increased* drug use. The commercials sent the message that lots of teens (all those trying to tempt the ad's star) are doing drugs. Berger (2013) also writes of how Koreen Johannessen tried to combat the binge drinking that 44% of students do. Stunts like putting a coffin on campus with stats on drinking deaths didn't work. However, when Johannessen ran a student newspaper ad citing student feedback, which revealed 69% of students have no more than four drinks when they party (below the binge-drinking practice), heavy drinking dropped by nearly 30%. Johannessen essentially used students as the messengers, but also ensured the right message came across through them.

Consider how you could empower appropriate messengers to deliver your message to others. For example, rather than sharing a message with students, you might train student body representatives and top athletes to deliver the message to their peers. Rather than stand as a lone conservative sharing your message with a liberal audience (or the other way around), you might forge a bipartisan team that supports your message and then deliver that message together.

More

The next two sections ("Exposure for Your Books" and "Exposure for Your Other Writing") include suggestions relative to promoting written work. However, you might apply some of those sections' tips to promoting other works (your speech, your interview, etc.), too.

EXPOSURE FOR YOUR BOOKS

You wrote your book or book chapter because you want it to be read so it can help people. It would be a shame if the impact of your words was limited by meager readership. While your publisher will likely promote your book in a variety of ways, do not rely on that alone. Rather, apply the following tips, along with the previous section's tips, to add to your book's promotion.

Social Media

In addition to the social media announcements covered in this chapter's "Exposure for Your Everything" section, tweet a link to your book and a compelling statement or question (such as, "Is the teaching profession set up to encourage teacher failure?") directly to high-profile reporters. They might want to cite or profile you and your book in an upcoming article.

Author Pages

As soon as any book or book chapter you authored has been published, you will want it attributed to you on an "author page" you set up with each popular book site. Set up and manage an author page with each of the following:

- **Amazon** (https://authorcentral.amazon.com)
- **Barnes & Noble** (https://help.barnesandnoble.com/app/answers/detail/a_id/3611/kw/author; submit author bio and book affiliations to titles@bn.com)
- **Goodreads** (www.goodreads.com/author/program)

Do not count on new publications being automatically associated with your author pages. Often, they are not, or they are associated with a duplicate name that does not sync with your author page, or another mistake is made. This is especially true of books for which you wrote a single chapter (which should be attributed to you as one of multiple contributing authors). Check your author page after each publication and follow the site's guidelines to ensure new books are attributed to you properly.

Your publisher will likely give you an author page, as well. Maintain this page in the same way as your other author pages.

The above-mentioned sites usually allow you to post news like upcoming speaking engagements. I find a way to post a link to the presentation page of my website in these cases so readers get an up-to-date account of speaking engagements without me having to list them on multiple webpages.

TIME-SAVING TIP

As you set up multiple author pages, multiple profile pages for different organizations, etc., you will find it hard to keep these up-to-date with new career developments. For this reason, whenever possible, I post a link to a single webpage where I keep all of my latest developments. For example, if there is an "Event" field, I post a link to the page of my website where I post all my upcoming appearances. If there is a "Publications" field, I post a link to the page where I list each new publication. If there is merely a bio field, I provide a general bio and end it with "See www. JennyRankin.com/bio for complete bio and CV." This way I only have to keep one area current, without having to maintain every profile page individually.

Bookseller Promotions

Some book sellers facilitate authors' promotion of their books, such as through book giveaways, conversing with readers, or hosting online discussions about your books. Explore each site to know your options.

Marketing and PR Teams

Whenever I have a newsworthy item (such as an article I published or an upcoming speaking engagement) related to my book's topic, I email my publisher's assigned marketing contact and copy my editor with a brief, tweetable mention about it. They often ensure this news is added to their newsletters, social media channels, etc., which helps promote the book. This practice also keeps you on the team's minds when future opportunities crop up, such as when a journalist asks for an expert to quote.

Experts Mentioned

I go through the reference list of every book I write. When the book is published, I contact authors cited (I usually find either a Twitter handle or a university email address) and let the author know I cited his work. Often, I'll hear back from these experts, who sometimes purchase the book or mention it in social media or elsewhere.

Reading Lists

Reach out to groups (related to your book's topic) that maintain reading lists. You can often find these lists by exploring organizations' websites. For example, the *Twice-Exceptional (2e) Newsletter* lists books for helping 2e children at www.2enewsletter.com/topic_resources_books.html, and the Collaborative Inquiry Toolkit lists books related to data use and collaborative inquiry at www.mnpscollaboration.org/reading-list.html. Use the contact page or another avenue to suggest your book be included. Be sure to explain why (using a few sentences summarizing the book and reflecting its value to the group's efforts).

Also look for such lists in relation to events that make field news. For example, following the 2017 tragedy in Charlottesville, the Collaborative for Academic, Social, and Emotional Learning (CASEL) posted a list of resources for educators promoting respectful school climates and helping students recover from the tragedy (www.casel.org/safe-and-respectful-environment-for-learning). There was even an invitation on the webpage to suggest additional resources for the list, and CASEL promoted the list in its newsletter.

Book Reviews

Submit your book to be reviewed. Nonfiction book reviews we're familiar with – such as *The New York Times* and *Kirkus Reviews* – typically only review general-interest books. Thus, it would only be worth submitting your book to these if it's one a non-educator would enjoy. However, specialized sites and publications in our field review books that cover their topics. For example, when I wrote the book *Engaging & Challenging Gifted Students*, it was reviewed by the *Twice-Exceptional (2e) Newsletter*, *Mensa Bulletin Magazine*, and *Mensa World Journal*. These were different publication types (a newsletter, magazine, and journal), yet they all featured book reviews and were all devoted to that book's topic (giftedness). Visit the websites and print materials of organizations and publications devoted to your specific topic and submit your book to those with a book review column. "For books by new or relatively unknown authors, negative reviews increased sales by 45 percent" (Berger, 2013, pp. 80-81), so don't worry too much about the outcome.

When a book review comes out, add a snippet of it to the editorial reviews for every format (paperback, hardcover, etc.) of your book on sites like Amazon, Barnes & Noble, and Goodreads. Let your editor and publisher's marketing/PR team know, as well, and post links to the review on social media. I also let the review's author know I am doing this, which lends me the author's blessing and possible feedback on which snippet to use.

You'll also want the kind of informal reviews people post online, such as on bookseller sites. "A five-star review on Amazon.com leads to approximately twenty more books sold than a one-star review" (Berger, 2013, p. 8).

If I know a colleague has read my book, I email her the link and directions to add a review for the book to prominent online sellers. See the "Sample Email" text box (note the underlined words are hyperlinks the reader can follow to the precise webpage where he can add reviews) and compose a similar email. Colleagues are busy, so making it easy for them to post reviews will increase the odds they will do so. According to Amazon bestselling author Norman Eng, "The more reviews you get, the more Amazon's algorithms will notice and promote your book. Most books published by academics have less than ten reviews, but 20 is better. With 50, you're going to get noticed."

SAMPLE EMAIL I SEND COLLEAGUES WHO READ MY BOOK

Hi [Colleague's Name],

Thank you very much for reading my book; I hope you enjoy[ed] it. If you want to post a short review of the book online, here are links for you to do so on <u>Amazon</u>, <u>Barnes & Noble</u>, and <u>GoodReads</u>. Thank you so much for your time and feedback!

Have a great day,

[Your Name]

Book Awards

Submit your book to win awards. This isn't about chasing accolades; rather, winning awards brings added credibility and attention to your book, and this means more readers who can use your words for good. See the awards that read "Book Award" in the "Category" column in this book's "List of Honors" eResource.

Blog

Around your book's publication date, write a blog post about it for your website (and any other places for which you regularly write). If you've synced your site with a tool like www.MailChimp.com, this post will automatically be emailed to everyone who subscribed to your blog via your site's signup form.

Articles

Approach publications (such as those on this book's "List of Writing Opportunities" eResource) about writing an article that focuses on one of your book's chapters (with some teaser text, depending on what your publisher allows) or key points.

Conferences

Notify your editor and publisher's marketing team when you commit to attending a conference. Your publisher might have a booth (as many do), and this could impact how your book is displayed. Your publisher might also schedule you for a "meet and greet" or book signing at the booth or arrange for other opportunities like a radio interview. No matter what, visit the booth and give those working it the chance to take your photo with your book, editor, or readers, as they will likely want to post this on social media.

If you ask in advance, most publishers will send you fliers (about your book), which you can distribute to your session's attendees. These sometimes have discount codes on them, which the audience appreciates.

Bring your books to all your related speaking engagements. My mentor, the prolific author Gail Thompson, taught me the value of holding up my books at such events and having copies handy for interested attendees to take a look at after the talks.

If you are a conference's keynote or featured speaker, inquire as to whether you could do a book signing or "meet and greet" at the event right after you present. Some authors sell their own copies at events (check with event organizers and your publisher before you do).

Email List

If you are working on a book that has not yet been released, pass around a "Please Notify Me When Your Next Book Comes Out" signup sheet (collecting email addresses) at each of your related speaking engagements. You can then send these folks an email when your book is released, including a link to a related blog post and a link to where they can purchase a copy. I house all these email addresses in my MailChimp (www.mailchimp.com) account, which makes it easy to send polished emails to growing lists of people.

Interviews

A new book is interview-worthy. See the "List of Broadcasting Opportunities" eResource described in "Chapter 9. Speaking on Air and Recordings" and reach out to likely interviewers. Let them know you have a new book and include an extremely succinct account of what the book is about, why it makes a difference for students, and your professional background.

Timing

While just after your book's publication is a natural time to promote it, also pursue interviews when major developments in your field take place (Routledge, 2017), and write pieces that tie your book topic to recent events.

Contacts

When you make a strong connection with someone in a high-profile position (for example, the president of an association) related to your book's topic, mention how your books relate to his work. Ask your publisher (via your editor or marketing contact) if it can send a copy of your book to this person. Follow up with the reader if there are particularly relevant sections he shouldn't miss.

Give a free copy of your book to other key people. Sometimes your publisher is willing to do this for you (at no cost to you) if you provide compelling rationale. If not, you can send people some of the extra free copies you got from your publisher, or buy copies using an author discount. As I mentioned in "Chapter 10. Connecting", Norman Eng gave me a copy of his book after attending a class I taught at the AERA Annual Meeting; as a result, his book is cited throughout this book. If you're confident your book it good, giving a copy away can help the receiver while likely leading to more book sales.

Audiobooks

Consider creating an audiobook. When author Valerie Geller produced an audio edition of her book, an option that is free if you join www.audible.com, her book gained further marketing power (Routledge, 2017).

Research Respositories

Add a flier for your book (publishers will typically provide this to you if asked, or you can make one yourself) and add it to research repositories. These are covered in the "Exposure for Your Other Writing" section (on pages 302–303).

Author Identification

Associate each new book with all your author identification accounts. These are covered in the next section.

EXPOSURE FOR YOUR OTHER WRITING

In addition to ideas provided in this chapter's "Exposure for Your Everything" section, below are some additional tips specific to non-book written work.

Research Repositories

You can add your publications (papers, articles, etc.) to sites known as research libraries, databases, registries, or lists. Such repositories lend your work greater exposure and increase its likelihood of having an impact. However, you may only share your work in this way if doing so will not violate any agreements you have made. Honor each repository's and publication's specific policies, which typically support the following:

- If you wrote a paper published in a journal, and you signed away your right to reprint or share the paper outside of the journal, you cannot upload this paper to a research repository. You can, however, check to see if the publisher will allow you to upload the paper's abstract with citation details and a link to the paper's original location. This way the paper can still receive added exposure through the site.
- If you wrote a published book, and you signed away your right to reprint or share the book's content, you can upload (to a research repository) a flier announcing the book, but you cannot upload the book itself.
- If you wrote an article for a publication that left you with rights to share the article as you want, you can upload the article to a research repository. In this case make it clear (in the document) where the article was first published.

Even if you do not retain the right to share your publication, many journals automatically share their papers with repositories for you (as is the case for over 1,000 journals indexed in ERIC). Whenever you have the right to upload your work to a research repository, or when you can upload a flier or abstract directing people to the work, I recommend considering the repositories listed in the following text box (some of which also serve as academic social networking sites).

RESEARCH REPOSITORIES

- **Academia** (www.academia.edu) is accessed by over 53 million members (Academia, 2017a), and papers uploaded to the site have been read by 850 million people around the world (Academia, 2017b). Papers received a 69% increase in citations over the course of five years when they were uploaded to Academia (Niyazov et al., 2016).
- **AERA Online Paper Repository** (www.aera.net/Publications/Online-Paper-Repository) is where the thousands of AERA Annual Meeting (conference) presenters can upload the research papers they presented there.
- **ARNIE Docs** (www.arniedocs.info) is offered by ESP Solutions and affiliated with AERA Division H, Department of Research and Evaluation (DRE), and National Association of Assessment Directors (NAAD).
- **Banco de Dissertações e Teses da CAPES** (catalogodeteses.capes.gov.br) is a Brazilian research database from South America's largest country.
- **Bepress** (www.bepress.com) offers Digital Commons, where higher education faculty can publish and manage work produced on campus.
- **Connecting REpositories (CORE)** (https://core.ac.uk) aggregates open access research papers worldwide.
- **EdTech Docs** (www.edtechdocs.info) is also maintained by ESP Solutions but is specific to educational technology.
- **EBSCO Academic Databases** (www.ebsco.com/who-we-serve/academic-libraries) contains papers relating to schools in the U.K., Canada, Australia, New Zealand and Ireland; this includes the British Education Index (BEI).
- **ERIC** (https://eric.ed.gov) is sponsored by the U.S. Department of Education, Institute of Education Sciences (IES). Over 48,000 new publications are added to ERIC every year (ERIC, 2017).
- **Figshare** (www.figshare.com) is popular in the U.K., Australia, and New Zealand.

- **Guardian Higher Education Network** (www.theguardian.com/ higher-education-network) is a directory of blogs and other resources relating to a range of higher education topics.
- **Humanities Commons** (https://hcommons.org) is a Modern Language Association project funded by an Andrew W. Mellon Foundation grant.
- **Reddit Journal of Science** (www.reddit.com/r/science) is an academic branch of Reddit, which facilitates information sharing online.
- **ResearchGate** (www.researchgate.net) allows you to share and collaborate on research at any stage in its completion. ResearchGate has more than 13 million users (ResearchGate, 2017), and approximately 6,000 new members sign up each day (Mangan, 2012).
- **SSRN** (www.elsevier.com/solutions/ssrn) of Elsevier – which includes Education Research Network (EduRN) – has more than 2.2 million users and 6 million citations (Elsevier, 2018).
- **What Works Clearinghouse** (https://ies.ed.gov), run by Institute of Education Sciences (IES) within the U.S. Department of Education, reviews and summarizes education research.
- **Zenodo** (https://zenodo.org) is funded by the OpenAIRE Consortium and CERN.

For some repositories, you set up a free account and then upload your own work or select work you authored. For others (such as ERIC), you must submit your work for consideration, and the work appears in the repository only after it is approved.

Many of these sites offer analytics, so you can track who is viewing which papers. These statistics can be used when you need to provide evidence of your online presence and exposure (such as for a book proposal or a potential job).

There is some controversy concerning these types of sites, particularly when it comes to uploading one's own research for others to access. Critics question whose hands scholars are putting their work into, and whether these networks will eventually start charging money for their use. Others worry about having their work or ideas stolen and published by others, particularly when in-progress research is shared.

My stance is one in favor of using such networks for published work (when publishers allow for sharing via these venues, or via an uploaded book flier or abstract with link to a published study) and removing my work should I disagree with future policy changes. I do not use these sites for works in progress, but you might feel comfortable doing so. See Espinoza Vasquez and Caicedo Bastidas (2015); Jeng, DesAutels, He, and Li (2017); and Jordan (2014) for help determining how you want to use these tools.

Author Identification

Register for accounts in Google Scholar (https://scholar.google.com), ORCHID (www.orcid.org), and SCOPUS (www.scopus.com). To save time, link publications to your account in Google Scholar or SCOPUS first, then import that information into ORCHID to automatically link the same publications to your ORCHID profile. Tie each of these three accounts to each new publication you produce. This increases online discoveries of your work.

Social Media

During the first week your new piece is published, include "#TellEWA" in a compelling tweet about it. The Education Writers Association (EWA) uses such tweets to select "EWA Story of the Week" content, which it shares with readers and journalists in the field.

Every day or two within the first two weeks of your publication, search for the title of your article or paper in Twitter (or whatever automatically populates tweets when readers click the Twitter "share" icon that accompanies your piece), LinkedIn, etc. This will reveal people who have shared your work but did not know your handle or account name in order to copy you on the share.

"Like" all of the shares you find. This alerts readers to your whereabouts on social media and can earn you new followers. Retweet/post these shares whenever it feels appropriate (don't share more than one or two at a time, look for shares that add to dialogue, etc.).

WHEN TO POST

These statistics are provided by TrackMaven (2014):

Twitter

- The most effective day to tweet (to get the most retweets) is Sunday, followed by Thursday.
- The most effective time to tweet is 10:00–11:00 PM EST.

Facebook

- The most effective day to post on Facebook (to receive the most interaction) is Saturday, followed by Sunday.
- The most effective time to post on Facebook is 12:00–1:00 AM EST.

Blog

- The most effective day to publish a blog post (to receive the most interaction) is Saturday, followed by Sunday.
- The most effective time to publish a blog post is 10:00–11:00 PM EST.

Email

- The most effective day to email (to get the most opens) is Thursday, followed by Wednesday.
- The most effective time to email is 2:00–5:00 PM EST.

Currated Content

Note which e-newsletters you read curate content from other publications (usually with a title, brief description, and link to the content's original location online). *Mensa Weekly Brainwave* is one example. Reach out to these publications and suggest your recent write-up be included in such a way (make it easy by writing a succinct description they can use). Some publications even provide directions for making such suggestions.

Reposts

Take note of which sites post content that first appeared elsewhere (such as with "Reprinted with permission from..." or "Originally published by..." displayed at the bottom). Let these sites know when you write something they might want to post on their sites, as well (as long as this does not violate any copyright).

Blog Directories

If you maintain a blog, submit it to blog directories like www.blogscholar.com or www.blogarama.com/education-blogs (you can find hundreds more by searching online). You might look into an RSS feeds generator (like www.rssground.com) for this task. Not only can people find your blog through these directories but increasing the number of backlinks to your work increases your blog's search engine ranking and thus makes it easier for people to find your blog when searching for related topics.

Images

For any online content, include a related image. "Some bloggers find that a large proportion of their traffic comes from Google Image Search. That means people are searching for images using keywords, finding images on a blog, and then finding their way to the blog" (Psychology Today, 2017). You can add the image yourself on your own blog or post, or you can suggest an image if someone else is uploading the content.

EXPOSURE FOR YOUR SPEAKING ENGAGEMENTS

Most tips for sharing your speaking engagements and broadcasting appearances were already covered in the previous sections. Some additional tips are below.

Social Media

Announce your appearance (in an inviting, "Join us!" style) beforehand on social media with a link to where guests can register or watch the event. Event organizers are often happy to provide an image you can use to call more attention to these posts.

If a recording of your appearance is housed online after the broadcast, share the link on social media. This gives you another chance to catch viewers who missed the initial airing.

If your speech is online with a designated title (for example, your TED Talk has a single name), periodically search for its title in Twitter (or whatever automatically populates tweets when readers click the Twitter "share" icon that accompanies your presentation), LinkedIn, etc. This will reveal people who have shared your speech but did not know your handle or account name in order to copy you on the share.

"Like" all of the shares (of your appearance) you find. This alerts audiences to your whereabouts on social media and can earn you new followers. Retweet/post these shares when it feels appropriate and not self-gratuitous.

Local Media

Contact local media about your visit. "Local media are always looking for uplifting stories tied to supporting teachers and students in their communities"; even if a story doesn't result from this outreach, it can establish you as a resource for reporters, who can then ask you to contribute to future stories (Boyle, 2017, p. 1).

Connected Educators Month (CEM)

If your event takes place in or near October, or if it is permanently online and you can refer to it in October, list the event for CEM, an initiative led by the American Institutes for Research (AIR). Simply visit www.connectededucators. org and use the "Add an Event/Activity" function. Support for this project was removed at the time of this writing but could return under a different government administration.

HUNTING AND HARVESTING

GUIDE TO HUNTING AND HARVESTING

This book directs you to many opportunities to share your expertise with the world, but you can hunt and harvest to land even *more* great opportunities. This involves finding opportunities through memberships, online communities, events, internet searches, and social media. See the "eResources" section near the start of this book for details on accessing the "Guide to Hunting and Harvesting".

CONCLUSION

I hope over the course of reading this book you have come to view me as a supportive friend. I hope you'll remember that I (through this book) am here for you anytime, and you can return to me again and again to add to your repertoire of expertise-sharing avenues.

If you found this book helpful, please share it with your colleagues to help them expose the world to their education expertise, too. Whatever your opinion, I would be grateful if you posted a review for the book on www.Amazon. com, www.BarnesandNoble.com, and www.GoodReads.com so others can learn from your impressions.

FINAL SCRAPPY TIP

When you post book reviews, publishers might contact you for permission to include your review in a future edition of a book.

If you've now pursued even 1% of the opportunities presented in this book, you have already shared your education expertise with new audiences who can apply your words to helping students. Don't lose steam, and you will continue to expand your influence on children's lives.

As your influence grows, never forget from where you came. Remember what it was like to yearn and struggle to get your expertise out into the world and help those who stand where you once stood (have to turn down a radio appearance because it doesn't fit your schedule? introduce the interviewer to someone you know who would be great for the opportunity). The more we help our peers to share quality information, the more we help our field and students.

As you close the pages of this book, please pour yourself a glass of something celebratory and pat yourself on the back. You are the kind of education expert not content to limit the reach of your expertise to the usual, comfortable outlets. You know you'll have a greater impact on students if you step onto the world stage, so you have officially launched that endeavor. With your mindset and determination there's no limit to the number of students you will help, the number of other education experts you will help, and the influence you will have on our field and our world. *Thank you*. Few lives leave behind such a legacy, and you should feel very proud.

REFERENCES

Academia. (2017a). *Academia*. Retrieved from www.academia.edu

Academia. [noreply@academia-mail.com]. (2017b, June 13). *The Academia community just hit a big milestone!* [email].

Associated Press (2018). *About us*. Retrieved from www.ap.org/about

Badgett, M. V. L. (2016). *The public professor: How to use your research to change the world*. New York, NY: NYU Press.

Berger, J. (2013). *Contagious: Why things catch on*. New York, NY: Simon & Schuster.

Boyle, D. [acquisitions@ascd.org]. (2017, November 7). *ASCD AuthorPULSE: Building relationships with local media*. [email].

Briggs, M. (2016). *Journalism next: A practical guide to digital reporting and publishing*. Lost Angeles, CA: Sage.

ERIC. (2017). *Who contributes content to ERIC?* [infographic]. Retrieved from https://eric.ed.gov/pdf/ERIC_Contributers_Fall2016.pdf

Espinoza Vasquez, F.K., & Caicedo Bastidas, C.E. (2015). Academic social networking sites: A comparative analysis of their services and tools. In *iConference 2015 Proceedings*, 1–6.

Etzioni, A. (2010). Reflections of a sometime-public intellectual. *PS: Political Science and Politics*, *43*(4), 651–655. Retrieved from www.jstor.org/stable/40927030

Grant, A. (2016). *Originals: How non-conformists move the world.* New York, NY: Penguin Books.

Heath, C., & Heath, D. (2008). *Made to stick: Why some ideas survive and others die.* New York, NY: Random House.

Jaschik, S. (2016). Professors and the press. In M. Gasman (Ed.), *Academics going public: How to write and speak beyond academe,* (pp. 9–19). New York, NY: Routledge, Taylor & Francis.

Jeng, W., DesAutels, S., He, D., & Li, L. (2017). Information exchange on an academic social networking site: A multidiscipline comparison on ResearchGate Q&A. *Journal of the Association for Information Science and Technology, 68*(3), 638–652. doi:10.1002/asi.23692

Jordan, K. (2014, November 3). Academics and their online networks: Exploring the role of academic social networking sites. *First Monday: Peer Reviewed Journal on the Internet 19*(11), doi:http://dx.doi.org/10.5210/fm.v19i11.4937

Mangan, K. (2012, April 29). Social networks for academics proliferate, despite some doubts. *The Chronicle of Higher Education.* Retrieved from www.chronicle.com/article/Social-Networks-for-Academics/131726

NBC Learn. [@nbclearn]. (2015, August 26). *If you or another educator want to be involved in our next #NBCLearnChat, let us know!* [Twitter moment]. Retrieved from https://twitter.com/nbclearn

Niyazov, Y., Vogel, C., Price, R., Lund, B., Judd, D., Akil, A., et al. (2016). Open access meets discoverability: Citations to articles posted toAcademia.edu. *PLoS ONE 11*(2): e0148257.doi:10.1371/journal.pone.0148257

Psychology Today. (2017). How to promote your blog. *Psychology Today.* Retrieved from www.psychologytoday.com/how-to-promote-your-blog

Reddick, R. J. (2016). Using social media to promote scholarship. In M. Gasman (Ed.), *Academics going public: How to write and speak beyond academe,* (pp. 55–70). New York, NY: Routledge, Taylor & Francis.

ResearchGate. (2017). About us. *ResearchGate.* Retrieved from www.researchgate.net/about

Routledge. (2017). *Promoting your book: Metadata surveys.* Retrieved from www.routledge.com/resources/authors/promoting-your-book.

Routledge, Taylor & Francis Group. (2017). *Author directions: Navigating your success in social media: 5 key tips for authors using social media.* Boca Raton, FL: CRC Press.

Sandberg, S. (2013). *Lean in: Women, work, and the will to lead.* New York, NY: Alfred A. Knopf.

Stein, K. (2016). How to write an influential press release. In M. Gasman (Ed.), *Academics going public: How to write and speak beyond academe,* (pp. 105–117). New York, NY: Routledge, Taylor & Francis.

TrackMaven. (2014). *A complete guide to the best times to post on social media (and more!).* Retrieved from www.slideshare.net/TrackMaven/when-to-postslidesharepdf/18-TrackMavenEmailWhen_to

Index